To   Sybil

43 years later – the whole story!

Love

Betty

ONCE A WICKED LADY

A BIOGRAPHY OF MARGARET LOCKWOOD

HILTON TIMS

ONCE A WICKED LADY

A BIOGRAPHY OF MARGARET LOCKWOOD

HILTON TIMS

VIRGIN

First published in Great Britain in 1989 by
Virgin Books
A division of W. H. Allen & Co Plc
Sekforde House
175–9 St John Street
London EC1V 4LL

For my mother-in-law, Ena Sampson,
a dedicated Margaret Lockwood fan.

British Library Cataloguing in Publication Data
Tims, Hilton
    Once a wicked lady: a biography of Margaret Lockwood.
    1. Cinema films. Acting. Lockwood, Margaret
    791.43′028′0924

    ISBN 1–85227–180–9

Set in Times by Input Typesetting Ltd, London

Printed and bound in Great Britain by Mackays of Chatham PLC, Kent

CONTENTS

*I*LLUSTRATIONS

With Stewart Granger in *Love Story*, 1944 (*Gainsborough/National Film Archive*)
With James Mason in *The Wicked Lady*, 1945 (*Gainsborough/National Film Archive*)

Between pages 146–7
Margaret's daughter Julia (Toots), born in 1941
Toots growing up
With Toots in *Hungry Hill*, 1946
With Toots in *The White Unicorn*, 1947
Signing a seven-year contract with J. Arthur Rank, 1946
With James Mason, receiving the first *Daily Mail* National Film Award from Lady Rothermere, 1946 (*Daily Mail*)
With Patricia Roc in *Jassy*, 1947 (*Gainsborough/Jim Simpson*)
With John Mills and J. Arthur Rank at the 1948 *Daily Mail* National Film Awards presentations (*Daily Mail*)
With Muriel and Sydney Box at Cannes 1946
In *Jassy*, 1947
With Keith Dobson at the première of *An Ideal Husband*, 1947 (*The Times*)
With Griffith Jones in *Look Before You Love*, 1948 (*Gainsborough*)

Between pages 178–9
In *Cardboard Cavalier*, 1948 (*Rank Organisation/The Times*)
With Dane Clark in *Highly Dangerous*, 1950 (*Rank Organisation*)
With Paul Dupuis in *Madness of the Heart*, 1949 (*Rank Organisation*)
With Orson Welles in *Trent's Last Case*, 1952 (*Wilson-Neagle*)
With Herbert Wilcox and Anna Neagle on the set of *Trent's Last Case*, 1952 (*The Times*)
With Forrest Tucker in *Laughing Anne*, 1953
Recording songs from *Laughing Anne*
With Dirk Bogarde preparing for *Cast A Dark Shadow*, 1954
With Agatha Christie and Herbert Leon, rehearsing *Spider's Web*, 1954
With Toots during *Peter Pan*, 1959
As Peter, 1950
With Richard Todd in *An Ideal Husband*, 1965
With John Stone in *And Suddenly It's Spring*, 1959 (*Cornell Lucas*)
With John Stone in *Justice*, 1973 (*Yorkshire Television/The Times*)
In *Justice is a Woman*, 1969 (*Yorkshire Television/The Times*)
In *The Slipper and the Rose*, 1976 (*Paradine/National Film Archive*)
Outside Buckingham Palace, 1981, after receiving the CBE from the Queen (*The Times*)

*A*CKNOWLEDGEMENTS

The idea for this book came, as so often, in an unlikely place at an unexpected moment. Spending a weekend in Ostende, I was browsing through an album of old film star postcards at a market stall and paused at a double page of Margaret Lockwood studies. Suddenly, behind my shoulder, a British voice said: 'Look, love. Margaret Lockwood.' Another voice replied: 'I used to think she was so lovely. I wonder what became of her?'

I knew what had become of her. We both lived in the same town, Kingston upon Thames, and since her retreat from the public eye she had granted me two long interviews, the only ones she has given in recent years, during which she looked back fascinatingly, humorously, sometimes a little sadly, over her life and career. Her autobiography, *Lucky Star*, had been published in 1955 and is long out of print. She told me she had no intention of bringing her memoirs up to date – the prospect of writing was too daunting – and she courteously declined to collaborate in the writing of this book. I knew the combination of misfortunes and sadness which had precipitated her sudden retirement in 1980 and I respected her wish not to share in any probing I might initiate.

The warmth and enthusiasm with which the many who did respond to my questions raked over their memories testify to the regard and affection in which Margaret Lockwood is held.

I am particularly indebted to Miss Patricia Roc, Miss Dulcie Gray, Mr Michael Denison, Mr Dermot Walsh, Mr Griffith Jones and Mr Richard Todd for their trouble and care in making their reminiscences available to me.

The book could not have been attempted without invaluable help from the following:

Mr Felix Barker, Mrs Hazel Bartholomew, Miss Joan Bennett, Miss Chili Bouchier, Mrs Muriel Box (Lady Gardiner), Mr Eric Braun,

Miss Sam Clark, Mr Theo Cowan, Mr Douglas Fairbanks Jr, Mr
Bryan Forbes, Mrs Marlena Frick, Miss Cheryl Goodman, Miss
Phyllis Gordon, Mr Peter Graves (Lord Graves), Mr Hughie Green,
Mr John Hickey, Miss Dorothy Hyson (Lady Quayle), Miss Morag
Kennedy, Mrs Vee Lyons, Mr Bob Morgan, Miss Lisa Rohumma,
Mr Royce Ryton, Sir Peter Saunders, Miss Denise Silvester-Carr, Mr
Jim Simpson, Miss Carolyn Sloan, Miss May N. Stone, Mr Michael
Thornton, Miss Anna Tims, Mr Oliver Tims, Miss Christine Wheeler,
Mr Charles Wilson, Miss Googie Withers, Miss Dorothy Wooder and
Miss Joyce Wright.

My special thanks must go to Miss Margaret Mitchell of New
Malden Library who has been indefatigable in tracking down valuable
source books, many of them rare and a challenge to locate; and to
the unfailingly helpful staffs of Kingston upon Thames Central
Library, the Local Studies Room of Richmond-upon-Thames Library,
Upper Norwood Library, the British Film Institute Library, the India
Office Library, Mr Jonathan Franklin of the British Architectural
Library, the Theatre Museum Archives and Miss Dorothy L. Swerd-
love of the Billy Rose Theatre Collection at the New York Public
Library.

Finally, my sincere gratitude to Mrs Gill Rowley for her confidence
in initiating the book; to my agent Mrs Carolyn Whitaker for her
encouragement and practical advice; and to Miss Gill Gibbins whose
patience, enthusiasm and consummate skills as my editor have been
an unfailing source of strength through the good writing times and
the bad.

$\mathscr{P}$ROLOGUE

Once she callously murdered her best friend; once she poisoned her husbands; and once she was a wicked lady.

In a career of 45 films, which took her to the peak of stardom and enthroned her as Britain's queen of cinema, Margaret Lockwood was 'wicked' in only three of them, so it is a matter of mild annoyance to her that she is best remembered as *The Wicked Lady*. 'I wear it round my neck like a label,' she has said. Only once afterwards, in *Bedelia*, did she ever play this type of character again.

The Wicked Lady was an inexpensively made, populist exercise in escapism for a war-weary audience, its script banal, its production unimaginative. It was not even conspicuously well acted. What set it apart from all other previous British films were Margaret Lockwood's character and performance. They came as a revelation, both of the star herself and of the audacity of which a British actress could show herself capable.

No woman before Margaret Lockwood had ever dared to project on film a spirit of such wanton sexuality or displayed such ruthless independence of will and action. The impact was all the more potent for being embodied in an actress whose screen personality was largely identified with the genteel, demure, anodyne virtues of an idealised, very English type of womanhood.

Margaret Lockwood had been a major star for seven years before *The Wicked Lady* immortalised her as Britain's all-time favourite screen actress. True, she had dabbled gingerly in villainy, first as an unprincipled hussy in *The Stars Look Down* and later as the murderous, though marginally sympathetic mistress of *The Man in Grey*. But to her as much as to her fans, those roles had seemed wayward castings against type. However successful she was in them, her popularity was founded on playing 'nice girls'. *The Wicked Lady* transformed that image at a stroke and imposed on her the one she will carry, albeit reluctantly, into the history of British cinema.

Her claim to a place in that history is of far greater significance than that one role, however, but it is seldom given its rightful recognition.

Margaret Lockwood was effectively Britain's first custom-tailored film star, her career an almost exact parallel of the rise and decline of the cinema's golden age.

From her first working day on a studio stage at the age of eighteen, when Chance plucked her out of a non-speaking, walk-on part to play the second female lead in *Lorna Doone*, she never needed to bid or jostle for attention. The young Margaret Lockwood was different. She was noticed. At a time when the majority of aspiring, even established, young actresses making their names on stage or screen tended to be 'bright young things', Margaret's air of quiet dignity, a quality of stillness and discipline in her, a professionalism beyond her years and a steely capacity to learn and work hard, marked her out as a refreshingly 'different' personality. So did her speaking voice, innocent of the affectations drilled into novice actresses by the stage schools of those times.

She arrived in the British film business at precisely the right moment, when it was starting to take itself more seriously, attracting investment and encouraging important new talent. An apprentice Carol Reed, poised to launch himself as a director, was the first to divine her special quality on the set of *Lorna Doone* and their subsequent association through seven films laid the foundations of her stardom. Less apparent and well-known was the decision of Edward Black, executive producer of Gainsborough Pictures, to create in the 1930s a star system to rival Hollywood's. Having formulated a policy, he scoured the studios for potential stars. Margaret was the first he signed to a long-term contract; the second was Michael Redgrave.

With such films as *Bank Holiday*, *The Lady Vanishes* and *The Stars Look Down*, she was already by the end of the 1930s the pre-eminent young actress in British films. Hollywood confirmed Black's instinct by borrowing her for two films. Had war not intervened, she might well have stayed there.

What, then, was Margaret Lockwood's special quality? She was never a great actress; few of her films gave her the scope to be, at least until the final years of her screen career. She was reserved and unadventurous and her private life, what little of it she chose to reveal, was totally lacking in the glamour and titillation expected of her Hollywood counterparts. Yet her fans adored her with an adulation never accorded any other British film star before or since. Her personal appearance tours round the country at the height of her popularity were on the scale of royal progresses.

Theo Cowan, an intimate qualified to judge both professionally and personally, has analysed her appeal as 'an aggressive ordinariness. She represented the "possible dream" to thousands of women who could look at her and say to themselves "That could have been me." '

When her film career declined, Margaret Lockwood's work for stage and television brought out something of the serious dramatic talent which the cinema had failed so lamentably to exploit, but her innate caution still restricted her choice and range of parts. Thus, to an extent, she created her own disappointments and lost opportunities. Her career could have been even more illustrious than it was had she not hesitated again and again to take on roles that broke away from the safe, trodden path, from the guarded, unfulfilled characters she frequently portrayed.

For the reasons, you must look deep behind the public face and seek not Margaret Lockwood, the actress, but Margaret Lockwood, the woman, whom happiness so often eluded, whose self-doubt confined her talent and who from childhood sacrificed so much to her need for affection and approval.

PART ONE

ℐNDIA

In the noonday of imperial India three daughters of the Raj were born. Nature endowed each of them with the promise of uncommon beauty. Destiny ordained that each would become an actress, each a great star of the cinema.

Estelle Merle O'Brien Thompson was born in 1911 to a Eurasian mother and a British engineer father. Her early life was spent in reduced circumstances in Bombay and Calcutta. She would change her name to Merle Oberon. In 1913 Vivian Mary Hartley made her debut in the shadow of Mount Everest amid the cool, restorative foothills of Darljeeling, the favourite retreat of the memsahibs of Calcutta where her father was a businessman. She would know fame as Vivien Leigh. The trio was completed in September 1916 when the heat of Karachi was at its sultriest, with the birth of a daughter to an expatriate railway official and his Scottish wife. This child, too, would consider changing her name when a public career beckoned. But dissimulation was alien to her character. She rejected the passing whim of 'masquerade' and became known to the world by her rightful name: Margaret Lockwood.

Lockwood is a sturdy Yorkshire name, immortalised by Emily Brontë in the greatest of all Yorkshire novels, *Wuthering Heights*, but by the time Margaret was born to it her branch of the clan had long since abandoned its territorial seedbed. Keeping the family name, though, was a decision which characterised her realistic, unpretentious sense of identity.

In the male line, the christian name of Francis traditionally recurred in each new generation. So, with less frequency, did the name Day, retrieved at intervals as a secondary forename for both male and female descendants. Margaret's grandfather, Francis Day Lockwood, had qualified as an architect, and moved from South Yorkshire to settle in London. By the time the nineteenth century was moving into its last quarter the Lockwoods were professional, prosperous and securely middle class. Success in business had ensured that succeeding generations would be well educated and fitted for the professions.

Francis was 27 and living in lodgings in Keppel Street, Bloomsbury, just behind the British Museum, when he married Sarah Maria Elizabeth Miller, daughter of a private gentleman, at the nearby parish church of St George in February 1879. His bride was just nineteen and gave as her residence at the time of marriage the same Keppel Street address, a common enough subterfuge in Victorian times to disguise elopement or absence of parental approval or to discourage unwelcome curiosity about a person's true circumstances. The accommodation was undoubtedly a temporary arrangement. Francis had already made provision for a marital home in a more congenial rural setting ten miles from central London at Richmond, taking a lease on No. 2 Heron Court. It was an impressive address, a Georgian enclave in the heart of fashionable Richmond overlooking the Thames, for the past century a favoured retreat for the *haut ton* of London as well as for artists. It was a curious coincidence, in the light of the Lockwood family's attachment to the name of Day, as well as the far-flung direction in which Francis's first-born's future was to lie, that one of the first occupants of Heron Court in the late eighteenth century had been Sir John Day, a judge advocate of Bengal. Half a century before, Lady Hamilton had taken one of the houses in the Court, living there with her daughter by Nelson at the nadir of her fortunes 'amid alarmingly mounting debts' while urging the government to honour Nelson's wish to leave her as 'a bequest to the nation'. Other notable residents had included Sir Henry Lytton Bulwer – brother of the author of *The Last Days of Pompeii*. When the Lockwoods had moved on, No. 2 became the home for many years of General Sir Harry Prendergast, one of the first holders of the Victoria Cross, awarded to him for gallantry in the Indian Mutiny.

Francis's bride was pregnant and on 28 September 1879, not quite seven months after her marriage, Sarah gave birth to a son. For the first weeks of his life the boy was nameless. No doubt it was parental indecision or disagreement over suitable names which caused Francis to delay registering his son's birth for a month and a day. Even then, the space for the child's name was left blank, the names Henry Francis being added some time later to the birth certificate.

The Lockwoods lived at Heron Court for less than a year. Francis Day, now practising in Richmond, moved his family to a newly built house, which he called Chartreuse, on Mount Ararat Road in an area of Richmond where solid Victorian houses were rapidly expanding the town for the solid Victorian business class. Again, they didn't stay long. A year later Chartreuse had a new owner and from that time Francis Day Lockwood retreated into obscurity.

In later life young Henry would look back on an unhappy boyhood, claiming he was orphaned at an early age and brought up by an uncle. Both statements exaggerated the truth, but of his youthful unhappiness there can be little doubt. Before she was out of her twenties, his mother had become a chronic alcoholic and it was drink which caused her tragically early death in April 1893, at the age of 32. Sarah was then living at 81 Manor Street, Chelsea but there is no evidence that her husband was with her. Her death from 'chronic alcoholism, cirrhosis of the liver, alcoholic neuritis and asthma' testifies to her wretched condition. The registrar was notified by one M. Pope also of 81 Manor Street, present at the death.

Henry was thirteen when his mother died. Seven years later, when he himself married for the first time, his father appears still to have been alive but was described on the marriage certificate as a 'colonial official'. Service in the empire was one of the most fruitful openings available for professional men, and an architect would have been able to command a very worthwhile livelihood in one of the dominions or colonies. Perhaps a child, left motherless at school in England, his wardship entrusted, however informally, to a relative, might be forgiven for regarding himself as technically 'orphaned'.

The only evidence that Henry Francis passed the rest of his minority in the guardianship of an uncle is his own hearsay. The 'uncle' – in fact, a cousin of the boy's father – was Sir Frank Lockwood, one of the most eminent and successful barristers of his time. His father, Charles Day Lockwood, had been a stone quarrier at Levitt Hagg, near Doncaster in Yorkshire, before moving to Manchester and establishing himself with conspicuous success in business. He educated his son at the exclusive Manchester Grammar School and at Gonville and Caius, Cambridge. Called to the Bar in 1872, Frank rapidly gained a reputation as a crowd-drawing counsel with his extrovert personality and highly theatrical performances in the courtroom. A few weeks before his cousin Francis Day's marriage in 1879 he defended – unsuccessfully – the murderer Charles Peace in one of England's most famous criminal trials at Sheffield Assizes. Shortly afterwards he took silk, was appointed Recorder of Sheffield and elected Liberal MP for

York, where a window in the Minster commemorates him. Multi-talented, Frank was also a skilled draughtsman and his courtroom sketches of judges, witnesses and litigants won him a sideline market in journalism, not least in *Punch* to which, for a time, he was a well-known contributor. His career as both lawyer and politician was crowned by the office of Solicitor-General in the governments of Lord Rosebery and Lord Salisbury during the late 1890s.

Frank's theatrical flair wasn't confined to the courtroom. Tall, powerfully built and blessed with a commanding presence and resonant voice, he enjoyed taking part in amateur dramatic performances, an inclination which made him a prominent West End first-nighter. He counted many illustrious theatrical names among his friends and, according to his obituary in *The Times*, 'might also have been eminent as an actor. Indeed, in his way he was a finished actor . . . declaiming with a force and finish which the greatest of our actors might envy.' When Margaret Lockwood began attracting notice as an actress, publicists would cite this as a family precedent for her talent, sometimes going so far as to bend her genealogy and transform Frank rather than Francis into her grandfather.

Margaret herself claimed in her autobiography, published in 1955, that it was Sir Frank's disapproval of her father's hankering to go on the stage that led him to pack Henry Francis off to India 'to make for himself a more established and less fanciful career'. She had been duped by family legend. Sir Frank died suddenly following a severe bout of influenza in December 1897, at the age of 51. Henry was still in London, a mere stripling of eighteen, with no thought of sailing to India for at least another four years.

If Sir Frank had indeed 'brought up' the boy or in any capacity acted as his guardian, there would appear to have been an estrangement between them. Henry did not attend Sir Frank's funeral, at which the mourners included Arthur Wing Pinero, the leading playwright of the day, and the actor-manager Herbert Beerbohm Tree, nor was mention made of Henry in his 'uncle's' will – he left an estate valued at what was, for those days, a respectable fortune of £31,500, including a Kensington house in fashionable Lennox Gardens and a country seat, Cloughton Hall, complete with grouse moor, near Scarborough in Yorkshire.

Henry Francis Lockwood came of age in September 1900. Two months after his 21st birthday he was married at Kensington Registry

Office to Jessie Ramsey, the 21-year-old daughter of a manufacturing chemist with a well-to-do address in Beauchamp Place, Kensington.

Henry, now living at Lee in south-east London, gave his occupation as 'clerk'. Perhaps, with his father posted overseas, as seems likely, Henry had decided to wait for his coming-of-age before marrying, so that he wouldn't need to obtain parental consent as the law required. Certainly it was no runaway match: the bride's father was present at the ceremony and acted as a witness. But the marriage was destined to be short-lived.

What happened remains a mystery. Jessie simply disappeared from the records, whether by death, divorce or annulment isn't documented, either in England or in India where, soon afterwards, Henry arrived. By 1905 he was firmly enough established to be registered in the official directories of the Raj.

Like so many fellow-expatriates without specific qualifications seeking wider horizons and more promising opportunities in the sub-continent, he had found work with the state railways, concentrating from the start on an administrative career. His first job was with the Southern Mahratta Railway as acting district traffic superintendent at Bellary, the chief military garrison of south India, 300 miles from Madras, on the Deccan plain. If Sir Frank Lockwood had indeed voiced ambitions for 'a more established and less fanciful career' for Henry they were about to be realised. Over the next ten years the young man travelled the length and breadth of the sub-continent in short-stay posts at key rail centres, indicating a steady if not spectacular progress in responsibility and status.

Henry's second wife made her appearance in 1908, a year after he had moved to the East Bengal State Railway as an assistant traffic superintendent. Barrackpore, on the east bank of the great Hooghly river, fifteen miles north of Calcutta, was an important railhead, the point at which the tracks out of Calcutta fanned away across the northern and eastern parts of India. It was a pleasant, gracious settlement, a haven for the British from Calcutta's dirt and din. The Viceroy's summer palace, built a century earlier and surrounded by a magnificent park, was the nerve-centre of social life.

Marie Anne Lockwood, at 40, was eleven years older than Henry and a Roman Catholic. On 5 June 1908 she gave birth to a son who three weeks later was christened Frank Day in the Catholic church of Serampore on the opposite bank of the Hooghly.

Henry was on the move yet again, this time to Gorakhpur, 500 miles north in the United Provinces. Broadening his experience, he had accepted a post in the printing department of another railway company, the Bengal and North Western, but leaving the salubrious air of Barrackpore was a hardship for him and a death sentence for his wife. Gorakhpur was a backward city, remote, mean and unhealthy. Childbirth at her comparatively late age had weakened Marie Anne and the upheaval of moving over a vast distance to a new home within weeks of the birth hardly allowed her time to recuperate. She died on 24 September of heart failure. At the age of 29 Henry was left a widower with a three-month old son. He didn't linger amid the painful memories of Gorakhpur. Within a month he had returned to his former employers, the East Bengal State Railway, as assistant traffic superintendent at Saidpur, 150 miles north of Calcutta and that much closer to a sizeable European community.

In the tightly knit, socially defined culture of the Raj at the zenith of its self-awareness, the difficulties for a young man responsible single-handed for the upbringing of a small child could be intense, problems not so much practical as sociological. There were servants in abundance anywhere in India, an *ayah* to act as surrogate mother and even, if required, a hired wet nurse. But for a European child there were only two options open for ensuring it received the all-important influences of an upbringing in its own society and tradition: sending it 'home' to England into the custody of near-relatives – and there were no female relations close enough for Henry to consider this as a possibility – or remarriage.

On the face of it, Henry's choice of bride for his third marriage in eleven years was an unlikely one. He was favoured with some of the characteristics which had so distinguished his 'uncle' Frank – commanding height (six foot three inches), extrovert personality, a resonant voice and the sort of good looks which draw second glances. There were those, not least his new bride, who considered him 'the best-looking man in the East'.

Margaret Evelyn Waugh was, by the standards of those days, hovering dangerously close to the dreaded condition of 'old maid'. At 29, two years Henry's junior, she was short and plump, with a determined set to her homely features, her hair drawn back severely into a bun. Even more unlikely for a man of Henry's personality, she had a dour nature, lacking in humour, but her credentials as a home-maker were impeccable.

She was the eldest of the eleven children of James Nichol Waugh, a Scots-born serving soldier, and his Irish wife. Her mother, worn out by annual child-bearing, had died at the age of 30 just after the birth of her last baby, and the eleven-year-old Margaret Evelyn had assumed the role of 'little mother' to the large family. Shortly afterwards James Waugh was posted to India, taking his children with him. By the time she met Henry Francis Lockwood, therefore, Margaret Evelyn was a veteran expatriate with only hazy childhood memories of 'home'. She had qualified as a nurse and was working in Calcutta when she was introduced to the good-looking widower from up-country. They were married on 8 April 1911 at St Andrew's Church of Scotland in Calcutta; having already gone through ceremonies in a registry office and a Roman Catholic church, Henry was content to leave the denominational decision to his bride.

Margaret's upbringing must have conditioned her to the impermanency of a soldier's life. It was just as well. No sooner had she established a routine in her new home at Saidpur than yet another posting took Henry further up-country to the small junction town of Katihar on the western side of Bengal. He had again switched from the East Bengal State Railway to the Bengal and North West Railway and barely a year later completed his transfer of company livery by joining the North West State Railway as traffic officer at Ferozepore.

Marriage had taken Margaret more than a thousand miles away from Calcutta and a world away from the life she had been used to there. Ferozepore in the South Punjab was an outpost of the railway empire but it was, in its small and, for a European, backwater way, a pleasant enough place to settle, with wide, well-paved roads and attractive gardens girding the town's ancient walls. In any case, she had more immediate concerns, coping with a lively four-year-old stepson and, by now, pregnant with her own child. On 12 October 1912 a son was born to the Lockwoods. Three weeks later he was baptised Henry Evelyn Francis. It was perhaps a small augury of the dominance Margaret would exercise over family matters that the boy should be given one of her own christian names. In fact he grew up to be known not as Henry or any variation thereof but as Evelyn, abbreviated for family purposes to Lyn.

Henry Lockwood now began to show signs of settling down. The family stayed at Ferozepore for three years, the longest he had remained in either a job or a home since his arrival in India. Remote as they were from the mainstream of European life, the family must have felt even more distanced from the cataclysmic events that were engulfing Europe and 'home' with the outbreak of war in 1914.

For men like Henry, far removed from the immediate conflict, there were decisions of conscience to be made. Many returned to England to enlist but just as many in vital services were judged to be of equal value to the war effort by remaining at their posts and keeping – in his case literally – the lines of communication running smoothly. As the war progressed India's railways became a crucial factor in the system for transportation of supplies and men to the Middle East and one of India's two most important terminals for that system would be Henry's next destination: in 1916 he applied to join the North Western State Railway and was appointed district traffic superintendent at Karachi. Margaret Evelyn was pregnant again. The family hardly had time to set up yet another home before she gave birth to a daughter. The date was 15 September 1916. In the sultry heat of Karachi Margaret Evelyn Lockwood pondered names as she nursed her baby. There was no doubt, of course, that her own should be passed on. For a second name she looked to her favourite sister. Her only daughter would be Margaret Mary Lockwood.

*E*NGLAND

It would become a cause of some irritation to Margaret Lockwood that reference books would sometimes add five years to her age. Even an institution as meticulous in detail as the National Portrait Gallery in London recorded the year of her birth as 1911 when it issued a postcard of her in 1986 to mark a British film exhibition. It has never been in Margaret Lockwood's character to dissemble about age, however much she may have resented its encroachments in later life, and the truth resides in the records of the Diocese of Lahore for anyone to authenticate. In the week of Christmas 1916, on 20 December, three months after her birth, she was baptised Margaret Mary at Trinity Church, Karachi by the chaplain, the Rev. A. O. G. Maunsell who had also officiated at Lyn's christening in Ferozepore four years previously.

The Italianate Anglican church of the Holy Trinity with its ungainly tower, generally regarded as a local eyesore, was a focal point of the extensive European quarter of Karachi, its large churchyard providing an oasis of green against the boundary of the military cantonment. Close by were the civil lines where Henry Lockwood had been allocated a company bungalow.

In the hierarchical structure of India's colonial administration, railway employees were allotted housing of a size and degree of appointment commensurate with their rank. Karachi, in railway terms, was the most important sub-district after Lahore, the divisional headquarters. Its port made it the busiest railhead on the Indian Ocean after Bombay. It had extensive railway workshops and it controlled one of the most romantic railways in the world, the north-bound track which climbed through the fabled North West Frontier to terminate at Chaman, three miles short of the border with Afghanistan. Henry's job had raised him to a comfortable status. The Lockwoods accordingly merited a medium-rank home, a spacious, airy bungalow set in pleasant gardens which would be impressive by English standards, if not by those of the Raj.

Karachi was a congenial posting. Situated on the great fan of the Indus river delta at the foot of the Pab Mountains, it had a warm, slightly humid climate, its mean average temperature of 80°F tempered by ocean breezes. Its most uncomfortable season, close and oppressive, fell in September and October, its hottest – though rarely more than 85°F – between April and June. The city had developed rapidly since the end of the nineteenth century and was very much a product of the Raj. The native quarters girded the port area and the mangrove swamps to the south; the Europeans laid out their broad avenues and raised their solid Anglo-Indian public buildings on the landward side. The city's eastern extremity was the vast military cantonment – barracks, hospital, parade ground, rifle butts and reservoirs. Beyond stretched the limitless wastes of the great Sind desert.

Margaret's first conscious surroundings were green and shady . For an airing, her *ayah* or her mother would take her to the nearby grounds of Frere Hall, Karachi's civic pride. King George V, as Prince of Wales, had opened the Victorian Gothic building ten years before and unveiled the particularly fine statue of his grandmother Queen Victoria in its grounds. In the other direction lay the racecourse and, to the rear of the civil lines, the golf links and polo ground. Later, when Margaret was walking, there were trips to the 40 tree-shaded acres of the Botanical Gardens on the banks of the Layari where, as a special treat, the children would be allowed to visit the small zoo. Sometimes there would be shopping excursions to the Empress Market beyond Holy Trinity Church and the stores along Elphinstone Street.

Social life for the sizeable expatriate community was solidly structured and varied, though layered according to class demarcations. At its apex the Sind Club was the preserve of the *pukka sahib* and his *memsahib*; for their subordinates, the Karachi Club did duty. Henry, if he chose, could indulge any acting aspirations he may have had with the Amateur Dramatic Club, or air his religious philosophies at the Theosophical Society. Or he could sail, boat or play golf with the appropriate clubs. The social high-water mark of the year was the race meeting at the course just a step down the road from the Lockwood bungalow.

With his extrovert personality, Henry was an eminently clubbable man, popular with his colleagues and friends. His wife, on the other hand, tended to shy away from the social commitment expected of a public official in his position. Essentially a domestic body, she preferred to stay at home, managing her small household, looking after the three children and avoiding the hard-playing, often hard-drinking company of the colonial enclave.

As the Great War entered its third and critical year Karachi's importance as a communications link grew and Henry's responsibilities expanded correspondingly. Supply ships and troop transports berthed continually at Erskine Wharf and James Wharf, fed by greatly increased rail traffic from the interior. Sitting in his office at the City Station, Henry, though far and safely removed from the campaigns in Europe and Mesopotamia, could nevertheless reassure himself that he was 'doing his bit' and making a vital contribution to the war effort. When the hard day was done he would drop into the adjacent North Western Hotel, the city's premier watering hole, for a sundowner before heading home along the McLeod Road, probably to catch up on the latest war news in the final edition of the *Daily Gazette* before dinner.

With their father preoccupied outside the home, inevitably the children's lives began to revolve more and more dependently round their mother who, in any case, was disposed by nature to be a dominant force in family affairs ('decisive' was the kinder word Margaret would use in her autobiography). But admirable though she was in the disciplines of motherhood and housekeeping, she was not a demonstrative or a giving woman. Lyn at the age of six was already developing a self-protective shell of taciturnity – 'the quietest little boy I have ever known', Margaret would recall – and Margaret too quickly acquired a deep-seated shyness which she would never entirely succeed in surmounting. Both children found difficulty in making friends from an early age.

When the war ended in November 1918, Frank, Henry's eleven-year-old elder son, was sent 'home' to England for schooling, a home that was a foreign land to him. But there were other, less overt signs that this ostensibly close-knit family was drifting towards a break-up. Henry's work frequently took him away from home on visits to outlying posts of the North Western Railway empire, and he had begun to drink fairly heavily. Margaret Evelyn, meanwhile, helped out the nursing staff at the military hospital on a part-time basis. Lyn was now approaching the age at which his future education must also be given serious consideration. The discussions drifted on through 1919, often heated, gradually strengthening Margaret Evelyn's conviction that the interests of the children – and herself – must take precedence over Henry. In the case of Margaret, not yet of kindergarten age by the standards of those times, much less eligible for prep school, Margaret Evelyn argued that her health would thrive better in an English climate even though it had never given cause for concern.

It was a common enough practice for colonial parents to dispatch their children to school in England, indeed certain boarding schools had founded their reputations and profitability on the traffic. Nor was it unusual for a mother to accompany the children over and be on hand while they adjusted to the upheaval. Almost as common, though not openly admitted, was the practice for such mothers, once they had set foot back in England, not to return to their colonial homes. With lifestyles – or even husbands – not always to their liking, maternal responsibility offered a convenient, socially acceptable escape route from marriage.

That was Margaret Evelyn's decision. It must have been a particularly difficult one for her to make. Unlike so many wives of her class, she was virtually a product of India. It had been her home for the greater part of her life and now, at 38 and approaching her difficult middle years, she was consciously rejecting all that was familiar and secure to return to a land of which she had only the sketchiest memories and with which she no longer had any active links. She was leaving behind in India her two sisters, the only members of the extended Waugh family with whom she had stayed in touch.

In the spring of 1920 the Lockwoods sailed for England. By chance, at the same time another family set sail on an identical mission. Once it was accomplished Vivien Leigh's mother returned to India with her husband. Margaret Lockwood's mother didn't.

Margaret, at three-and-a-half, was the model of a healthy, well-developed little girl, scarcely needing the benefits of a temperate climate. Her features were already hinting at beauty to come. Photographs capture a contemplative look in her eyes beneath dark, well-defined brows; her abundant hair, dark and unusually thick, is cut tidily and fashionably in a bob style with a fringe; she seems a decorous, amiable child, alert and assured. She was, however, small for her age. It was Lyn who had inherited their father's imposing height and Margaret's lack of inches would prove a cause for some concern until she was well into her teens.

Henry arranged for Lyn to enter the junior school of Dulwich College in South London, a prestigious public school founded by the Elizabethan actor Edward Alleyn, a contemporary of Shakespeare and principal rival of the Bard's leading player, Richard Burbage. According to legend his foundation of the college was by way of atonement for an intemperate life.

Ahead of the Lockwoods, when they came ashore, stretched a whole English summer before the new school year commenced – time for the children to acclimatise themselves to their new environment. They went first to the Isle of Wight where Henry rented a house for a traditional seaside holiday and it was there, at Shanklin, that the most momentous event so far in Margaret's short life occurred. She was taken to the cinema for the first time.

The film was an early Charlie Chaplin, the period of *Shoulder Arms* and *Sunnyside*. The three-year-old girl was enthralled: 'That first film began an interest in the cinema that has never flagged.' The trademark Chaplin walk fascinated her and for days afterwards she practised incessantly until she was satisfied she had perfected it.

England must have seemed as strange and novel to Margaret Evelyn as it did to her children and the prospect of adjusting to their new life alone, without Henry to turn to, daunting. However, she betrayed no sign of alarm, addressing herself to the challenge of finding a permanent home with the practicality and acumen that were always her strongest suit. The neighbourhood of Dulwich College seemed the most obvious place, so it was there that she began house-hunting.

The Lockwoods, though not wealthy, were financially comfortable. Still, with two homes half the world apart to maintain now, school fees to be found for the boys and more in prospect for Margaret's education, money needed to be husbanded. All Margaret Evelyn's instincts had been drilled in economy and in any case she couldn't tolerate extravagance. She took a lease on a maisonette in Upper Norwood.

Lunham Road was – and still is – a peaceful side road in an area established in the 1870s as London's newly affluent merchant class moved further out along the new railway routes. It was an attractive area which had caught the artist's eye of the French impressionist, Camille Pissarro in the 1880s. He lived for a time in a house on Westow Hill, which later developed into Upper Norwood's main shopping street. In 1920 Upper Norwood still retained something of its semi-rural 'village' character, perched on the southern heights which commanded panoramic views across the City of London, as did the back windows of No. 2 Lunham Road, a semi-detached Victorian house of honey-coloured brick, three storeys high above a basement area and with a steeply sloping garden at the rear.

Margaret Evelyn had chosen a perfect location for children to thrive in. The uplands air was fresh and invigorating. There was a quiet charm about these eminently respectable streets and roads, with ample open space and wooded slopes for them to play on. And best of all, perhaps, for young adventurers there was the Crystal Palace in its great park dominating the whole neighbourhood.

Built in London's Hyde Park for the Great Exhibition of 1851, the vast glass structure, one of the architectural marvels of the age, had been dismantled the following year and re-sited at Sydenham as a 'Versailles' of music and culture, surrounded by gardens to rival those of Louis XIV. For the second half of the nineteenth century it had been a fashionable venue but it was dilapidated now after years of decline and use during the First World War as a landlocked naval station officially re-named HMS Victory VI. All but a trace of its splendid terraces and landscaping had been obliterated.

Patched up and re-opened to the public the same year the Lockwoods came to live in its shadow, the palace's fairy-tale reputation was now a thing of the past. But to young imaginations like Lyn's and Margaret's it still provided a world of make-believe and magic on their doorstep. The boating lake remained intact and there was still a small zoo, an amusement park and a maze. Exhibitions and shows were held and a circus came every New Year. But most enticing of all for the Lockwood children, its old skating rink had been converted into a cinema.

That first summer of their new life was drawing to a close when Henry said his farewells and set sail back to India. He was given promotion again, so the Karachi years were over too. His new post took him to Lahore, headquarters of the North Western system, as deputy traffic manager. By the time his next long leave brought him back into the family circle, Margaret, coming up to her eighth birthday, had developed her own individuality, vivacious within the privacy of home but, to outsiders, reserved and not quick to make friends.

Under her mother's restrictive influence Margaret was beginning to acquire an unconscious self-sufficiency which enabled her to pass long hours on her own, content with solitary thoughts and pastimes. The closest contact she forged in those early years was with a neighbour in the flat below. Mrs Leigh Bennett, a kindly, perceptive woman, was able to penetrate the little girl's natural reserve and respond to the lively, questioning spirit that lay behind it. Margaret possibly sensed in her the reciprocal interest and generosity of expression which her own mother found so difficult to show. Soon she was in the habit of visiting Mrs Leigh Bennett every day, encouraged to chatter about her interests and the happenings of her day. She would recite poems she had learned at school, act out scenes she had devised herself, recount and comment on the Bible stories she'd heard at Christ Church Sunday School at the end of the road. Gradually Mrs Leigh Bennett discerned an unusually realistic attitude in a girl so young, seemingly at odds with the talents latent in her, with the performer beginning to emerge.

Highland Road intersected with Lunham Road opposite the gate to No. 2 and soon Margaret Evelyn found more spacious accommodation there in a house a few yards further up the hill, at 18A. Highland Road would be Margaret's address until she was 21 and a rising star of British films, but she never forgot 'the lady downstairs'. Even at the height of her fame she kept up a tradition when shooting ended on a new picture of inviting Mrs Leigh Bennett over to the studio to see a rough cut and have lunch. 'She does not appear to notice she has become famous,' Mrs Leigh Bennett once remarked. 'In fact she behaves exactly as she did when she was unknown.'

When Henry next set eyes on his daughter he must have felt pleased with the way she had developed. Though small for her age – she wouldn't start filling out until she was sixteen – she had grown into a strikingly pretty girl, her chiselled features crowned by a swirl of dark hair which she wore in plaits. She had poise, good humour and a becoming shyness. Her elocution was excellent, her bearing restrained. She was, in short, a credit to her mother's upbringing. Only one facet of her personality possibly gave him cause for mild reproof: she had an insatiable interest in the cinema.

Ironically, it was Margaret Evelyn who had connived at this and encouraged her. Puritanical though she could be, she, too, had developed a passion for the movies, going to the cinema as often as three or four times a week and only too willing to take the children along when she judged a film to be suitable for them. Margaret later recalled: 'At that time, when the cinema was so new to the public, we were regarded as something between freaks and Bohemians in going to the pictures so often. Somehow it wasn't "quite done" and my mother was considered quite odd.' This despite the fact that in 1916 Queen Alexandra, the queen mother, had bestowed the royal seal of respectability on the newly popular moving pictures by 'commanding' the first screening of a feature-length film, a production by the British pioneer film-maker Cecil Hepworth called *Comin' Through the Rye*.

The movies were, in fact, the only outlet Margaret Evelyn had from the self-imposed restrictions of her domestic regime. Life was centred on the children. She had no social circle of her own. So, through those impressionable early years, Margaret was immersed in the shadowplay of the cinema. It coloured the real world and inspired her own dream world. The stars were her exemplars. She spent countless hours re-enacting scenes and stories she had seen on the screen, casting her closest schoolfriends and a generally uncomplaining Lyn in supporting roles, reserving the star performance for herself. The fantasies intruded into her school hours at nearby Belvedere College – she was frequently in trouble for inattention – but they served her well when it came to school plays and concerts: Margaret and her principal acting accomplice, a girl called Varna Julier, were invariably the star turn together.

Varna, daughter of a neighbour in Highland Road, was virtually Margaret's only close friend. Margaret Evelyn allowed her to bring other little girls home to join in her 'performances' but, through a stubborn and misguided refusal to observe the social niceties of those times, effectively prevented Margaret from forming wider friendships. She would agree to Margaret asking some girl or other round to tea but adamantly refused to write the expected invitation note to the child's mother. The result was that Margaret's verbal invitations were more often than not ignored. 'I had a woebegone time making friends,' she recalled, 'Nobody seemed to want to play with me, I was so dreadfully shy. Somehow I didn't "belong".'

Margaret Evelyn made no efforts to get to know other mothers in her daughter's school circle – and what little these ladies knew of the Lockwoods didn't entirely meet with their approval. 'They thought my mother quite wrong in taking me and Lyn to the cinema so often, "filling our heads with rubbish".' So Margaret, captive in her innate shyness and her mother's isolationism, was conditioned to be self-reliant, uneasy with outsiders and inhibited about striking up relationships. It was a personality flaw that would bedevil her entire life, professional as well as private, and subconsciously leave its mark on the course of her career. Yet the drawback had a positive side. While she seldom allowed working relationships with colleagues to develop into close friendships, and, indeed, unwittingly incurred hostility in some who regarded her as stand-offish, it did help form her single-minded approach to work, earning her the reputation of 'a true professional'.

EXTRACURRICULAR ACTIVITIES

During Henry's leave in 1924 Margaret's future schooling was decided and a few days after her eighth birthday in September she entered the preparatory wing of Sydenham High School, a public day school for girls considered then, as now, among the best of its kind in south-east London. It was conveniently close to home, a ten-minute bus ride away on the northern edge of the Crystal Palace park.

Margaret's record at Sydenham High School was not auspicious. Apart from reading and elocution, at both of which she excelled, she had little interest in or disposition for the general curriculum, and because of her diminutive stature she was a non-starter at sports. Extra-mural activities increasingly claimed her attention and intruded on her school work; this, surprisingly, with her mother's connivance. She encouraged Margaret in her piano lessons with Miss Margaret Overbury, a teacher living two roads away with a studio above the music shop in Upper Norwood's main street, Westow Hill. She approved of Margaret's dedication to elocution lessons, conceding that she 'had a flair for this sort of thing'. Yet she was meagre in her praises for any manifestation of ability in her daughter.

Margaret meantime added dancing to her syllabus and took to informing any classmates who would listen: 'I'm going to be a famous actress one day, you see.' Nevertheless drama had not, at this stage, entered her dreams or calculations. For all her embryonic talent for impersonation and creating roles, she saw herself primarily as a dancer, her stage metier in musical comedy, an ambition reinforced by occasional theatre visits to the local music hall, the Lewisham Hippodrome, where Jack Buchanan, in particular, was one of the stars who fired her aspirations, and Evelyn Laye also became an idol.

In time growing success in her 'performing' studies had an effect on her confidence. She began to develop a more outgoing personality

20

and a wider circle of friends. She soon became the ring-leader of her class, acquiring the authoritative veneer with which she would protect herself as actress and star. Sunday School at Christ Church had primed her well in religious studies and for a spell she had gone through a phase of wanting to become a missionary. But the allure of show business had burned too deep into her psyche. She was a natural performer. She knew it, and so did Margaret Evelyn.

It was Margaret Evelyn who initiated the first tentative step her daughter took towards a professional career. Discovering that the Italia Conti School, one of London's most prestigious theatrical academies, included dancing in its curriculum, she decided that Margaret should be enrolled. Twice a week mother and daughter travelled to Holborn. Margaret made steady progress and when the legendary Miss Conti herself took to dropping in on classes, the small, dedicated, dark-haired girl immediately caught her eye. She was scouting potential fairies for a charity production of *A Midsummer Night's Dream* which was to have two performances at the Holborn Empire, a famous London music-hall. Margaret was one of the girls she picked.

The experience of appearing in an authentic theatre was intoxicating. All Margaret's instincts were gratified. Now she was certain where her future lay. But the euphoria was short-lived. Margaret stayed only one term at the school before she was obliged to drop out, for a reason as trivial as it was humiliating. The twice-weekly journeys by train and bus made her travel-sick. It was a congenital disorder which would cause her discomfort throughout her life and, to some degree, restrict her career potential. So . . . back to the parochial routine of Upper Norwood and, as a substitute for the lustre of the Italia Conti cachet, enrolment at the local Haddon School of Dancing.

The die, however, had been cast and Margaret felt self-confident enough to start taking initiatives of her own. Hearing of a ballroom dancing competition to be held at the Crystal Palace, she persuaded a fellow pupil at the Haddon School to partner her and entered for no fewer than four classes – the quickstep, slow foxtrot, foxtrot and waltz. They won all four and returned home in triumph with four silver medals.

Important though dancing was to her, it didn't eliminate her obsession with the cinema, which reached its apogee when the Hollywood silent version of *Peter Pan* arrived at the Crystal Palace cinema. Somehow she contrived to see it every night for a week and its star Betty Bronson became her idol. The name of the director, Herbert

21

Brenon, meant nothing to her but if she had been able to foretell her future she might have diverted some of her attention from Miss Bronson to his technique. Within a few years he would be directing one of her first movies.

Margaret had just turned thirteen in the winter of 1929 when Miss Grace Cone, who presided over the respected Cone School of Dancing in London's West End, sent out a call to the Haddon School for pupils with promise to audition as fairies for a pantomime production of *Babes in the Wood*.

Ten girls were selected and Margaret was one of them. Without too much difficulty, her mother was persuaded to let her compete but insisted on accompanying her to the audition. The challenge was a microcosmic illustration of the duality in Margaret's temperament: innate shyness yielding to determination, even assertiveness, in matters of ambition. She went into her dance and was picked. Nobody seemed aware of a muted undercurrent of crisis which was preoccupying the formidable Miss Cone. When, some time later, she asked the chosen few if any of them could sing, Margaret's hand was the first to shoot up. She was heard, then asked to speak a few lines. A *sotto voce* consultation between Miss Cone and her aides heightened the mystery. Then Miss Cone thrust a script into Margaret Evelyn's hands with the peremptory order: 'We'd like her to try to learn this tonight.'

It was a leading role, the part of the girl babe. The child who had already been cast for it had contracted measles.

Margaret travelled back to Upper Norwood on a cloud. Even Margaret Evelyn kept repeating excitedly: 'This is your big chance.' There was little sleep that night. By morning Margaret, always a quick learner, was word-perfect.

The production was to be in one of the West End's leading theatres, the Scala, a stage on which, twenty years later, Margaret would create her most enduring theatrical memory – as Peter Pan. For now, though, a suitable stage name had to be invented. In those days, when the right 'name' was an essential ingredient in projecting 'image' and making instant contact with the public, Margaret Lockwood was not even a contender: too prosaic, too staid, too long. The starting point for a choice was the certainty that she was going to be a song-and-dance artiste. Several permutations were tried and discarded. Finally, incorporating one of the family names and corrupting her own, she settled on Margie Day. It was a short-lived pseudonym yet oddly the name persisted throughout her life, with biographical data frequently listing her 'real name' as Margaret Day.

As rehearsals progressed Margaret's confidence and self-regard increased. In the final run-up to opening night she posed in costume for publicity photographs. She stood on the pavement outside the theatre entrance, gazing entranced at her own likeness in the show-cases. When the programmes were delivered she read, in a euphoria of achievement, her new name in print for the first time. A star by the name of Margie Day seemed certain to be born.

The day of the first performance arrived. She reported early to the stage door. And so, three hours before the curtain was due to go up, did the girl she had replaced, miraculously restored to health and fully rehearsed. Margie Day, crushed by disappointment, found herself relegated to the ranks of fairies at a fee of 30 shillings a week, but she was nothing if not resilient. Her conditioning of self-containment and instinctive sense of dignity carried her through.

'Nobody will ever know how terribly upset I was,' she wrote many years later. 'That was my first taste of the misery of disappointment, and I thought the world a very cruel place.' Though she was in no mind to realise it at the time, the episode had immense repercussions on her future: in recompense she was taken on as a pupil of the Cone School.

Long after she had become a star, the school's principal left one of the most graphic memoirs of Margaret at this turning point in her life.

Her face was pretty and petite with very large expressive eyes and framed by long dark hair. As a child she had a nice little figure, well proportioned and with long arms and legs. Although delicate, she had a sturdy look of health about her.

She was extremely promising from the start and I recollect telling her mother that I believed she would go to the top. In fact, I even forecast that she would be at her best in films.

She had a strong, clear-cut, dynamic personality which clearly would not be satisfied with anything but success. Although she also gave promise as a dancer, it was as a dramatic actress that I visualised her future. She was fundamentally good to teach, provided she fully understood what was required of her and what she was doing.

She wanted to know the reason behind everything – the mark

23

of a discerning artiste – but if she wasn't interested then she just would not bother to try.

The Cone School provided an all-round training in stage-craft but it was on singing and dancing that Margaret concentrated. Gradually she was eased into public appearances, with Miss Cone recommending her for minor engagements at small private functions – smoking concerts or Masonic ladies' evenings – which entailed journeys to far-flung venues all over London. Combined with her regular school work, it was a gruelling routine for a thirteen-year-old who suffered from travel sickness but curiously she seemed to thrive on it.

Margaret Evelyn always accompanied her, an apparent support always illogically and confusingly contradicted by her outward attitude. While appearing to encourage, even to connive at, the thrust of Margaret's vocation, she would damn any manifestations of it with faint praise if, indeed, she praised at all.

At Sydenham High School Margaret's merely average academic performance inevitably suffered and towards the end of the summer term in 1929 the headmistress summoned her mother, tactfully suggesting that Margaret's – and the school's – interests might be better served if she were withdrawn and placed full-time in stage school. Margaret Evelyn's response was surprisingly submissive. She agreed.

So, as winter approached, Margaret's formal schooling was terminated at the age of fourteen and she became a full-time pupil at the Cone School, travelling each day up to Grosvenor Street, off Oxford Street in the heart of London, where the syncopations of tap-dancing and declamations of Shakespeare punctuated the more commonplace rituals of the three Rs. She was surpassingly content.

There were major changes, too, at home in Highland Road. Margaret Evelyn's two favourite sisters, Mary and Kitty, with Kitty's daughter Betty, had followed her 'home' from India and moved into No. 30. Kitty had a tragically early death, leaving young Betty to be brought up by her two aunts. Mary was Margaret Evelyn's companion for the next decade, a confidante for Margaret and a buffer in the often tense, repressed relationship between mother and daughter.

Grace Cone – Miss Gracie to all her staff and students – was, as she indicated in her memoir, quick to recognise Margaret's special abilities and surreptitiously groomed her by lining up auditions. Gradually, but according to a prescribed strategy, Margaret was acquiring professional experience in cabaret and concert work which was crowned by her selection for appearances in tea-time shows at the smart Regent Street store, Dickins and Jones, and in one of the West End's most sophisticated night clubs, the Café de Paris. By now Margaret Evelyn had more or less subordinated her daily routine to the demands of Margaret's engagements, often chaperoning her every evening of the week and discharging the duty without complaint, if not with whole-hearted enthusiasm.

Henry, now nearing retirement and at the peak of his career as a divisional superintendent, was home on leave again in 1931 and none too pleased at the direction his fifteen-year-old daughter's life was taking, refusing to take 'all this play acting' seriously. In the past he had adopted a fairly indulgent line over it to Margaret herself, treating it as a pastime and something of a joke. Now, realising how consuming a part of her life it had been allowed to become, he switched to stern paternal disapproval, particularly resenting the claims it made on Margaret Evelyn's time while he was on leave.

Strong words were exchanged but, as an absentee father and husband, merely dropping in on his family every four years or so, he was objecting from a weak position. Nevertheless Margaret Evelyn decided that it would be advisable to win him round with practical rather than rhetorical argument. She persuaded him to attend one of Margaret's tea-time performances. His daughter's competence came as a revelation and Margaret Evelyn seized the chance to press her case. With a talent as promising as this, she urged, it was their duty to give Margaret a chance. Henry capitulated.

'If she's happy and makes a success of it, I suppose it will be worth it . . .'

*C*AVALCADE AND *R*ADA

In the summer of 1931 the West End theatrical grapevine was humming with rumours of a new work by Noel Coward, darling of the Shaftesbury Avenue box offices.

Cavalcade was the word on every back-stage tongue, a word obscure at that time but which passed into common usage after Coward chose it for his title. This, according to the talk, was going to be a spectacular in every sense; a vast patriotic canvas chronicling the fortunes of an ordinary British family amid the pageantry of the nation's imperial glory from 1899 to the present day and incorporating Queen Victoria's funeral, the call to arms in two wars, even the Titanic disaster. A cast of hundreds! Forty-three speaking parts, 23 scenes, sets to include a railway station complete with full-scale locomotive, and Trafalgar Square. It would be the most ambitious, technically the most complex production ever staged, and among those hundreds were walk-on parts for a number of children. Miss Gracie sent Margaret, just past her fifteenth birthday, along to audition.

The Master himself presided over the auditions as he would over rehearsals. One of the children he singled out was Margaret, mainly, she assumed, because her physical slightness made her look younger than her years and her long hair gave her a period air. Coward, at one of the four dress rehearsals, uttered the first forbidden swear word Margaret had ever heard. She was shocked, little knowing in her unworldliness that even more shocking words existed and that one of them was soon to be her undoing in the production.

By now Margaret Evelyn had decided that Margaret was old enough to dispense with her chaperoning services. After all, she had got her first professional engagement in a West End production – and the most talked-about production of the season, at that. Each day, as Margaret turned the corner under Christ Church tower and tore down the steep of Gipsy Hill to the station, a panorama of the city

26

lay before her. It must have seemed that London lay at her feet. She had come an unimaginably long way since the days when she'd dragooned Christ Church Sunday School-mates into her dream world of play-acting. Soon she would be making her professional debut on London's grandest, most legendary stage, the Theatre Royal, Drury Lane.

Opening night was 13 October 1931 and the children in the 250-strong cast were allowed to stay for the whole of the long evening so that they could share in the curtain calls. This gigantic anthem to national fervour – some would call it jingoism – climaxed with the entire company on stage singing the National Anthem, the Union Jack glowing massively in the darkness behind. The first-night audience went wild. Curtain after curtain was demanded. The auditorium was a tumult of people cheering, clapping, waving programmes, standing on seats to roar approval. *Cavalcade* made history that night. Even the critics applauded and the public's response, little short of delirious, ensured a long run ahead.

Margaret, standing in a rear rank, straining on tip-toes to catch a glimpse of the excitement, felt its charge lifting her into a euphoria she had never guessed was possible. She felt intoxicated. This was the moment, the fulfilment, towards which all her intuitions had been thrusting her.

Somewhere in that tumult sat Margaret Evelyn. Hardly knowing what she was doing, Margaret raced back to the dressing-room to change and collect her belongings, then down to the stage door where her mother was waiting in the crush.

'Wasn't it wonderful?' Margaret shouted.

Margaret Evelyn's face was stony. 'It was *terrible*,' she snapped.

The cruelty of that moment, the deliberate slap-down in the hearing of so many strangers, would remain with Margaret for the rest of her life. 'Mother embarrassed me terribly that night, as she was always doing,' she recalled bitterly.

Now that she was past the age of fourteen, Margaret was no longer subject to the strict licensing regulations which governed child performers, dictating the number and frequency of their appearances on a professional stage (she had needed a licence for *Babes in the Wood*). The show was giving her an invaluable early lesson in the discipline of nightly performances and self-reliance. She still found difficulty in mixing spontaneously, a reserved presence on the fringe of the company, but quietly, at her own pace, she was developing the confidence

27

and independence which home life had stunted, making the journey to and from the theatre on her own, gaining in assurance, learning to cope with the cut-and-thrust of backstage life. Independence ended, however, once the homeward train reached Gipsy Hill. Unfailingly, Margaret Evelyn would be waiting at the top of the platform stairs.

One evening, backstage at Drury Lane, Margaret got caught up in some high-spirited exchanges among the company youngsters. The girls were giggling over something a boy had said and Margaret had to keep asking what it was. The boy had used a four-letter word. One of the girls whispered it in her ear. It meant nothing to her and she asked the girl to repeat it. This time she heard but was none the wiser. Later, as she bounded up the station steps to her mother, she shouted, 'Mummy, what does "fuck" mean?'

Too late, she realised it meant something she had no business knowing. Rigid with shock, her mother snapped, 'Where did you hear that word?' and, hesitant now, Margaret told her.

They walked up Gipsy Hill in silence. Inside the house Margaret Evelyn immediately sat down and wrote a letter to the Drury Lane management. Without a word she went out again to the post box. When she returned, she spoke for the first time since they'd left the station.

'I've told them you are not going back. You have left for good.'

Margaret's dreams crashed. She pleaded and argued but in vain. She knew how futile it was to try to turn her mother from an implacable decision. She'd never known such heartbreak. So . . . back to the Cone School, bitterly aware that *Cavalcade* was the hit of the season – and a natural question about a word she didn't understand had cost her her role in it.

That night she was ready to believe that she would never appear on a stage again, but in another of her unpredictable about-turns, Margaret Evelyn then discussed the incident sensibly, using it to point a lesson in life. 'We've chosen a life for you that can be a splendid one but it can also be a cheap and sordid one if you let it. Whenever anything like this happens, there's only one answer – walk out. Once you let this career cheapen you, you're finished.' Good advice, common sense, Margaret realised . . . if only Margaret Evelyn didn't react so violently, so uncompromisingly. She longed for some sign of approval.

The summer of 1932 found Margaret drifting. She had left the Cone

School – at fifteen, she'd abandoned schooling altogether – and was keeping ambitions afloat with the cabaret and concert work for which she was in modest demand.

Out shopping together in the West End one day Margaret Evelyn suddenly asked, 'What do you want to do now?'

Margaret knew what she meant. It was a question she had been asking herself for months and the answer came readily: 'Go to RADA.'

The *Cavalcade* experience had sharpened her interest in 'straight acting' and she was now committed to the idea. In the intervening months she had read every book and magazine on the theatre she could lay her hands on, shrewdly assessing the challenges and rewards of drama. Above all, she had deduced that the most practical course she could take would be via the Royal Academy of Dramatic Art.

Again Margaret Evelyn's reaction was unexpected. She not only agreed immediately but set about investigating the procedures for getting in. They were both realistic about the prospects of Margaret being admitted. She had talent but so did an average of three other candidates competing for every vacancy. In a situation like this the positive side of Margaret Evelyn's dominance was a bonus. She expressed no doubts that Margaret would be accepted, bolstering her confidence.

For her audition Margaret chose one of Rosalind's speeches from *As You Like It*. The principal of RADA, Kenneth Barnes, heard her. Dressed in a plain sweater and skirt, with her abundant hair braided into two long plaits, her physique still small and almost child-like, she must have cut an unlikely, un-actressy figure. What impressed Sir Kenneth more was 'the feeling that she was out for business, not just pleasure'.

Somehow she managed to endure a week of suspense, waiting for every postal delivery – and cast down twice a day – before the letter offering her a place arrived.

The Royal Academy of Dramatic Art was a relatively new force in British theatre, but, established for only two years, it had already acquired a reputation for the quality of its students and the excellence of its courses.

Around the time Margaret enrolled another aspiring young actress – still to decide on the name by which the world would eventually know her – was cutting short her brief student days there. The future Vivien Leigh was already a wife and mother but consumed with an ambition to act. Merle Oberon, too, had been inching her way upwards in bit parts in British films and was now working on *The Private Life of Henry VIII* which in a year's time would rocket her to international stardom.

Margaret enrolled for the Spring term of 1933 as student No. 4577, Lockwood, Margaret Mary. The brief life of Margie Day was over. From now on there was going to be no nonsense with names. She'd be Margaret Lockwood, plain and simple.

Kenneth Barnes recalled later: 'Self-contained, ambitious, she really understood what training and studentship means and was aware of the considerable demands on the personality which are necessary if an actress is to achieve correct expression. Very intelligent, she had a keen sense of technique and was a pleasure to teach.'

By the end of her first term any lingering uncertainties about the decision she'd taken were swept aside by achievement. Competing for a scholarship, she tied for first place with an Australian student who, being in greater financial need, was awarded it. For Margaret, the fact that she had proved herself eligible was reward enough. At the end of term she won one of the prizes for diction. This news was cabled to Henry in India as proof, Margaret said, that her decision to become an actress had been justified – though, considering the expense and relative insignificance of the tidings, there was perhaps an element of 'So there!' implicit in the message, too.

Another important decision was taken soon after she arrived at RADA. She was being teased about her long schoolgirl hair, so Margaret Evelyn agreed she could have it cut. No styling or shaping, though. Her mother sliced off the long plaits with a razor.

Revelling in the work, thriving on the spirit of the academy, Margaret romped through the normal two-year course in half the time.

Shopping in Westow Hill one Saturday in 1933, she stopped to chat to two old schoolfriends from Sydenham High. She'd never been close to Rhoda and Betty Leon, sisters whose home was nearby, but on parting they invited her to a party at their house that evening. On an impulse she accepted.

The Leons were prosperous, though they were an unpretentious, close-knit family. French-born Emile Armand Leon had worked his way up from commercial clerk to managing director of a City commodities firm, the British Iron and Steel Corporation. Daisy Alice, his wife, was English. The house Margaret went to that evening, of honey-coloured brick, standing detached in spacious grounds discreetly distanced from its neighbours, was imposing even by the stock-broker standards of Upper Norwood's most desirable neighbour-hoods, the Leons' standard of living considerably more affluent than the Lockwoods'. No. 13 Harold Road was no more than a brisk five-minute walk from Highland Road yet it was in a different world. Approaching the stately front porch, probably taking in the balus-traded parapets and decorated stucco plaques set into the brickwork, Margaret couldn't fail to be impressed. She wasn't quite so impressed, though, by her first meeting with the son of the house.

Rupert William Leon was a tall, gangling nineteen-year-old. His fair hair hung lank across his forehead and though his build was spare, accentuating his height, Margaret noted that his hands and feet were unusually large. At his side she looked even more diminutive than usual.

Rupert had recently left school, joining his father's firm on the bottom rung of the ladder as a clerk. He was immediately attracted to Margaret but any interest she showed in return was strictly the politeness required of a guest in his father's house. At the end of the evening he offered to walk her home and she consented, even though she had made up her mind she didn't particularly like him. He was courteous and correct, walking on the outside of the pavement, making sure to take her arm crossing the road. At the front door of No. 30 he tried to kiss her. She dodged and slipped inside and never gave him another thought.

$\mathscr{F}$EATURED BILLING

T he climax of every RADA student's year is the annual production – in those days a single performance held in a West
End theatre. All graduating students were eligible to audition
but only the best could count on being chosen. Competition was
fierce: the show served as a shop-window for emerging new talent and
for the most ambitious among them the only important members of
the audience were the theatre producers and agents who came to
scout.

When the scenes chosen for the 1934 production were announced,
Margaret set her sights on the title role in *Hannele*, a tear-jerking
play by the German dramatist Gerhardt Hauptmann. It was to be
directed by Leontine Sagan, a formidable name since the sensation
caused by her recent production of the controversial play *Mädchen in
Uniform*. The scouts in the audience could be guaranteed to pay it
particular attention.

Margaret reached a short-list of three at auditions – 'One of the
most wonderful moments of my life.' It was a difficult role and the
selected scene from the play's climax a challenge to bring off in
isolation. The heroine, a German waif, is known to be dying. Frail
and nearing the end of her life, she has visions in which she hears the
voices of angels. In Sagan's production the scene was all the more
effective for being played in a suffused light, calling for all the powers
of expression and vocal persuasion Margaret could summon. She won
the part and her performance on the night won her an ovation and a
diploma, though not, disappointingly, the coveted Gold Medal for the
year's outstanding student.

Margaret Evelyn rarely bothered to attend any of Margaret's performances now but she made an exception that night. She would have
been less than human not to feel a mother's pride in her daughter's
hour of triumph, but she was careful to suppress it. When Margaret

joined her afterwards, asking the inevitable question, she told her: 'It was dreadful. I couldn't see you half the time and I couldn't hear anything.'

Whatever her private feeling might be, she seemed compelled to slap Margaret down if she sensed any danger of success or praise turning her head. 'Always one to bring me down to earth,' Margaret would say, remembering that evening. But if she could sour the moment, Margaret Evelyn couldn't rob her daughter of the laurels. Leontine Sagan was extravagant in her praise. And one man in the audience was convinced he'd been watching a star in the making.

Herbert de Leon had recently set up business as an agent and he had been transfixed by Margaret's solo.

'It was a great occasion,' he wrote subsequently, 'how great I did not realise when I first entered the theatre. Watching Margaret as the suicidal waif rising to a high pitch of hysteria in a scene played in semi-darkness was an amazing experience. I knew a star was being born and I was determined to do all I could to help her.'

The similarity of his name to that of Margaret's well-to-do neighbours was coincidental. Herbert was no relation of the Leon family.

Born in Panama in 1905, he and his brother Jack had been brought to England as children. After leaving school Herbert had trained as a singer in London, Paris and Vienna and for some years had earned his living professionally. Jack, meanwhile, had founded the Q Theatre at Kew Bridge on the outskirts of London, quickly establishing it as one of the capital's most innovative 'little theatres' and a nursery for undiscovered talent.

Herbert was drawn to the world of theatre in which his brother was making a reputation. In 1929, four years after the Q opened, he started his own film agency, expanding later with another agent into the theatre. Essentially a loner, he soon broke away and set up on his own. By 1934 he was on his way to becoming an influential figure on the West End scene, with a wide circle of contacts. He'd developed a sharp eye for talent. At the time he first saw Margaret he'd just taken on a striking red-headed Irish girl from the Birmingham Repertory Company and placed her in a West End play. Her name was Greer Garson.

The day after the RADA performance he contacted Margaret and invited her to call at his office.

'I was convinced the Gold Medal would be hers and frankly I was amazed to read the next morning that she'd not received any award at all. The fact that she didn't, however, made no difference to my opinion and I asked her to come and see me.'

Still the innocent at large, though, thanks to her mother's indoctrination, a guarded one, Margaret made her way to Shaftesbury Avenue and nervously climbed the stairs to this stranger's office. Herbert faced 'a small, ingenuous, rather naïve girl on the other side of my desk. There was a vague surprised air about her that seemed to ask "What am I here for?" She showed none of the breathless eagerness or youthful insistence one so often finds in the young actresses seeking their first chance. At that time Margaret was quite unaware of the full value of her latent talents and this to me was part of her charm.'

Then and there they came to an agreement. No contracts were signed. It was one of Herbert's unorthodoxies as an agent that neither he nor his clients ever put signatures to a formal agreement. No contract existed between Margaret and Herbert for the entire 45 years he represented her. His philosophy was that if clients didn't wish to stay with him, he didn't want them to, and it formed a bedrock of trust and integrity unique in the London theatre. Herbert de Leon would mould her career, guide her star, give to the world the Margaret Lockwood it came to know. He was no Svengali, but she would play Trilby to him, counting on him more than any other man in her life: agent, mentor, business manager and, ultimately, surrogate father. She came to trust and depend on him as she trusted and depended on no other person.

The absence of that 'breathless eagerness or youthful insistence' Herbert had noted was what set Margaret apart. There was nothing 'actressy' about her; no airs and graces. Even her speaking voice was clear of the affectations and exaggerations which elocution teachers deemed proper for the delivery of 'stage' English in those days. They'd tried for a time to graft the notorious RADA 'voice' on to her diction. 'You must practise your Ys, dear – love-lay, *not* love-lee,' as she recalled many years later. She'd resisted them, realising the artificiality of assuming speech patterns nobody outside the Academy used. The result was that her speaking voice retained a genuine middle-of-the-road accent with which most people, whatever their own, could identify.

That Margaret was nervous throughout the interview was due not so much to her temerity in taking an independent decision which would dictate her future as the prospect of telling Margaret Evelyn what she'd done. She knew what to expect and she wasn't disappointed. Margaret Evelyn flirted with melodrama that evening, berating Margaret and ranting about the white slave traffic. She clearly resented any action Margaret took without her prior sanction. Less predictably, Rupert's reaction was just as alarmed, if more considered. 'You should be more careful,' he told her. 'Who is this man?'

By now Margaret and Rupert had worked out an understanding. A few weeks after their first unpromising encounter, Margaret had decided to call on Rhoda and Betty without, she insisted, a thought for Rupert. Arriving home while they were having tea, he again insisted on walking her to her door. This time they talked more openly and Margaret realised there was a shyness about him which struck a chord with her. Suddenly she warmed towards him.

Rupert had recently acquired a second-hand car. Fascinated by the prospect, Margaret couldn't refuse an invitation for a spin. From then on Rupert was the first and only man for her.

Margaret Evelyn knew they were meeting but they maintained a low profile for fear of antagonising her. Saturday was a regular date and on a lucky weekend they would occasionally contrive a Sunday together too. It was a thrifty courtship – there was a limit to the entertainment they could afford on Rupert's 30 shillings a week pay – but they found their pleasures in each other's company, tearing off into the country in the car or sometimes going up to London for dancing in the afternoon followed by tea at a Lyons Cornerhouse. Rupert had one or two foibles which struck Margaret as slightly odd – he wasn't enthusiastic about her being an actress and he disliked her wearing make-up – but he didn't press them and Margaret was too content to worry.

Margaret Evelyn dealt her daughter another embarrassment the day after her interview with Herbert by going to see him herself. She wanted to find out 'what his game was'. Placated, she came away convinced, at least, that her daughter wasn't about to be sold into the particular form of slavery she'd feared.

Herbert wasted no time in finding her work. Margaret was offered the leading role in a new play at the Q Theatre, *House on Fire*, playing a girl returning home from convent school to a disrupted family, and events her sheltered life hadn't prepared her for. The run was for one week only but it was a start and, on the Q stage, a valuable exposure.

Herbert persuaded a leading West End producer, Sydney Carroll, to drive out one evening and vet her. He was impressed, with reservations. Her lack of stagecraft showed up in the final act, which required an abrupt change of dramatic gear from the quiet schoolgirl of the first two acts to a young woman thrust into adulthood by suffering and shattered by the sudden death of her mother. Margaret couldn't quite bring it off. Carroll told Herbert that but for her inexperience in that climax he would have offered her a contract. Instead he found her a small part in the new play he was scheduling at his Ambassadors Theatre. Called *Family Affairs*, it was to have one of the great ladies of the theatre, Lilian Braithwaite, in the lead. It was more than Margaret had dared hope for. Within weeks of leaving RADA she was heading for the West End.

Herbert had a hunch about the cinema, an intuition that this was where Margaret's long-term future lay. Films were the new opium of the masses. With the arrival of the Talkies only four years before, commercial and artistic interests in British entertainment were shifting towards the new film studios now springing up all round London. He sounded out his contacts. British International Pictures were casting a screen version of Charles Dickens's *The Old Curiosity Shop* and in due course Margaret got a call to test for the lead of Little Nell at Elstree.

The cameraman shooting the test took one look at her and insisted she had her unfashionably thick eyebrows removed before he would go ahead. Margaret was horrified but after some argument agreed. Her brows were shaved and replaced with pencilled ones, never to be allowed to grow back. The effect of this trauma on her performance in the test can only be imagined; the film hasn't survived. But her main worry was how she was going to break the news about her eyebrows to Margaret Evelyn. She was also learning how to handle her mother, though. A telephone call from the studio prepared the way for the shock when they met, as arranged, at Victoria Station. Margaret Evelyn surveyed the damage with distaste. And said no more about it.

Herbert next arranged for Margaret to be interviewed by Alexander Korda, poised to make his reputation with *The Private Life of Henry VIII* and a star of Merle Oberon. After a few desultory questions, Korda dismissed her from his office, clearly unimpressed. He would mete out the same indifference to Vivien Leigh a few months later. Margaret wasn't dismayed. Plenty was happening; irons warming in various fires and rehearsals about to start for *Family Affairs*. She was content enough to be working in the theatre – and the West End theatre, at that. She was untouched even when the Little Nell part went to another actress. Margaret was considered too old for it; probably a diplomatic excuse since, at seventeen, she still retained a childlike quality though, to her relief, she had suddenly started to gain inches.

At least Herbert had a screen test in her portfolio. He began circulating it.

Family Affairs opened in August 1934. It was anchored in the British stage conventions of its time, a portrait of family life among the middle classes with carefully measured doses of laughs, tears and dramas. The cast, headed by Lilian Braithwaite as a dominant grandmother, was a strong one, with such established or soon-to-be worthies as Athene Seyler, Jack Livesey and Robert Eddison.

Margaret's role was little more than a side-issue, billed ninth in a cast of twelve. Yet if she didn't steal the show, she managed to pilfer a little of the limelight from her seniors and betters. 'There is', the *Times* reviewer noted, 'a little sketch of a secretary by Miss Margaret Lockwood which has more of the sparkle of truth in it than anything else in the evening.'

She was earning £12 a week, a heady enough wage for a teenager, and she splurged her first week's salary on a £12 gold watch. Time-keeping and the telephone, recently installed at 30 Highland Road, were basic essentials for a working actress, she reasoned.

Herbert submitted her test to the producer Basil Dean at Ealing studios, who, along with Korda, was generally regarded as one of the white hopes of the British film industry. He was already a formidable name in the London theatre in 1928 when he saw an early Talkie for the first time on a visit to New York and came away convinced that sound was going to revolutionise the cinema. Not all producers, even in Hollywood, were as far-sighted at that time. Back in England he co-founded the Associated Talking Pictures company (ATC) in 1929, producing a handful of films with mixed success, and gambling every-thing he had on building the first British studio specifically designed and equipped for sound at Ealing. He'd finally struck gold by starring Gracie Fields in her first film, *Sally in Our Alley*. In 1932 it grossed a record £100,000 at the box office, instantly transforming the nation's most popular music-hall name into its favourite movie star.

Dean liked what he saw of Margaret in the test and decided to sign her.

He'd just completed his latest Fields vehicle, *Sing As We Go*, and

37

was about to embark on a project he'd long been developing, an adaptation of the R. D. Blackmore classic, *Lorna Doone*. It had always been one of his favourite stories but suddenly he now had an ulterior personal motive for activating the project. It was an open secret in close-knit, gossipy show-business circles that there was a new woman in his life.

Already twice married, he'd fallen for a young unknown actress he'd spotted in provincial repertory. From the moment he met her he was determined to make her a star. In her mid-twenties, Victoria Hopper was 21 years his junior. She was lovely and had considerable charm but her talent was fragile and her quiet, unassuming personality would need sensitive handling if she were to carry the responsibilities of a demanding role in a big production. Her first film, a remake of *The Constant Nymph*, a stage hit and silent movie in the 1920s, in which she played the fey adolescent heroine Tessa, had been moderately successful but the public's response to her hadn't quite matched Dean's expectations. With the title role in *Lorna Doone* he was convinced he had the perfect vehicle for persuading audiences to take her to their hearts.

Victoria Hopper had just become the third Mrs Dean when he viewed Margaret's test. There was only one role left uncast and she got it – one day's work playing a village girl in a country dance sequence. Herbert's timing had been impeccable. Chance had got her into films, and chance hadn't finished with her yet.

John Loder had the male lead as Jan Ridd and the second female lead, his sister Annie Ridd, had been assigned to Dorothy Hyson, a seasoned Dean player on both stage and screen, daughter of the musical comedy star Dorothy Dickson.

The lucky break that brought Margaret Lockwood into films at starring level, a fable in the firm tradition of movie mythology, has been well documented but never placed in its true context. She was rehearsing her brief dancing scene when the casting director, Aubrey Blackburn, suddenly took her on one side and warned her to hold herself ready for a possible change of plan: Dorothy Hyson had been taken ill and wouldn't be doing the Annie Ridd role. Dean was desperate. He couldn't afford to hold up the £32,000 production while the agencies were combed for a replacement actress. Blackburn had suggested Margaret. Barely remembering her existence, Dean called for the screen test to be run again. By the end of the day she had leaped from bit part to second female lead.

In interviews and biographical details ever after Margaret scrupulously credited Dorothy Hyson's misfortune for her own good fortune. Not even she was fully aware of the real circumstances. Miss Hyson, who gave up a brief, promising career to marry the actor Anthony Quayle, was certainly incapable of taking on the role at that moment. She had been driven to the brink of a nervous breakdown by Basil Dean. The memory of him could still make her shudder more than 50 years later.

'I was under contract to him,' she recalled, 'and Basil Dean was a very frightening man. He loved domineering people, particularly young actresses. He seemed to take a delight in making them break down and cry.

'Oh, yes! He was a sadist. I'd been working on *Sing As We Go* on location in Blackpool. At the same time he put me into his new play in the West End, Dodie Smith's *Touch Wood*. Travelling between London and Blackpool and working day and night was exhausting and then, a month after the play opened, he was making me do *Lorna Doone*. I couldn't take much more.

'He'd been giving me an awful time. I just couldn't face any more of it. I had a mini-breakdown. It was Basil Dean who caused it.

'My agent eventually got me out of the contract. I was so relieved.'

Dean belonged to the old disciplinarian school of producer-managers. He was respected by his peers and feared by many of his underlings, particularly young actresses he'd given a chance who were terrified of offending him. One such would be the fledgling Vivien Leigh. Within months of Dorothy Hyson's experience, she too would fall victim to his bullying. The fates that seemed to be driving the Lockwood and Leigh life-lines in tandem were again at work. Even as Margaret was making *Lorna Doone*, Vivien was essaying her first tentative screen role – a much less important one – in a Cicely Courtneidge comedy, *Things Are Looking Up*. Again it was Aubrey Blackburn, an ace talent spotter, who recommended Dean to give Vivien Leigh her first contract and put her into Gracie Fields's next film, *Look Up and Laugh*. On the set Dean indulged his pastime of humiliating raw young ingenues, brutally calling attention to what he considered Vivien's inadequacies in front of the crew and bombarding her with insults until the tears flowed. Gracie Fields, his most valuable asset as well as a strong enough personality to stand up to him, came to Vivien's rescue, warning him to ease up.

Margaret, a tailor-made victim, was, however, spared the Dean

39

treatment. It could have been her professionalism, unusual in so young an actress, that saved her. For all her shyness and vulnerability, there was a steely character beneath the surface naïveté and, even then, she had a knack of knowing precisely what was expected of her. Nevertheless she recalls being terrified on the set at first. 'Basil Dean had the reputation of being a bit of a martinet. But I found him very kind indeed and enjoyed working for him.'

Dean, in any case, had more important things on his mind for once than terrorising an insignificant young actress. He was absorbed in making sure that the new Mrs Dean appeared to best advantage. 'Everyone', Dorothy Hyson remembers, 'knew the film was purely a vehicle for Victoria Hopper.'

As filming proceeded Margaret found herself making friends with the young assistant director, a Dean protegé. His name was Carol Reed. Fair-haired, quiet-spoken and earnest, Reed was something of a loner. Now 27, he had joined ATP within a year of Dean forming the company as dialogue coach at the newly opened Ealing studios. His ambition was to be a director and Dean, always a shrewd assessor of ability, had put opportunities his way as an assistant. But Carol was a man in a hurry and while working on *Sing As We Go* a few months before *Lorna Doone*, he'd given Dean an ultimatum: a film to direct or he would quit. By now he was too valuable for Dean to lose. A deal was struck. Carol would get his own picture after *Lorna Doone* had wrapped. He and Margaret found they had much in common: a certain solitariness, outwardly shy, a dedication, almost to the exclusion of any other interest, to their vocations. They got on well together.

Margaret had stepped on to the sort of treadmill which had worn Dorothy Hyson into her breakdown, working in the studio all day, appearing on stage at night. She was certainly tired by the end of the day but adrenalin kept her going, a compound of excitement and satisfaction.

Rupert volunteered to drive her to the studio each morning, dropping her at the gate and then continuing to his own office in the City. Awakened, like Margaret, by a 5 a.m. alarm, he would be waiting in the car at 5.30 outside her front door. It was on one of those early morning drives through the stirring city that he summoned the courage to tell her he was in love. Joyfully, Margaret told him she felt the same way. As they sped through the empty streets they traded fantasies. She was going to be a famous actress; he would be a millionaire. She wasn't yet eighteen; he celebrated his twentieth birthday while she was working on *Lorna Doone*. Rupert didn't intend to voice his reservations about her way of life. He privately hoped, even believed, that acting was a phase she was passing through, soon to be outgrown. Margaret, for her part, thrust aside misgivings she felt about the way her mother would react to the plans they were making. Time, each believed, would clear the obstacles. They were on top of the world and neither of them wanted to glance down.

Lorna Doone seemed to be turning into the major production Basil Dean had envisaged during those summer weeks of 1934. The press was giving it a lot of attention, with the emphasis, not surprisingly, on Victoria Hopper. Much of the filming was on location on Exmoor, using the actual sites described in the book: the original Doone farm, the church at Oare where the tragic wedding of Lorna and Jan Ridd took place. With his passion for detail, Dean had the church interior duplicated in the studio down to the last stone.

Margaret's scenes were confined to the set. Every moment of the seven-week shooting schedule was an education for her. Too lowly in the unit pecking order to qualify for a peep at the daily rushes, she asked Carol Reed how the film was shaping, angling for an opinion on her own showing.

'It stinks,' he snapped, immediately unnerving her. She was so hurt that they were barely on speaking terms for the rest of the shooting. It was only towards the end that she realised he'd been referring to the film, not her own performance. When they were talking again, he told her about his arrangement with Dean and promised to find her a part in the first film he directed.

Herbert meanwhile was capitalising on Margaret's featured billing in the picture. Dean was showing no further signs of interest in her for the moment, as he normally did with bright young actresses he'd 'discovered', so Herbert started touting her CV round rival producers.

Samuel Woolf, managing director of British Lion, took the bait. One of the pioneering figures of the industry – he'd been in film distribution since the cinema building boom year of 1910 – he offered a three-year contract. When Herbert explained the financial terms to her, Margaret could be forgiven for thinking she wasn't only on course for her own fantasy of being a famous actress but taking over Rupert's of becoming a millionaire, too. She would be receiving £500 for 50 days' work with £10 a day for any extra time she was needed in the first year, rising to £750 plus £15 a day in the second. It was the equivalent of £4,000 a year, a fortune for those days. And barely six months before she'd been a merely average student at RADA.

To celebrate she went shopping in Bond Street, buying a wardrobe appropriate to her new status. But she had to ask Margaret Evelyn for the money. From the time she'd received her first pay cheque for *Family Affairs*, her mother had taken charge of her finances. Half her earnings were paid into Margaret Evelyn's account, half into one of her own which she wouldn't be allowed to touch until she came of age. She was dependent on her mother for every penny she spent, and accountable to her.

As long as she could remember her mother had wanted a refrigerator . . . 'Only we can't afford one.' Now, for the first time in her life, she was in a position to give her something she longed for. Setting aside some of the cash for her new clothes, Margaret arranged for a local shop to install a fridge for Margaret Evelyn's birthday, delivery carefully timed so that she would be out of the house.

Margaret made sure she was in the kitchen when she heard the front door opening. Margaret Evelyn noticed the gleaming new appliance immediately. Stonily, she said, 'What's this?' and then read Margaret a lecture on wasting money: 'I've managed all these years without one . . .' Once again Margaret was crushed.

British Lion came up almost immediately with a part in *The Case of Gabriel Perry*, a Victorian courtroom thriller, based on the play *Wild Justice* by James Dale. It was an interesting and off-beat script. A stern but devoted head of family in a provincial town has secretly gambled himself to the brink of ruin. In a fit of desperation, he murders an old woman and the crime is pinned on a mentally retarded youth. The discovery of an incriminating clue in his home forces him to confess to his wife, swearing her to secrecy. The family is then subjected to the latent underside of his personality, cruel, calculating and devious. At his trial he is acquitted but retribution catches up with him at the hands of his nearest and dearest. Margaret's role as the daughter of the house was little more than decoration but, as the only young woman among the lead players, she realised it could be built into an effective display case.

Filming was at British Lion's Beaconsfield Studios in Berkshire, 40 miles from her home. For the first time she enjoyed 'film star' treatment, with a studio car to pick her up at dawn for the drive into the country and deliver her to the Ambassadors in time for the evening performance of *Family Affairs*. On the set she was surrounded by a cast of theatre veterans, several destined to become well-known character players in British movies.

Henry Oscar was repeating his stage success as the father, Olga Lindo was his wife, and as new to the mysteries of movie-making as Margaret herself were Ralph Truman, Raymond Lovell and the dauntingly imperious Martita Hunt. The studio paths of all of them would criss-cross over the next decade. Margaret, the only one among them to be movie-bred, studied and learned from their techniques. It was a bonus, too, to be working with the director Albert de Courville. For years he'd been the leading producer of West End musical revue. Switching to the cinema, he'd moulded Jessie Matthews into one of the two (with Gracie Fields) most popular stars in British films.

Despite her enthusiasm and energy, the treadmill was now racing faster than Margaret could keep pace with, just as Dorothy Hyson had found. Filming by day and appearing at the theatre by night was overtaxing her. She wasn't getting home until midnight: an eighteen-hour working day. More and more, she found herself falling asleep on the homebound train, frequently travelling beyond Gipsy Hill station and having to find her way back in the dead of night.

A compromise was reached with the Ambassadors management: on the days she was needed in the studio her understudy would go on for the play. It wasn't an arrangement that appealed to the professional in Margaret but she had no other choice. Before it went into effect, however, *Lorna Doone* had its première in February 1935. Basil Dean had been persuaded against his better judgment into organising a full-dress charity première at the Prince Edward cinema in Soho. It was to be a one-off screening several weeks ahead of the public opening and he wasn't convinced it was a good idea.

The film's credits gave Margaret fourth billing but the artwork for posters and display publicity stopped short of her name. Victoria Hopper, of course, was billed in letters as big as the title itself. Below it the names of John Loder and Mary Clare were just decipherable. There was no invitation to the première for Margaret. As far as Dean was concerned, she'd ceased to exist on the last day of shooting. In any case, she'd be otherwise engaged at the Ambassadors, a stone's throw away from the Prince Edward. In the event, she wasn't. Filming that day kept her later than usual at Beaconsfield, increasingly worried that she'd be late for the theatre. She finally had to ask to be released and made a headlong dash for the West End in the studio car. She was too late. As she sped in, an angry stage manager told her that the understudy had gone on and that he'd deal with her in the morning.

Disconsolate, Margaret found herself walking in the direction of the Prince Edward. A lone figure in black tie was pacing the empty foyer, a forlorn, nerve-racked Dean, as downcast as she was. The sophisticated première audience was *laughing* at his masterpiece. Plucking up her courage, she asked him if she could slip inside. He nodded. She was in time to catch her first scene, stunned by the size of her image on the screen and the unfamiliar sound of her own voice. Despondently, she watched the film to the end, then slipped away and caught the train home.

The critics were kinder than the audience. *The Daily Telegraph*, forecasting a wide public for the film, found 'Blackmore's tale grips and holds the interest.' The *Daily Mail* probably did it no favours at the box office with the view that 'it should win the affection of film-goers because it is utterly sincere and utterly English. A film drama of great dignity and unfailing good taste.' The *Daily Herald* decided it was 'a picture which British filmdom can be proud to have prod-uced.' The learned *Monthly Film Bulletin*, however, caught Basil Dean out in an unfortunate lapse of the detail he obsessively lavished on his productions. 'The screen work is somewhat patchy and in one of the interior scenes it is surely an anachronism to see one of the Ridd family reading with horn-rimmed spectacles in the seventeenth century.'

None of the critics noticed Margaret. She remained as anonymous in the press cuttings as she did in the publicity material. *Lorna Doone*, she always said afterwards, was 'the worst film ever made'.

QUOTA QUICKIES

In the year they had been going out together Rupert hadn't once set foot inside the Highland Road house. Whenever he called for her in his car, Margaret would be waiting to join him at a pre-arranged signal on the horn. When he returned her home there would be an unobserved kiss and then she'd jump out and hurry indoors. He was never invited across the threshold. Time and again she found excuses to evade the necessity of introducing Rupert to her mother. Margaret Evelyn would, she knew, receive him with all the correct proprieties but also with reservations to be aired in no uncertain terms after he'd left. In a sense Rupert was a symbol of independence for Margaret, the first man with whom she'd formed a relationship without Margaret Evelyn's vetting and approval. Some of that would be sur-rendered if her mother were allowed to become a party to the situation.

Margaret Evelyn, watching from behind the curtains, had observed the lanky, fair-haired young man in his £5 car from a distance. She hadn't been particularly impressed but she'd said nothing, believing the friendship would take what she considered its natural course and fizzle out. In any case, she was enough of a realist to accept that a pretty, unconventional girl in the circles Margaret was now moving in was bound to attract some interest from the opposite sex. She had cautioned her often enough about it.

The couple hatched a plan of campaign. Rupert persuaded his own mother to invite the Lockwood ladies for tea.

Mr and Mrs Leon, a kindly couple, had taken Margaret to their hearts, making her feel as welcome in their home as any of their own children. She had grown fond of them in return, finding in their house a relaxed family atmosphere she'd rarely known at home.

One Sunday afternoon mother and daughter set out for the eight-minute walk to Harold Road. Margaret, knowing how much was at stake for her, was tense but tea passed off pleasantly enough, even if she sensed some constraint. Mr and Mrs Leon were at pains to make their guests feel at ease. After the sandwiches and cakes had been dispensed and tea-cups replenished, Mr Leon passed round the cigarette box. Margaret had started to smoke but it hadn't yet become the habit of a lifetime. Nervous, she accepted a cigarette. As she waited for a light she innocently ignited the fuse for years of conflict and bitterness. The explosion came not from her mother but from a quarter she least expected, from Rupert himself.

She knew he had certain reservations about her style of life. He wasn't happy about her career. Acting, he'd told her, was not a suitable occupation for a lady. He disliked make-up so she'd learned not to wear it when they were out together, except for a light touch of lipstick. She had no idea, until that moment, that he hated to see a lady smoke. Suddenly he rounded on her, white with temper, magnifying his objection into a scene out of all proportion to the offence. Smoking, he lectured her, was an unladylike habit and he was surprised she hadn't realised he wouldn't approve. Pompously, he hoped she wouldn't do it again. The others heard him out in embarrassed silence. Margaret didn't know whether to be angry or apologetic.

Margaret Evelyn was outraged for her, setting her mouth in the grim line Margaret knew so well but managing to restrain herself from adding to her discomfiture.

The tea party on which so much had been staked broke up in frosty politeness. Once clear of the house Margaret Evelyn's anger broke. How dare 'that young man' speak to Margaret like that in front of her mother and his own parents? It was a ridiculous scene to cause over a cigarette. He was too domineering. 'If he's like that now, what's he going to be like later on?' She was as angry as Margaret had ever known her to be, for once with good reason, though her outburst was in its own way as much an over-reaction as Rupert's had been. It wasn't beyond the bounds of possibility that she was exploiting the incident for her own ends, and Rupert had provided a heaven-sent opportunity for her to diminish him in Margaret's eyes. The tirade ended with an ominous warning. 'Don't you ever bring him to this house. I don't want him here.'

Margaret was in tears. She'd never wavered in her loyalty to her mother. She craved approval from her. But she was in love with Rupert. There was one single ray of hope. At least Margaret Evelyn had stopped short of forbidding her to see him again. Rupert's name was seldom mentioned between them afterwards but Margaret, putting the incident behind her, continued to meet him, standing her ground for the first time in her life and quietly defying her mother. She had no way of knowing it was a decision that would lead to years of acrimony, but at least she now knew better than to light up a cigarette in Rupert's company.

Margaret Evelyn would probably have found some pretext for objecting to any young man Margaret favoured at that period. She might have been hoping for a better prospect, Margaret concluded later, so the tea party scene was a convenient lever for her antagonism. Yet by Lockwood standards or indeed most standards at that time, Rupert was a highly eligible young man: quiet, stable, well-bred, scion of an affluent family and set to make his way in his father's firm with no reason for doubting his chances of success or the security he'd be in a position to offer some day.

Perversely, it was likely that Margaret Evelyn in fact resented the Leons' material superiority to the Lockwoods' tightly-budgeted suburban economies. Neither could she forget her own lower-class background, a large family living on the meagre pay of an army sergeant, she herself having to earn her own living. She'd never mixed comfortably with her peers even after marrying Henry, never been mistress of a house quite as grand as Mrs Leon's. But at the root of her antipathy to Rupert lay possessiveness. She demanded absolute allegiance from her children and found it difficult to yield any claim on Margaret to an outsider, least of all to an eligible suitor.

By 1935 Margaret was increasingly in demand. Her name was still unknown to the public but her reputation was spreading where it mattered, among the producers. *Lorna Doone* was proving popular with the paying customer in spite of the première audience, and studios were taking note of the promising newcomer in it. British Lion, without a suitable property of its own to schedule for her, began to make a dividend on Margaret's contract by loaning her out to other companies.

For the past decade the industry had been under threat from the volume and superior quality of imported Hollywood films. Financing domestic production became increasingly difficult and there had been signs that the home industry could be crushed out of existence. The government was finally spurred to act in 1927 with the introduction of the Cinematograph Films Act, sometimes described as the Magna Carta of British film production, which laid down certain controls over the production and distribution of home-produced output. Its most significant provision was the requirement for cinemas to show a prescribed quota of British films each year, beginning with a modest five per cent but rising over the following ten years to twenty per cent. The result was a production boom.

Few people in the industry, particularly the cinema owners, welcomed the quota regulations. No amount of government legislation could change the public's preference for Hollywood movies but the cinemas were legally obliged to fulfil their quota of British productions. A loophole was soon discovered: the quota could be complied with by producing and showing short, low-budget B-features, often shoddily made, slotted into a supporting programme for a main Hollywood feature. Production on a shoestring often took no longer than two or three weeks and on the credit side, these B-features – or quota quickies – meant work for actors and technicians and served as a nursery for talent – actors, directors, cameramen – which would blossom in the 1940s.

Thanks to quota quickies, Margaret made more films in 1935 – six – than in any other year of her career. They familiarised her with studio techniques, camera angles and dialogue delivery, the trick of understatement in gesture and speech, all the craft of which she was to become mistress.

At the time she broke into films the majority of artists appearing in them had come from the theatre or music-hall. The favourite stars of the era – Gracie Fields, Jessie Matthews, Cicely Courtneidge and Jack Hulbert, Ivor Novello – simply transferred their top-billing stage names to the screen with minor technical modifications. The British cinema hadn't so far discovered and groomed a star it could call its own. Margaret, unmannered and possessing a technique which hadn't been schooled in the theatre, was a natural for the camera and the microphone. The first favoured her pretty, well-defined features, the second a pleasant, musical voice free of the curlicues and exaggerations which most young actresses of that time assumed. Inexperienced as she was in those early films, she brought a freshening quality to her performances.

Michael Powell, a director destined to become perhaps the most creative of the British cinema, was learning his craft on quickies. In *Some Day* he guided Margaret through her first leading role, playing opposite Esmond Knight in a 69-minute romantic trifle about a lift-boy and a servant girl whose first date inadvertently lands them in trouble with the law.

Hollywood itself was cashing in on the quickie boom, attracted by the favourable financing structure which subsidised it. Studios like Warner Bros invested some of their British profits in productions that would qualify as British quota, leasing the newly built Thames-side studios at Teddington for this purpose in 1931. They sent over a veteran film-maker of the silent era, Irving Asher, to run the production programme with the stipulation that he turn out around twenty films a year under the quota system and keep the studios in profit.

The films Asher initiated were among the most polished of the quickies, air-brushed with a Hollywood gloss. Each year he went back to Los Angeles to comb the shelves of Warner's story department for scenarios that had already been produced. Back in England he would make a choice from 50 or so scripts and metamorphose them into suitable subjects for British audiences. Costs were thus pared to a minimum and the Warner accountants kept happy. Moreover, there was no risk of the home studio's main market in the United States seeing the recycled material: quickies were never allowed to cross the Atlantic.

Some Day was a product of this system. A British author, I. A. R. Wylie, had written the original novel *Young Nowheres*, which Warner had bought and scripted. Asher found it shelved and re-exported it to Britain. Asher's quickies, Michael Powell has written, 'were a damn sight more honest and entertaining because they were not trying to be anything but what they were, and they were tailored from first-class scripts'. *Some Day*, however, was one exception and is usually omitted from Margaret Lockwood filmographies. But at least it brought her the first personal notice she ever had in a film, albeit not a particularly encouraging one. Dismissing the film as 'a feeble romance', *Picturegoer* recorded that 'neither of the two principals acts very convincingly'.

Her next director was a name that spelled magic for her – Herbert Brenon. In the silent era he had been one of Hollywood's most successful directors. He'd acted with, as well as directed, Theda Bara in *Two Orphans* and made the first screen versions of both *Beau Geste*, with Ronald Colman, and *The Great Gatsby*, a year after each novel had been published. But his greatest achievement in Margaret's eyes now was as the director of *Peter Pan*, the film she'd seen as a child every evening for a week. Brenon's career had waned with the advent of the Talkies but his reputation was still substantial when British International Pictures hired him to direct *Honours Easy*. Margaret was thrilled to be working with him.

Based on a 1930 West End play by Roland Pertwee, the film gave her a small but central role in a story about a feud between two powerful men. One of them is robbed. He accuses the other's son who, at the time of the robbery, had been about to spend an illicit night in a hotel with a married woman; honour bound, he had abandoned the tryst and returned to his forgiving fiancée. Margaret played the girl who provides the evidence of the son's innocence. Patric Knowles was the son, and the film's top-billed star, playing the married woman, was the Norwegian Greta Nissen whose career was on the decline after making a Hollywood name for herself in silents. *Honours Easy* was the last film she made.

The cameraman was 24-year-old Ronald Neame, one of the great cinema names of the future as producer, director and cinematographer with such classic titles as *Pygmalion, In Which We Serve, Brief Encounter, Great Expectations* and *Oliver Twist* among his achievements. Faded or raw as the talent surrounding her may have been, Margaret couldn't fail to pick up valuable lessons in craftsmanship from such an assortment of talent. The supporting cast included Chili Bouchier, a vivacious young actress, already at 24 a screen veteran of seven years and twice as many films. The name of Margaret Lockwood meant nothing to her when they met on the set but she retained a vivid memory of her.

'I found myself taking note and watching her closely,' she remembered. 'I knew straightaway she was going to be a star yet I remember being puzzled because I couldn't quite work out why.

'She was pretty, but there were dozens of youngsters more striking looking in the business, struggling to make their way. She had a very quiet personality, almost withdrawn. At that time she didn't show any exceptional talents.

'And yet there was "star" written all over her. I think it must have been some quality of authority and stillness she had, unusual at that age and at that time when the rest of us were chattering bright young things. It marked her out.'

Some, including Margaret herself, have attributed the speedy development of her career to luck. If chance timing and a gust of ill wind are the co-ordinates of luck, she did enjoy her share of it but, as Chili

Karachi, 1916: Margaret at six weeks of age, with her mother *(above)* and in the arms of her *ayah (above right)*. Margaret's brother Lyn *(below left)* was the 'quietest little boy I have ever known'. *Below right:* the teddy bear was Margaret's 'partner' in her first professional engagement in 1930.

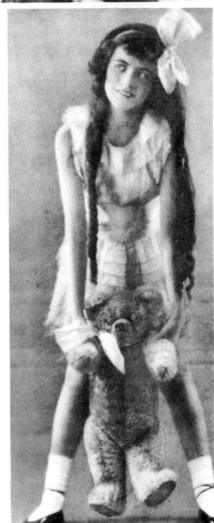

Right: Margaret was 'terrified' of Maurice Chevalier when they were teamed in 1936 for *The Beloved Vagabond*... a decade later *(inset)* they met again on equal terms of stardom.

'One of the most promising young players in British films' claimed this 1935 publicity shot from *Honours Easy. Right:* the unknown ingenue in *The Case of Gabriel Perry,* 1935.

Margaret in *Dr Syn*, the performance which in 1937 persuaded Gainsborough they had a future star on their books.

A rare 'cheesecake' shot for *Bank Holiday*, 1938.

he launch of a team to rival any that Hollywood could offer: Michael Redgrave and Margaret Lockwood in 1938 in *The Lady Vanishes*, with Dame May Whitty.

Checking the script of *The Lady Vanishes* with Alfred Hitchcock.

Margaret *(extreme right)* on the sidelines in *A Girl Must Live*, with Renée Houston and Lilli Palmer *(centre)*.

Margaret and director Carol Reed.

A mixed star wardrobe aboard the
Ile de France, Hollywood-bound in 1939.

Lunching with camera-shy husband Rupert Leon for a publicity photo-call before departure.

The Hollywood treatment: a studio photograph for *Rulers of the Sea*, 1939.

Bouchier perceived, it was her self-applied disciplines – hard work, study, determination – that laid the foundations for success. Those disciplines were now about to bear fruit.

Early in the 1935 Basil Dean was as good as his word to Carol Reed and offered him his first solo assignment as a director. Carol, in turn, remembered his promise to Margaret as they'd put the finishing touches to *Lorna Doone*.

The subject was to be Captain Marryat's nineteenth-century classic naval yarn for schoolboys, *Mr Midshipman Easy;* not at first sight an encouraging one for an ambitious young actress. Episodic and action-packed, the story chronicles the adventures and growth into manhood of a spirited teenager in a Royal Navy man-o'-war of the 1790s. The book had trimmed the action with satire and social observation but the screenplay, merely paying lip-service to the author's liberal senti-ments, wisely jettisoned most of them in the interests of high adventuring.

Apart from a brief appearance by the lad's mother, the only female role in the script was Margaret's character of Donna Agnes Ribiera, daughter of a Spanish grandee, with whom the young hero enjoys a flirtatious interlude after she has been rescued from brigands.

For the title role Dean had signed Hughie Green, already at fifteen a favourite in the music-hall and on radio with a popular act known as Hughie Green and his Gang.

The star career in films that everyone thought lay ahead of Hughie Green never materialised. Instead he found screen stardom in tele-vision twenty years later as founder and presenter of the long-running talent spotting show *Opportunity Knocks*. But *Midshipman Easy* was his first film and, he has claimed, so great was Dean's faith in his future that he was given the casting vote in the choice of leading lady from three contenders.

'I remember going down to Ealing Studios one day and sitting in the projection room while they ran films of the three for me. As far as I was concerned the choice was obvious. "I'll have that one," I said.

'They told me her name was Margaret Lockwood. You could say I made opportunity knock for her.'

Midshipman Easy held little enough promise for Margaret, targeted as it was at the juvenile market and not even the female end of it. But she was happy to be working with Carol Reed again. The ten-month run of *Family Affairs* ended just as she was offered the film and in spite of a preference for theatre she was realistic enough, under Herbert's guidance, to see better prospects in films.

A working bond had been struck between Carol Reed and herself on *Lorna Doone*. They had much in common. They understood each other. Like Margaret, Carol was something of a loner, immersed in his career; his quiet, courteous manner complemented her own. Like her, too, he had a side to his character that remained withdrawn and 'boyish' just as she at that period was still reserved and 'girlish'. Each had grown up without a father's influence. Carol was the illegitimate son – one of six children out of wedlock – of the great Victorian actor-manager Sir Herbert Beerbohm Tree, close friend of Margaret's 'great uncle', Sir Frank Lockwood. Tree, though 'respectably' married, maintained a second household with his mistress, May Pinney. His illegitimacy was a sensitive issue with Carol. Throughout his life it was a subject he never allowed to be mentioned and privately he always harboured resentment at being denied a legitimate father. Neither he nor Margaret knew at that time of the 'connection' between their families.

As a frame for Margaret's talent, *Midshipman Easy* hadn't much to commend it. Its importance lay in renewing and confirming a professional relationship that would be the keystone of her progress and eventual stardom. Carol Reed, even as he was laying the foundations of his own career, was to be the chief architect of Margaret's.

Production took her back to Ealing, with location work at Weymouth and Portland Bill on the Dorset coast. It was not without its tensions. Carol the perfectionist quickly realised that the responsibilities of being in command were a very different burden from those of being second or third in command.

'I found I didn't know at all the very things I thought I knew,' he wrote subsequently. 'I thought I had picked up a lot about cutting and camera angles but now, when I had to make all the decisions myself and was not just mentally approving or criticising what somebody else decided, I was pretty well lost. Fortunately I realised that this was the only way to learn – by making mistakes.'

He set himself the challenge of making as few mistakes as possible, constantly trying to conceal them from everybody else in the unit and affecting an air of confidence so that he would inspire it in his crew. It was a testing time and he was thankful to have Margaret, a kindred perfectionist, aboard. She was an admiring and reassuring ally.

Primitive as his direction of *Midshipman Easy* was, it implanted a theme that would recur through his films like a personal signature. The boyish element in his own personality made him specially sensitive in handling child characters and actors, and he filtered the incidents in *Midshipman Easy* through the eyes and understanding of the boy hero, a technique he would return to twelve years later in one of his greatest achievements, *The Fallen Idol*. Boy characters would also make key contributions to *The Third Man, The Man Between, A Kid for Two Farthings* and *Oliver!*, the last film he made, crowning a distinguished career with an Academy Award.

But in those early days it was Margaret who became the 'signature' of his apprentice films, so integral a part of them that she came to be almost a talisman for him. Hers was the name he first thought of when he was casting and such was his faith in her that he would organise a production schedule round her availability as, indeed, he had done with *Midshipman Easy*.

Rupert was still ferrying Margaret to and from whichever studio she was working at. Now he decided it was time she learned to drive herself. He gave her lessons on Sundays, the only day of the week they could count on spending together, and she proved an apt pupil. Soon she passed her driving test at the first attempt and bought herself her first car, a Standard Eight. The independence it gave her was a luxury she relished.

As soon as the four-week shooting schedule for *Midshipman Easy* ended, Herbert had lined up two more quickies for her.

Jury's Evidence was the first subject British Lion had offered Margaret since she had signed her contract with them and it took her back to Beaconsfield, now capable of driving herself the 40 miles. The story was based on a play by Jack de Leon, Herbert's brother, who had given her that first chance at his Q Theatre. Now a de Leon screenplay was to provide her first leading role with the prospect of her name above the title. And the first time she was required to die.

Margaret played a young wife who takes a job as a private secretary to a ruthless businessman. He falls in love with her; when her husband finds out there is a quarrel. Shortly afterwards she is found dead and the husband is charged with murder. The screenplay concentrated on the Old Bailey murder trial, with the jury, unconvinced of the husband's guilt, reconstructing the crime to prove that the law is capable of making mistakes even when there is circumstantial evidence to support the prosecution case.

Again Margaret found herself working under a gifted Hollywood hand: the director Ralph Ince had arrived in Britain the year before and already delivered six quickies. He, too, had made a name for himself in silents but it had been overshadowed by the more revered one of his elder brother, Thomas, one of the great pioneer figures of the industry. An even darker shadow had been cast eleven years earlier by scandal. Thomas Ince had met a violent death in a shooting mystery aboard William Randolph Hearst's yacht during a weekend cruise in a party which included Charlie Chaplin and Hearst's mistress, Marion Davies. The circumstances were never fully explained and the resulting scandal, following so closely on the Fatty Arbuckle rape trial and the unsolved murder of another director, William Desmond Taylor, which ruined the careers of two top stars, Mabel Normand and Mary Miles Minter, was duly written into Hollywood legend.

It was the second of the two quickies that was, for Margaret, the more significant: it brought her into working contact with a Hollywood star for the first time.

Douglas Fairbanks Jr brought an aura of genuine Hollywood glamour on to the set with him. As the son of Douglas Fairbanks Sr and stepson of Mary Pickford, the 'world's sweetheart', he was the crown prince of filmdom royalty. Though still only 26, he'd already made more than 40 movies. Eighteen months earlier, his much publicised marriage to Joan Crawford had ended in divorce and the early months of 1935 found him down on his luck. He was already deeply involved in an affair with Gertrude Lawrence and living beyond his means. At the same time he was trying to set up a company of his own, Criterion Productions, but finding difficulty in raising capital. His prospects weren't helped by a sensational court case in which Miss Lawrence was declared bankrupt, attracting massive publicity from newspapers chafing under the ban on reporting a burgeoning romance between the Prince of Wales and an American divorcée.

Fairbanks, as he bluntly admitted, was broke and at this point Irving Asher at Teddington studios came to his rescue with the offer of work in one of his quickies, to co-star the silent star Laura La Plante, Asher's wife.

'It was a film I made in a hurry, more or less as a favour to my old and close friend Irving Asher and his dear wife Laura La Plante,' he remembered. 'Also, I wanted to make some quick and easy money. The best part of the picture was having some location shots scheduled to be done in Monte Carlo.'

Those shots didn't involve Margaret and, indeed, as Fairbanks confessed more than half a century later: 'I'd forgotten she was also in the picture. How shaming of me!' She did, however, leave some impression on him at the time, which he was to recall a few months later when Criterion Productions finally, if briefly, got off the ground.

Man of the Moment was a flimsy romantic comedy about a prospective bridegroom who dissuades a girl from a suicide attempt and the complications they have to face when they fall in love. With its emphasis on the two stars Fairbanks and La Plante, it wasn't surprising that Margaret's supporting role got overlooked. She rated fourth billing, a setback after the attention she'd recently been accustomed to, but again she was being exposed to major film talent at work and adding another layer of varnish to her own.

Irving Asher hoped that with its star names *Man of the Moment* would get an American release, breaking Warner's bar on importing its British quota quickies. It didn't. Fairbanks in his autobiography reflected: 'Professionally, *Man of the Moment* was not at all what I should have done at that period . . . The actual filming . . . was quite easy on mind and body. Unfortunately, it was even easier on the exercise of talent.'

A few weeks later he finally secured backing for his new company. United Artists agreed to a distribution deal for four films with the condition that Fairbanks appeared in at least two of them. He'd already lined up the first, an adaptation of a popular Jeffrey Farnol Regency novel *The Amateur Gentleman*. The screenplay had been written by the novelist and playwright Clemence Dane who, like Margaret, was a former pupil of Sydenham High School. As his co-star, Fairbanks signed Elissa Landi. Miss Landi, blonde, cool and ladylike, who claimed in her publicity to be descended from Emperor Franz Josef of Austria, had recently undergone a spell of intense Hollywood grooming as 'the new Garbo' but her prospects had dwindled after a brief sequence of movies.

With his key casting complete, Fairbanks remembered Margaret. The role he offered her was small but the production was the biggest she'd so far been associated with and it was attracting a great deal of attention from the trade and the press. The director was Thornton Freedland, another American who had recently transferred to British studios; two years earlier he'd directed Fred Astaire and Ginger Rogers in the first film of their partnership, *Flying Down to Rio*.

The plot of *The Amateur Gentleman* involved the exploits of Fair-

55

banks as the son of a retired prize-fighter now turned innkeeper in his quest to prove his father innocent of a charge of stealing a nobleman's money. The young man worms his way into London high society, gains entry to the Prince Regent's court and, after a series of set-piece adventures, discovers romance, the culprit and the truth about his own high-born antecedents.

Margaret's role as a young society girl cast her in a sub-plot romance with Hugh Williams, recently returned from playing Steerforth in Hollywood's version of *David Copperfield*. In later life he doubled with equal success as actor and playwright, co-authoring with his wife a string of comedy hits including *The Grass is Greener*.

The production budget for *The Amateur Gentleman* was skilfully managed to create the impression of an important A-feature film. Interest in Fairbanks's entrepreneurial debut and speculation about his shot-in-the-arm stake in British cinema didn't harm its prospects, either. London's socialites, including Lord and Lady Louis Mountbatten and Douglas Fairbanks Sr, drove down to Elstree to watch the shooting. They were suitably impressed by the largest set built for a British film up to that time, a 13,000 square foot reconstruction of the ballroom at Carlton House for the Prince Regent's ball. Of Margaret, Fairbanks had this to say recently: 'She was shy but very well disciplined and seemed to all of us to have spent a good amount of time studying her craft. This was a welcome sign as so few of the young players took the trouble then to learn the foundations of their craft. They take even less time nowadays.'

As 1935 drew to a close Margaret had good reason to be pleased with the progress she'd made in just over a year. At the age of nineteen she had eight films to her credit. Only one, *Lorna Doone*, had so far been released and she was still unknown to the public, but that didn't worry her. She was ambitious as an actress, not as a potential star, a distinction that set her apart from the majority of young hopefuls besieging agents and producers at that time. Reserved, retiring, self-effacing as she still was, thoughts of stardom hadn't entered her calculations. She was consolidating her career according to her own estimates, quietly building it block by block and earning the respect of the people who were vital to it. That she had not, like so many of her contemporaries, had to start on the bottom rung of bit parts and walk-ons, striving to be noticed and 'discovered', was luck. That she had never been given an insignificant role, however insignificant the film, could be credited to her own, and Herbert's, hard work and skills.

ℬREAKTHROUGH

'**M**argaret Lockwood looking gloriously attractive in an old-fashioned blue dress, having "still" photographs taken on the set of *The Amateur Gentleman* at Elstree . . .'
Thus Margaret made her debut in the fan columns in November 1935. The item lifted the curtain on a name which wouldn't so much seize film-goers' attention as gently seep into it during the coming weeks. *The Case of Gabriel Perry* went out on release the same month – 'a gripping drama with an unusual twist to it, competently directed and well acted', according to *Film Pictorial*. A prescient reviewer waited until the last paragraph to mention: 'Margaret Lockwood makes her debut on the screen as the daughter and promises to become a personality in British films, if properly groomed and directed.' When the film was reissued four years later she received top billing.

On 23 December 1935, in time for the Christmas holiday, *Midshipman Easy* opened in the West End. Ill luck or bad scheduling brought another, more eye-catching naval epic, *Mutiny on the Bounty*, into the West End the same week but the Hollywood rival didn't blind reviewers to the virtues of the more modest British offering. A brilliant new director was acclaimed:

'The name of Carol Reed . . . will, or should be, on the lips of the entire film world. For that young man has shown a mastery of his job as remarkable as it is distinctive,' wrote *The Sunday Times*. 'The picture has that certainty of atmosphere, that correctness of touch and first-rate casting we can only find in first-rate control.' And, it added, 'Margaret Lockwood is a delightful heroine.'
The Observer thought it 'extraordinary to find an English picture that moves with such a pace from adventure to adventure, that suffers from so few inhibitions and flings out its extravagances so generously'.

The *Sunday Express* declared itself 'impressed by the vigorous, purposeful direction of an unknown young man, Carol Reed'.

The most astringent critic of those days, Graham Greene of the *Spectator*, wrote: 'It is the first film of a new English director, Mr Carol Reed, who has more sense of the cinema that most veteran British directors, certainly than Mr [Herbert] Wilcox or Mr Basil Dean.' Greene and Reed would later collaborate in two of the greatest British films of all time, *The Fallen Idol* and *The Third Man*.

The première of *The Amateur Gentleman*, her most prestigious film to date, had been fixed for 21 January 1936 at the London Pavilion. On 20 January King George V died. He had been an enthusiastic film fan and, with a nice aptness, the last picture this sailor king had watched had been *Midshipman Easy*. On the 21st, the newspapers were edged with black. Cinemas and theatres closed as a mark of respect. The première was cancelled.

It was a bitter disappointment, most of all for Fairbanks, who had staked so much on his first production venture. The film had, however, been previewed by the critics and as the nation mourned the notices appeared, unanimously praising it. But as Fairbanks has since recalled: 'We never quite gained the full momentum needed to start us off well', though business began to pick up later.

Before the new year of 1936 was more than three months old, Margaret's face, if not yet her name, was registering with critics and audiences throughout the country. No young unknown actress had ever achieved such a concentrated exposure to the public in a multiplicity of roles and guises.

A film of the mid–1930s could expect a fairly prolonged life under a release system not yet formally structured and subject to the tyranny of block booking. The general release of *The Amateur Gentleman* was delayed until the summer months and for as long as a year after its London opening it could be found showing in some cinema or other throughout Britain.

A similar lease system of booking applied to the quickies which served the independent exhibitor as a kind of bran-tub into which to dip whenever their British quota requirement needed to be topped up.

Some Day and *Honours Easy* both went into circulation in February 1936, the latter ('A stirring and fascinating marital drama – keyed to emotion's tensest pitch') turning up in many programmes as the supporting feature for one of the year's top box-office attractions,

Garbo's *Anna Karenina*, a match-making that couldn't help but bring Margaret to the attention of an ever-widening public. In March that year *Man of the Moment* started its rounds as a supporting feature, which meant that Margaret was on view in no fewer than five new films criss-crossing the country.

Quietly, behind the scenes, her worth was being assessed. She was professional if not yet fully polished; she was fresh and she had eye-appeal; she was different – a little subdued, perhaps, but definitely a personality. The time had now come to start moulding that personality into a star. It wasn't a term Margaret used herself, still less a status she coveted, but she had committed herself to being a 'famous actress' – a name actress – and if so-called stardom was a necessary part of the process she would resign herself to it.

The chance came in 1936 with *The Beloved Vagabond*, to star Maurice Chevalier.

The company producing the film had recently been set up by a former co-director of Alexander Korda's London Film Productions, the grandly named Italian producer, Ludovico Toeplitz de Grand Ry. Independently wealthy, he had advanced Korda the money to complete *The Private Life of Henry VIII*, then, fired by its success, had broken with Korda to launch his own Toeplitz Productions. His aim was to produce just two films a year but on a scale to rival anything Korda might attempt in quality and commercial potential. The first result had been *The Dictator*, for which he had imported expatriate British stars Madeleine Carroll and Clive Brook from Hollywood; it fulfilled all his hopes except at the box office.

Notwithstanding an uncertain financial future, Toeplitz pressed ahead with his second project, *The Beloved Vagabond*, based on a sentimental novel by William J. Locke. A London architect is enmeshed in a love affair with a woman married to a brutal husband. Seeing that no future with her is possible, he turns his back on her and fashionable London to wander aimlessly around Provence with a young French lad for company – an arrangement which could be offered and accepted in all innocence in those days. The architect meets a peasant girl, Blanquette, whose simple virtues make him take a fresh look at the life he has been leading. He falls in love with her but eventually returns to London – his mistress has obtained a divorce and marriage with her seems unavoidable. On the eve of their wedding Blanquette arrives on the doorstep and all is resolved in a conventional happy ending. Herbert had entered her in the stakes for the role of

Blanquette, together, it was estimated, with every other young actress on the casting books. Three days after finishing *The Amateur Gentleman* in 1935 Margaret had signed the contract. 'I'm so thrilled,' she told reporters. Co-starring with Chevalier, one of the idols of the western world, was guaranteed to thrust her into the public eye and the press made much of the fact that, at nineteen, she was the youngest leading lady in British films.

The director, Kurt Bernhardt, had been an important name in the German cinema until he fled to France when the Nazis came to power. Later, as Curtis Bernhardt, he became one of Hollywood's most polished directors of 'women's pictures', working with Bette Davis, Joan Crawford and Barbara Stanwyck on some of their most successful tear-jerkers. The great Paris couturier Schiaparelli was engaged to design the costumes, the composer Darius Milhaud to supply the music soundtrack. No detail was spared to ensure a quality production. Everything about *The Beloved Vagabond* pointed to success and, for Margaret, a breakthrough into the front rank.

There was a trend in the 1930s to film multi-lingual versions of certain British productions with a view to the Continental market and *The Beloved Vagabond* was to be shot additionally in French, with a French actress replacing Margaret. Location work would take her to the South of France – the first time she had been abroad since arriving in England – and she faced breaking the news to Margaret Evelyn with some trepidation. Surprisingly, she raised no objection, appearing instead to encourage Margaret, who suspected that her reaction was based on the hope that separation might cause a split between herself and Rupert. Although Margaret Evelyn knew they were still seeing each other she hadn't yielded an inch in her opposition since the tea party. Margaret had tried several times to talk her round, to convince her they were serious about each other, but whenever she broached the subject it seemed to drift from her control, into anger on her mother's side and tears on her own. She had learned bitterly never to mention Rupert's name in Margaret Evelyn's hearing. Her Aunt Mary was a sympathetic ally but one without influence: dependent on her sister and no less dominated by her than was Margaret, she had too much to lose to risk taking Margaret's part openly.

No less disturbing for Margaret was the prospect of being separated from Rupert for the first time. He was increasingly pressing her to marry him, pushing her further into a dilemma for which there appeared to be no solution. She wouldn't come of age for another year and even then she couldn't conceive of taking such a momentous step without her mother's approval. Experience may have taught her repeatedly that approval was something Margaret Evelyn dispensed grudgingly but always, in her heart, Margaret craved it.

In desperation, just before production of *The Beloved Vagabond* started, she wrote to her father in India, explaining the situation and asking his permission to marry. Henry didn't reply. Instead he returned her letter to Margaret Evelyn, asking her what was going on and telling her to deal with it as she thought best. There was a terrible scene. Margaret was shattered by her father's treachery and apparent lack of concern for her, and he never figured in her life again. She still was not resilient enough to withstand the stresses of these private conflicts. Departing for Nice was no release; it only seemed to exacerbate matters.

To add to her depression, the travel sickness which had curtailed her studies at the Italia Conti School returned. The weather was bad and the filming schedules erratic. Working with Chevalier awed Margaret – 'I was terrified of him' – and he didn't help the atmosphere by treating her with indifference. Margaret Evelyn, hoping the experience of mixing with people like Chevalier would broaden Margaret's horizons and cut Rupert down to size in her esteem, soon realised it had had the opposite effect. Separation had made both of them realise how committed they were to each other and it stiffened Margaret's determination. On her return to London she confronted her mother and asked her to consider meeting Rupert again.

The reaction was just as she'd expected. A grim tightening of the mouth and . . . 'Don't mention that young man's name to me. I don't want to hear anything about him.' Her tone nevertheless drove Margaret into a tactical error. Flaring, she retorted that she loved Rupert and was going to marry him whatever her mother said. The gloves were off. Margaret Evelyn was angrier than Margaret could ever remember her.

'You don't know what love is,' she sneered, 'and as for marrying him, you'll never get my permission.' Work, she raged on, was what Margaret should be concentrating on. 'And don't you ever dare mention his name in this house again.'

That night, distraught, Margaret told Rupert what had happened. 'She'll never let us marry. She hates you.'

Rupert was thoughtful. After a few moments he said: 'Let's run away together. As soon as you've finished at the studios we'll go to Gretna Green.'

It was a pipe-dream, of course – Rupert was in no position to support a wife. Margaret's income was probably more than enough to keep them in some style but her mother had control over it as long as she was under age. And Rupert, Margaret suspected, would quickly start resenting the thought of living primarily off her earnings as an actress.

In any case there was no prospect that she would be 'finished at the studios', nor that the studios wanted to be finished with her. True, the workload had eased and an industry slump was being forecast. The boom-time of the mid-'thirties, with new studios mushrooming and increasingly ornate picture palaces being built, had attracted a new breed of entrepreneur into the industry, people with high investment to back them – some of them in high society – who were seduced by the glamour as well as the profits of film-making. Small production companies with grand ideas had sprung up, secured by banks and finance houses, only to collapse when the first of their films failed to show an adequate return.

By the end of 1936 Toeplitz Productions was in serious trouble. *The Beloved Vagabond*, only its second film, was also its last. Douglas Fairbanks Jr's Criterion struggled on with three more productions after *The Amateur Gentleman* before it, too, was wound up towards the end of the year. The only area of production which seemed immune to the climate of failure was the quickie, cushioned by government regulations and shoestring financing but even its future now seemed shaky under threats of proposed revisions to the quota system.

Margaret found herself back in quickies. It seemed like a backward step, but work was work and she thrust her personal worries aside. *Irish For Luck* took her back to Irving Asher's Teddington studios, a lightweight screenplay cashing in on a vogue for stories with broadcasting background. Athene Seyler, with whom she'd appeared in *Family Affairs*, played an impoverished Irish duchess, Margaret was her orphaned niece and the handsome Patric Knowles, her co-star in *Honours Easy*, played a busker; all three team up in a radio act for the BBC. It was Knowles's last British film before moving to Hollywood for a long career as a popular second lead, often to Errol Flynn, whom he resembled.

Next, Margaret was loaned out to British National at Pinewood for *The Street Singer;* this was the title Arthur Tracy, better known in the music-hall, had bestowed on himself and the film was designed as a vehicle for him. Margaret's role reduced her to little more than a 'feed' for Tracy as a girl busker who mistakes him for a tramp and takes him under her wing.

Herbert de Leon, scenting the uncertainty in the studios, advised Margaret to keep her options in the theatre open. She had already made a low-key return to the stage earlier in the year for a two-week engagement at the Arts Theatre in a play called *Repayment*, soon forgotten. Now Herbert found her a part in *Miss Smith* at the Duke of York's Theatre. 'Entertaining . . . but not of any distinction,' reported *The Times*. No distinction, either, for Margaret, who took over a minor role a month after the play's June opening: its focus was almost exclusively on its star, Olga Lindo, playing a kind of precursor of Mary Poppins.

Driving home on the night of 30 November 1936, Margaret saw the sky over south London lit by flames. The Crystal Palace was ablaze. Sadly, she watched the great fire consume some of her fondest memories of childhood. Life, just then, seemed greyer than for many months past.

Cinema couldn't match such real-life spectacle but it could at least put it to profitable use. Sam Smith, managing director of British Lion, acted quickly and bought up the rights to all the newsreel footage of the disaster, then set his writers to working up a screenplay. The result was *Melody and Romance*, Margaret's first film of 1937. Again, broadcasting provided the setting and again she was teamed with Hughie Green, this time trailing his Gang along in a story which had all of them simultaneously seeking fame on radio. Among the supporting cast was an actor just making his way into films – Alastair Sim.

The film's climax had Green rescuing her from the Crystal Palace fire. 'I had to carry her out of the flames, so I took the opportunity to feel parts of her I wouldn't normally have got close to. She was shocked. But we always got on well together. I teased her a lot. I liked making her blush.'

As Margaret's 21st birthday approached, the pressures at home intensified. Rupert still clung to the Gretna Green fantasy. The idea seemed even less realistic now than when he had originally suggested it, but in some vague, out-of-reach way it had come to be a last-resort objective for them. Margaret would soon be 21, would become independent, assume responsibility for her own decisions and actions, yet knowing all that was approaching didn't seem to make solutions any easier. It wouldn't change Margaret Evelyn's attitude: she would still have to be faced and defied. Margaret dreaded the scenes she knew would follow; the possibility, even, of a complete break.

There was nobody she could turn to for advice or comfort, no close friends, no relations to support her. Aunt Mary knew what she had in mind but was tremulous about the consequences. Lyn, having decided on an acting career himself, had joined a repertory company at Westcliff-on-Sea well away from family difficulties. Frank, the half-brother she had never really known, was a policeman in Shanghai. Margaret grew more and more preoccupied and withdrawn and the strain began to show in her appearance. She was tired and tense; her complexion deteriorated, her hair was in poor condition.

That summer Carol Reed was casting for a sophisticated comedy called *Who's Your Lady Friend?* There was a good pivotal role in it for Margaret.

Carol had directed two films since *Midshipman Easy;* one of them, *Laburnum Grove*, added to his growing reputation, the other, a quickie called *Talk of the Devil* which he had also written, set it back again. He had just signed a three-year contract with Gainsborough Pictures, guaranteeing him a year-round £100 a week, rising to £150 – Edward (Ted) Black, Gainsborough's managing director and one of the shrewdest heads in the business, knew when he had a good investment. All the same, despite being clearly destined for higher things, Carol was still expected to take his share of routine work.

'You were handed a script and told you had to shoot so many scenes a day,' he recalled. 'It was a six-day week and you were seldom through before eight any night. If you didn't make up your lost time you were liable to be taken off the picture and somebody put in who could push it through on time.'

Who's Your Lady Friend? was a bread-and-butter assignment on loan-out to Dorian, another of the maverick independent companies. The comedian Vic Oliver and the singer Frances Day – a name that must have struck chords with Margaret on-set – were the stars. Also in the cast, making her screen debut, was Oliver's wife, Sarah Churchill, Winston Churchill's daughter, earnestly assuring interviewers that she wished to succeed on talent, not because she was the wife and daughter of famous men.

The screenplay, based on a German stage hit and film *Der Herr*

Ohne Wohnung, was a marital mix-up comedy. Oliver played an eminent cosmetic surgeon who sends his secretary (male) to meet a celebrity patient off the train. The secretary's girl-friend – Margaret's role – happens to see him with the strange woman (in fact he's collected the wrong one) and thinks he's two-timing her. Misunderstandings fan out to embroil the surgeon and his wife.

Preoccupied with her personal love problems, Margaret was in no mood to be playing brittle, fast-paced farce. Her mind wasn't on the job. She viewed some of the rushes – the first time she had ever done so – and was appalled by what she saw. Her performance was arch, artificial, bad. Carol thought so too. He tried to help her tone down her mannerisms but the results were still unconvincing. He was puzzled by the change that had come over her; this wasn't the actress he had had such faith in.

The whole production was jinxed. Chief cameraman Jan Stallich suddenly collapsed on the set with acute appendicitis. Rushing to his aid, the chief electrician, Jack Ford, tripped and injured himself badly. It looked as though the picture would have to be abandoned, and Carol was distraught, but the cast, including Margaret, offered to work overtime without pay and the film was completed on schedule, saving Carol's face. By then, everyone was suffering from the strain. 'I was never so happy to finish a picture,' Margaret said, dismayed at her own performance and aware that Carol had lost confidence in her.

Some consolation was at hand with the première of *The Beloved Vagabond* in March 1937. The critics were lukewarm about the film, but not about Margaret. She was, they generally agreed, its saving grace, and she garnered more column inches than the great Chevalier himself.

'Easy to enjoy and even easier to forget,' said *The Times* of the film, then added: 'Chevalier has handled, with his particular charm and grace, the not too formidable situations with which he is faced. Miss Lockwood, however, can act and she is so persuasive that the audience begins actively to care.' The *Daily Sketch* hailed her as 'definitely one of our coming stars. She is gracious and charming and has that certain quality that should take her to the top.' The *Sunday Times* critic was won over by 'the altogether delightful presence of Margaret Lockwood . . . her beauty and natural ability are undeniable and I have the feeling this picture will be a tremendous help to her in gaining the recognition she deserves'.

She had made her mark. Within two months the first 'star' interview with her appeared in a fan magazine. 'Margaret Lockwood is the essence of youthful innocence and romance, dark, vivacious, with eyes that twinkle mischievously,' gushed the *Picture Show* columnist.

There were signs that she had already mastered the art of fielding awkward questions. Asked if she was in love with anyone, she replied 'a little guardedly' in the interviewer's opinion: 'No, I don't think so.' Persisting, he managed to extract some cogent pointers to her feelings which, had he known the situation, might have guided him to a scoop.

'Miss Lockwood assured me that she would never marry an actor. She was most definite about this. In fact, a little too definite for anybody who is not in love. She is quite certain she will never marry anybody either connected with the stage or screen. I fancy there is some lucky fellow somewhere about. But one thing she was also definite about was that if she did marry she would never give up the screen.' Another full-page interview followed two months later in *Picturegoer*. This time her defences were up: references to her private life were firmly avoided.

According to Margaret, 'I expected great things to develop from my performance [in *The Beloved Vagabond*] but nothing happened, no great offers were forthcoming.' Still, when *The Beloved Vagabond* opened in New York, the first time one of her films had been seen by American critics and audiences, *Variety* commented: 'She has a pleasing personality and a voice that is less British than the average. Her wistfulness reminds one of Janet Gaynor' – a current favourite in *A Star is Born*.

In June 1937 Margaret had been loaned out to the Gaumont-British Picture Corporation for the female lead in *Dr Syn*. Its star was the great George Arliss, at 69 nearing the end of his career, and he had the title role in what was to be his final film. Margaret played his daughter and her romantic interest was John Loder from *Lorna Doone*.

Russell Thorndike's stories of eighteenth-century smugglers on the Romney Marshes led by the sinister vicar of Dymchurch, in reality a former pirate believed to have been hanged, had enjoyed lasting popularity since the 1920s. Margaret's ingenue role was one she could play blindfold but she never took any role for granted. Working with an actor of George Arliss's stature gave her an extra incentive. So did the director, Roy William Neill, yet another Hollywood exile. His speciality was above-average B-pictures and after a few more British productions he would return to Hollywood to direct Basil Rathbone's Sherlock Holmes series. He was a craftsman with a knack for fine detail, a technique Margaret could appreciate and respond to.

She treated George Arliss with a proper degree of awe, self-effacing in his presence and grateful for his occasional kindly advice. He, in turn, was impressed by her and made a point of telling Maurice Ostrer and Ted Black, the Gaumont-British production executives, that she was 'a nice little actress' whom they shouldn't let slip through their fingers. Three days into shooting Ostrer and Black viewed the early rushes. With Arliss's advice in mind, they took special note of Margaret and liked what they saw. Her contract with British Lion had only a few weeks left to run. Ostrer and Black decided to buy it out.

The timing couldn't have been better. British Lion, overtaken by the slump, had struck a financial reef and was foundering. *Melody and Romance*, finished earlier in the year, was the last film made by them for twelve months. They had nothing in prospect for Margaret.

Ostrer and Black offered her a three-year contract with Gainsborough Pictures, the production arm of Gaumont-British, guaranteeing her £3,000 a year. Herbert was confident he could hold out for £4,000. Such a sum was wealth beyond the dreams of a twenty-year-old actress only three years into her career. In those days a new three-bedroom house in the London area cost £300; a luxury flat could be rented for £250 a year. Margaret Evelyn was incredulous. '£60 a week for a slip of girl like you' – but behind the scoffing words lay an inadmissible pride. Had she looked further ahead to the prospect of Margaret's independence, she might, even then, have helped them both by a show of friendship.

ℳARRIAGE

G ainsborough had been founded in 1924 by Michael Balcon and taken over four years later by the Gaumont-British Picture Corporation, which, besides producing and distributing films, owned a nationwide chain of 300 cinemas: the tiny Gainsborough studios at Islington in north London augmented the much larger facilities G-B operated at Shepherd's Bush on the western side of the capital.

Gainsborough's restructuring, in 1938, was largely financed by the three Ostrer brothers – Maurice, Isidore and Mark – who encouraged Balcon, in charge of production, to shift production emphasis to capture a slice of the lucrative American audience. Every British production company of any account during the 1930s had made strenuous efforts to do the same, but only Alexander Korda had any appreciable success.

For Gainsborough the gamble had been disastrous. Hollywood stars were imported, lavish budgets allocated, but the films met, at best, with indifference if not with outright antipathy from the all-powerful, studio-owned US cinema monopolies. By 1936 the company's losses were critical and Balcon left to join MGM's British operation. His successor was Ted Black, who had joined Gainsborough in 1928 as a studio manager.

Black was one of another remarkable trio of brothers. They came from the north-east of England and they each left a mark on British show-business, George and Alfred as theatre impresarios. A restrained, courteous man, deeply respected by his associates – to Margaret he was always 'dear Ted' – Ted Black possessed that most vital, and elusive, gift a film producer can have: an unerring instinct for the public's taste.

One of the first decisions he made at Gainsborough was to build up a star system which would rival Hollywood's, something the British industry had failed conspicuously to do – the top names of the mid–1930s had all come into films from well-established theatre careers, Anna Neagle being virtually the only example of an unknown who had been conscientiously groomed to screen stardom and Basil Dean's attempts to build his wife, Victoria Hopper, into a major star being all too typical of the right idea put behind the wrong talent.

Not that the studios were incapable of spotting star quality. Merle Oberon, Madeleine Carroll, Wendy Barrie, Charles Laughton, Ray Milland, even Errol Flynn, had all made lowly starts in a British studio but as soon as they became recognisable they side-stepped smartly in the direction of Hollywood. Ted Black knew this could and must be changed.

'It seemed to me', he wrote, 'that there was a great dearth of British stars, especially as the best of them usually found a permanent home in Hollywood as soon as they were successful enough. So I set out to create some new stars by putting fresh talent into well-made pictures.' Margaret's contract was his first move to implement the plan. Margaret Lockwood was going to be Britain's first custom-made film star.

Black had a perfect subject in mind to launch her, and a new co-star in mind for her to play against but first she needed to build her experience and her screen confidence. He put her initially into a modest romance of life among Cumbrian hill farmers, *Owd Bob*. Margaret must have felt some disappointment. Little seemed to have changed . . . the same passive, placid role she had played endlessly . . . John Loder for her leading man. The Scottish comedian Will Fyffe played her father.

'Owd Bob' was the name of a sheepdog, owned by a crusty farmer, which has traditionally won the annual sheepdog trials – until a young doctor, newly arrived in the neighbourhood, takes the trophy with his dog. The developing feud is complicated by the farmer's daughter falling in love with the newcomer. The film offered Margaret little challenge. 'She has trouble with the accent and her perm is too perfect,' sniffed one critic. But Ted, undeterred, was more concerned with Phase Two of his grand design.

Black's vision wasn't confined to establishing a stable of stars. He wanted at the same time to change the face of Gainsborough's films, breaking away from the raw comedy and routine melodrama that had been its staple fare. He was seeking a new sense of realism.

Bank Holiday was a different kind of screenplay. It showed people in everyday situations, held a mirror up for the audience to see themselves. The script was naturalistic and understated, skilfully orchestrating joys and heartaches, humour and human interest, strongly emotional and spiced with illicit romance. It followed the fortunes of a group of characters only loosely linked to each other, spending one August Bank Holiday weekend in a seaside resort – Brighton by another name.

Central to it was the story of a young London nurse who has reluctantly agreed to spend the weekend with her boy-friend. Not only is she troubled by guilt and doubt over her tryst but also by concern for the distraught husband of one of her patients who has just died in childbirth. She cuts short a weekend of minor disasters and embarrassments to dash back to London in time to save the husband from a suicide attempt. Sub-plots involving peripheral holidaying characters fed into the main story.

Carol Reed, lined up to direct, realised it was a subject that could advance his career, but he was dismayed to learn who his leading lady was to be. Disappointment over Margaret's work in *Who's Your Lady Friend?* still rankled. He didn't relish a repeat performance and made his objections clear to Black, stifling them only when it was hinted that he could be taken off the picture if he refused to accept her.

Unaware of these pre-production frictions, Margaret was filling in time between finishing *Owd Bob* and starting *Bank Holiday* with a brief return to Jack de Leon's Q Theatre in *Ann's Lapse*, a comedy which turned on a chain of absurd events caused by her character's loss of memory. 'Miss Margaret Lockwood found it difficult to manage the heroine's cruder remarks, but when she was given the chance she was engaging,' wrote *The Times* in a tepid review. It was her last stage performance for twelve years.

Shooting on *Bank Holiday* started in September 1937 at Islington. The atmosphere on-set was edgy for the first few days, with Carol no more communicative than he needed to be and Margaret correspondingly nervous.

'His attitude towards me was one of extreme wariness,' she noted.

But imperceptibly the mood began to change. From the first day filming forged ahead without a hitch and with gathering momentum. Carol's reservations about Margaret were dispelled when he saw the first rushes. Clearly, *Who's Your Lady Friend?* had been an aberration, a prolonged off-moment. Now she was justifying all the hopes he had originally had and he concentrated his direction on her, nurturing the quality of naturalness and serenity, the quietness of voice and calmness of delivery which set her apart from the brittle 'projected' personalities and diction of most of her contemporaries. (The critic James Agate, reviewing Anna Neagle's performance as *Victoria the Great*, had noted that her accent was 'overlaid by layer after layer of suburban refinement'.)

Margaret told a *Film Weekly* columnist a few weeks later: 'As the picture swung into production I experienced a quite unforgettable feeling of elation. We made the film at tremendous speed, scarcely stopping for retakes, and everything that went into the camera sparkled with life.'

What nobody on the set guessed was that she was living on a knife-edge of nervous tension. She had come to a momentous decision. Her 21st birthday, on 15 September, soon after starting work on the film, had finally made her legally free of Margaret Evelyn's authority. And she'd made up her mind, come what may, to marry Rupert at the first opportunity.

'I was working long hours at the studio, nervous lest I should spoil the important part I'd been given and unhappy because I couldn't marry and fearful of the tremendous rift I knew it would cause between mother and me when I did. I couldn't eat. My face was covered with spots and the most trivial things would make me cry.'

Again Rupert proposed they wed in secret. Again, thinking he still had Gretna Green in mind, she stalled, this time with the reasonable argument that she had become too well known and the newspapers would seize on it. Rupert countered by pointing out that after 15 September there was no need for Gretna Green or a runaway marriage: they could have a normal ceremony in any registry office.

It seemed to make sense. Except that it didn't solve the problem she dreaded most – her mother's reaction. Rupert now played his trump card. Nobody, he assured her, need ever know. They could slip away early one morning, get married, carry on as though nothing had happened and Margaret Evelyn needn't be told until the film was finished. By then they would be man and wife and she would have a husband to stand up for her. It was, of course, a supremely unrealistic stratagem but Margaret, too dispirited to come up with an alternative, fell in with it.

Rupert, elated, went ahead with the arrangements. The wedding day was to be Saturday, 16 October. He found a registrar willing to oblige in the small Surrey market town of Epsom, conveniently out of the way but not too far from Upper Norwood; they had often driven out to Epsom Downs, overlooking the famous Derby racecourse, to enjoy the bracing uplands air on their Sunday dates.

With plans carefully laid, Margaret somehow had to find an excuse to be absent from the studio that Saturday. At the beginning of the week she screwed up courage to ask if she could be spared so that she could attend the wedding of 'a friend'. It simply wouldn't have occurred to the professional in her to plead a diplomatic illness and not show up for work. Carol, however, refused permission.

Rupert, frantically phoning, managed to get a postponement and a dispensation for the ceremony to take place the following day, a Sunday. As that week passed, hour by counted hour, Margaret was in an agony of suspense. Then, as though the fates were conspiring, a totally unforeseen development added another nail-biting twist to the suspense. She had forgotten all about *Melody and Romance*, made eight months earlier and still awaiting release. With only two days left before her wedding day, and giving the performance of her life to keep Margaret Evelyn's suspicions at bay, she got a call from Beaconsfield: last-minute retakes needed to be shot on *Melody and Romance*. Only a day's work . . . but the only day all the people involved were free was a Sunday – this coming Sunday. Short of revealing her secret, Margaret could see no way out. She had to agree.

Early that morning of 17 October 1937 Rupert drove round to 30 Highland Road as usual and sounded the car horn as usual. Margaret ran to the door, calling her usual good-bye. At least she hadn't had to lie to her mother: she would be going to work, just as she'd told her. As she climbed into the car, Rupert pointed out that she would need a hat. She ran back into the house, back upstairs and grabbed the only one she possessed, her old school beret. Well-used and out of shape, it seemed all of a piece with the dowdy working clothes she always wore to the studios.

A registry office wedding required witnesses, so they had let two people close to them in on the secret, Kenneth Cluitt, an old friend of Rupert's, and Kathleen Marshall, an actress who had been in the *Family Affairs* company. Rupert detoured to collect them. At ten minutes to nine the car drew up outside Epsom Registry Office in the Sunday morning quiet of a small country town. All four sat silently for a few moments, sensing the tensions that precede every wedding as the moment of no return approaches. The enormity of what they were about to do, the implications, crowded in on Margaret. She was far from being the proverbial happy bride. She took a last look at herself in the rear-view mirror and put the beret on, noting how spotty her face was. Then she grabbed Rupert's hand and squeezed it.

The ceremony was as anonymous as any the registrar had ever performed. He didn't recognise the bride. When the time came to sign the register, she left the space for her profession blank. She avoided writing her own address by giving Rupert's instead, unknowingly emulating her grandmother. As far as was legally permissible, she obliterated all traces of her true identity. And again, unknowingly, by marrying at the earliest opportunity after her 21st birthday, she echoed the circumstances of her father's first marriage. Ten minutes later Mr and Mrs Rupert Leon were on their way to Beaconsfield.

Any passing thought Margaret Evelyn might have given her daughter at that hour would have been no more than a mental check that she was hard at work in the studio. And so, almost, she was. As the 'bridal' car drew up at the studio gate Margaret drew her wedding ring off and gave it to Rupert for safe-keeping. It wasn't only a symbol of the fulfilment and happiness a wedding ring confers, it was a reminder of a brooding shadow, too. It symbolised a deception.

At the end of a morning's work Margaret managed to slip away and join the other three for lunch. It was hardly a festive wedding breakfast: she and Rupert were debating how they could contrive to spend their wedding night together without arousing their families' suspicions. As dusk approached, luck came to their rescue. By 6.30 p.m. when Margaret was free to leave the studio, a fog had settled. She phoned her mother and explained that it was so dense she would have to spend the night in an hotel. With the ring back on her finger, the pair drove cautiously into London and registered at a small, anonymous hotel near Marble Arch.

The stress of this extraordinary – not least for being so ordinary – day had taken its toll. They were both exhausted, and Margaret had to be up at 5.30 the next morning for an early studio call. After work that Monday evening, according to plan, she returned home to 30 Highland Road and settled back into its routine as though nothing had happened.

Margaret made no attempt to prepare her mother for the revelation that was bound to come. The end of shooting on *Bank Holiday* was still the deadline agreed with Rupert for announcing their marriage, but when it came, several weeks later, she still couldn't find the courage. Rupert was forbearing. They continued to see each other every Sunday and for the occasional evening out, with Margaret Evelyn's tacit disapproval. They were over 21, man and wife, and still conducting themselves like artful children.

Suddenly Margaret had a valid excuse for further stalling: immediately *Bank Holiday* finished she learned she must start work on her next film with barely a week to catch her breath. A few weeks previously she had spotted by chance a newspaper item announcing that she was to star in a film called *Lost Lady*. Studio chiefs in those days often announced film plans to the press without feeling any obligation to inform their contract players. *Lost Lady* was based on a novel, *The Wheel Spins*, by Ethel Lina White.

A White fan, Margaret knew the book and knowing also that Gainsborough owned the film rights had been longing to play its spirited heroine, Iris Henderson. Her hopes of doing so weren't high: both Lilli Palmer and Nova Pilbeam were being tipped for the role. Then, out of the blue, it was hers. She was elated and looking forward eagerly to being told when filming would start.

Alfred Hitchcock was to direct. Under contract to Gainsborough, he had one last commitment to the company and he was anxious to discharge it so that he could take up an offer from David O. Selznick and leave for Hollywood. He had already rejected a couple of scripts and had been urging Ted Black to come up quickly with something more suitable. *Lost Lady*, adapted by an unknown pair of writers, Frank Launder and Sidney Gilliat, had been lying on a shelf in the story department for the past year. Initial attempts to produce it in 1936 had been aborted after a location unit sent to Yugoslavia had been ordered to leave the country: the government, fearful of upsetting Adolf Hitler, had taken exception to one scene in which a shot of goose-stepping soldiers dissolved into another of waddling geese. Early in November 1937, however, the cameras started rolling at Islington. *Lost Lady* became *The Lady Vanishes*.

Ted Black's eye for star quality had fastened on a young actor called Michael Redgrave, making a name for himself with John Gielgud's Old Vic Company.

After several years as an amateur, Redgrave had turned professional and joined the Liverpool Playhouse company in 1934, the year of Margaret's debut. He had made an immediate impact when he came to London in the autumn of 1936 and was soon being hounded by film producers, who were mystified and exasperated by his apparent lack of interest in their offers. A small part that year in Hitchcock's

The Secret Agent starring his mentor Gielgud was Redgrave's only experience of screen acting, and not one calculated to make him alter his attitude towards it.

'It may seem a little odd that . . . I should have been so aloof towards the cinema,' he explained in his memoirs, 'but I was a stage actor, and at that time there was a gulf between the stage and the screen. Not an unbridgeable gulf: Olivier and Ralph Richardson made films but only Charles Laughton took films, especially English films, seriously.'

It was the persuasive Ted Black who finally talked Redgrave into testing for the male lead in *The Lady Vanishes* and signing a contract. Gielgud, Edith Evans and Peggy Ashcroft all tried to dissuade him but Black prevailed, his one concession a clause allowing Redgrave six months free every year for theatre work.

Just as Margaret had learned of her casting from the newspapers, so Redgrave read one day that she was going to be his leading lady. They were introduced for the first time at a film charity ball at the Royal Albert Hall and urged to pose in an embrace for the photographers. The pictures which duly appeared gave a totally false impression of their initial reactions to each other. Margaret was suspicious of his 'actorish' disdain for the whole business of filming, which she thought unprofessional of him. Redgrave was apprehensive about her complete mastery of camera technique in which he wasn't just a novice, but a novice unwilling to learn.

'As a matter of fact', he told the Hungarian actor, Paul Lukas, who was playing the villain in the film, 'I find it intensely boring.' This was an attitude that irritated Margaret – 'though she was too kind to reproach me for it'.

It was perhaps fortuitous that the relationship between them in the script called for a degree of antipathy and exasperation, at least until halfway through it, when they started to fall in love. Redgrave admitted: 'I respected her professionalism, as I respected Hitchcock's, yet secretly I saw little to praise in it.'

Ted Black was satisfied, however. Margaret's performance was better than he'd hoped for and the rushes showed that the chemistry between his two protegés was working.

At that stage of production nobody foresaw that *The Lady Vanishes* was going to be an exceptional film, a classic. At under £80,000, its budget was negligible. Shooting was confined to a cramped 90-foot long stage and the schedule was tight. Filming lasted a meagre five weeks, ending early in December, but it was those very conditions, orchestrated by Hitchcock, anxious to be off and away, that helped give the film its pace, immediacy and quick-fire mix of suspense and humour, as fresh and endearing after 50 years as they seemed at the time of its original release.

Not so obvious are the changes it marked in Margaret. Compared with *Bank Holiday*, made only a few weeks earlier, she showed a new authority, a more cutting edge to her personality. She had been married less than a month when filming started but already she seemed to have shed some of her inhibition and found a new confidence. She also looked prettier than in any of her previous films.

That December Queen Mary attended the charity première of *Dr Syn* at the New Gallery Cinema. Three years before Margaret had furtively slipped into the première of *Lorna Doone*, uninvited, unsung. Now she was to present a bouquet to the Queen.

In her first days with Gainsborough, Maurice Ostrer had been annoyed by Margaret's apparent lack of interest in her appearance off-duty. He carpeted her after spotting her at Newmarket Races one Saturday, on a day out with Rupert, wearing an old raincoat and no stockings, gloves or hat. The following Monday Ostrer called her to his office and bluntly explained what he expected of rising young actresses on his payroll. Ted Black later recalled: 'Around the *Dr Syn* time it was a great trouble to get her to dress up and look presentable at premières and parties. Her ideas of dress seemed confined to a raincoat and beret. I had to reason with her, explaining that the public expected glamour from their favourites.'

Margaret never needed correcting twice. Fashion and dressing up would always be low in her priorities as an individual but for her public, from then on, no effort was spared. The *Dr Syn* première was her baptism as a star in full dress. Maurice Ostrer appointed himself her advisor and she went shopping in Oxford Street, choosing a white chiffon gown trimmed with rosebuds and a white fox fur. The bill came to £60, a week's pay. Despite having spent the money under orders from the boss she didn't dare tell Margaret Evelyn how much she had spent.

At home everyone approved when she gave them a preview, but since the première was not on a Sunday Rupert had no chance to see her in her finery. It was another niggling reminder of the sideline role he was being forced to play in their life together, but a more painful

77

one followed a month later. It was Christmas. Their first as man and wife . . . but because of Margaret's faint-heartedness they had to carry on acting out the pantomime of being 'just good friends'.

It was the most miserable Christmas of Margaret's life, made worse by the knowledge that she was the cause of such an unnatural situation. The misery of it compounded the lie they were living, adding yet more strain to the guilt they shared.

Rupert began to get impatient. Their marriage, unacknowledged, inadmissible, invalidated by the intransigence of one woman, was a sham. Spurred by the wretched Christmas spent apart, Rupert finally took a firm line with Margaret and told her that she had to confront her mother. She agreed but could no more find the courage than before. Was she ready, in her innermost self, for the commitment? Was Rupert? They had convinced themselves and each other that they were in love. But could they really know? In each case, it was first love. They had no previous experience to measure their feelings by.

In the end, the matter was taken out of their hands. Margaret's greatest naïveté, perhaps, was in failing to realise that she was no longer a young apprentice actress but a rising star, a public figure, with public interest in her increasing, fanned by the studio's publicity machine. Somehow rumours started circulating that she was secretly married. Carol Reed himself had suspected that the 'friend's wedding' she had wanted to attend during *Bank Holiday* was, in fact, her own, but kept his thoughts to himself. In the gossip-hungry circles of film and theatre, however, it was inevitable that the secret would leak out.

Bank Holiday opened in March 1938. Overnight the name of Margaret Lockwood became newsworthy. A reporter, trying to contact her, telephoned 30 Highland Road and spoke to Margaret Evelyn. His opening words stunned her. Indignantly she denied the 'rumour'. Of course her daughter wasn't married. But the reporter had done his research at Somerset House. In front of him he had a copy of a certificate of marriage between Margaret Mary Lockwood and Rupert William Leon at Epsom Registry Office on 17 October 1937 . . .

When Margaret returned home she was met in the hallway by an ashen-faced Aunt Mary.

'You'd better go straight to your mother,' she whispered. 'She knows you're married.'

It was a scene neither mother nor daughter would ever forget, more harrowing than Margaret, in her worst fears, had ever envisaged. She had steeled herself against anger, accusations and denunciations, but not against tears. It was the first time in her life Margaret had seen her mother in tears. On and on Margaret Evelyn stormed. How could she have been so ungrateful and deceitful? She had brought shame on them all.

'You've never done anything that I've forbidden in your whole life. How could you marry that man?'

Margaret heard her out before trying to explain and justify herself. It was useless. Reason was the last thing Margaret Evelyn wanted to listen to. In one last bid at reconciliation, Margaret begged her at least to meet Rupert and give him a chance to speak for himself. Margaret Evelyn's only reply was a vow never to allow her son-in-law to enter her house.

PART TWO

*T*HE *L*ADY *V*ANISHES... AND GOES TO *H*OLLYWOOD

O minous newspaper headlines on 14 March 1938 told the British people of Adolf Hitler's annexation of Austria, the first spark of the conflagration that was to engulf Europe eighteen months later. Had readers but realised, the news that morning signified the beginning of the end of life as Britain had known it – familiar, ordered, complacent – for the past two decades. Perhaps attention was more strongly caught by news on the inside pages of the same newspapers of a new British film – *Bank Holiday*, a valedictory, as it turned out, for those years of peace and simple, conventional pleasures.

That day Margaret became a star. The critics proclaimed her unanimously: 'Margaret Lockwood suddenly stands out as an actress,' (London *Evening Standard*).

'Margaret Lockwood is particularly successful. I regard her as one of the best of our younger film actresses. Beware of Hollywood! Miss Lockwood must be kept in England at all costs to appear, as she deserves, in bigger and better pictures,' (*Daily Herald*).

'Three cheers for a fine British picture, well cast, most ably directed by Carol Reed and, above all, establishing Margaret Lockwood as a lovely, sensitive and clever young star. She is admirable. Her performance has remarkable skill and charm,' (*Daily Sketch*).

'In particular it is a triumph for a thirty-year-old English director Carol Reed and a twenty-year-old [*sic*] English actress Margaret Lockwood. Of Miss Lockwood I need only say that her possibilities have been sticking out a mile ever since she played her first big part two years ago.

'She has beauty, dignity and an unaffected charm and she is mercifully free of vowel mutilation and that odious trick of the British ingénue – ending every other word on a breathy higher note, supposed to suggest vivacity or emotion whereas, of course, all it really suggests is adenoids,' (*Daily Telegraph*).

The critics' enthusiasm for the film wasn't quite matched by London's film-goers. Events in Europe were making people edgy, *Bank Holiday* wasn't obvious escapism and the box office for the opening weeks was sluggish. But it was the kind of film that thrives on word-of-mouth publicity and by the time it went into general release – on Whitsun Bank Holiday – the returns were building respectably.

Ted Black, meanwhile, had been building his ideas for Margaret into a structured plan. Delighted with the results of the Lockwood-Redgrave partnership in *The Lady Vanishes*, he saw in it Britain's answer to the romantic teaming Hollywood had employed with so much success – a British William Powell and Myrna Loy, or Charles Farrell and Janet Gaynor, or Tyrone Power and Loretta Young. He released details to the press of two important subjects lined up for them. It was a measure of his faith that they were both to be in colour, a process Gainsborough had never before been able to afford.

The first, to go into production that summer, was to be *The Blue Lagoon*, a bold choice in view of its risqué storyline. The second would be a costume epic based on the exploits of the Scottish outlaw, Rob Roy. But within days of Hitler's march into Austria, all such projects were put into abeyance as the British people found themselves facing a real prospect of war.

All over the country civil defence emergency plans were activated. Gas masks were rushed to distribution centres. Plans to evacuate the likely target cities were drawn up. The London night sky was dissected by searchlights as anti-aircraft units held exercises. The panic quickly evaporated but an air of uncertainty and trepidation intensified as Europe waited for Hitler's next move. For its part, Gainsborough decided that until the situation clarified plans to send a location unit to the Caribbean for *The Blue Lagoon* should be dropped, production temporarily shelved. A camera unit had been dispatched to the Scottish Highlands to shoot background footage for *Rob Roy*, and both Margaret and Michael Redgrave had got as far as costume tests, before this, too, was postponed. As a result Margaret suddenly found herself with the first prolonged period of free time on her hands since *Lorna Doone* four years before.

Once news of her marriage was out, Margaret had set about re-organising her personal affairs. Not least because of her mother's attitude, but also because being known to be living apart from Rupert could have fuelled all kinds of speculation, their first priority was to find a home of their own.

Dolphin Square was then one of the most glamorous addresses in London. It had been open only a year, a model of futuristic planned living on the Chelsea Embankment overlooking the Thames. It was a cathedral of Art Deco design, a self-sufficient township of 1,250 service apartments with shops, a restaurant, squash courts, a swimming pool and gymnasium.

Margaret and Rupert leased a flat on the eighth floor with two bedrooms, a large drawing-room including a dining area, and a balcony commanding a spectacular view over the city. It was just the right setting for a film star; indeed many, then and now, have chosen to live there. 'A tiny service flat in town for use while she is filming,' was how one fan magazine in June 1938 described it. Margaret told the interviewer: 'I took this flat because I liked the swimming pool and it's quiet here.' No hint that she was sharing it with a husband. 'Her main thoughts', readers were informed, 'concern getting on with her career, saving money for her old age and enjoying the best things of life in the right spirit.' Rupert, if he had read it, wouldn't have found much reassurance in those quotes.

Margaret now took over control of her own finances. Gainsborough had redrafted her contract on the strength of *Bank Holiday*, boosting her salary to £6,000 a year – the equivalent of £140,000 in late–1980s values. She was already one of the top-earning British stars. Re-ordering her financial affairs called for some delicacy. Margaret Evelyn now had to relinquish the 50 per cent of Margaret's income she had always, whatever the sum, kept for rent, board and sundry services. Rupert's income remained a pittance compared with his wife's. Margaret arranged for mother and husband to receive a monthly allowance of £30 each, handing over responsibility for the rest of her finances to Herbert, who launched a programme of investment.

Now, with time unexpectedly on her hands, she and Rupert took off on a delayed honeymoon, driving down to Devon to stay at a quiet hotel at Slapton Sands near Dartmouth, out of reach of studio or parental pressures.

A number of Hollywood companies had over the years been buying themselves into British production, mainly as a means of securing studio space for the quickies and B-pictures they found it profitable to make in Britain, thereby circumventing the quota system.

MGM and Twentieth Century-Fox had made substantial invest-
ments in Gaumont-British, Gainsborough's parent company, and Fox
had exclusive access to Gainsborough's studio facilities. Fox's policy
through the 1930s had been to produce films which would be acceptable to audiences on both sides of the Atlantic, renting any studio
space available, latterly at Pinewood. Several important, if not always
commercially successful, films had resulted, most notably the first
British production ever shot entirely in Technicolor – *Wings of the
Morning*, a big international hit. In 1938, however, Pinewood closed
down and Fox was obliged to transfer its dwindling production to
Gainsborough's sound stages at Islington.

While Margaret and Rupert were on holiday, MGM and Gaumont-
British/Gainsborough announced a new distribution deal under which
The Lady Vanishes would be the first release. On paper it looked like
just another business agreement but it would have a significant influence on Margaret's immediate future since in return for the British
distribution rights MGM guaranteed a coveted American release for
any co-productions through its own chain of cinemas. It was an entrée
to the US market that no other British producer, except the independent Korda, had ever been able to secure. Even such a breakthrough
as that, however, looked hopeless in the current uncertain atmosphere. In September, though, Britain's Prime Minister, Neville
Chamberlain, flew back from his talks with Hitler flourishing the scrap
of paper that constituted the Munich Agreement. 'Peace in our time'
had been bought at the expense of the Czech nation. Britain rejoiced.
There would be no war after all, and life could continue.

The Blue Lagoon was taken down off the shelf and re-scheduled
for the summer of 1939, but with a revised cast. Fox, now involved
at Gainsborough, pressed for Michael Redgrave to be replaced by
Richard Greene, a handsome young British actor they were grooming
for leading man status alongside Tyrone Power and Don Ameche.
More immediately, though, a Fox-Gainsborough co-production was
hurriedly set up for Margaret to star in and Carol Reed to direct.

A Girl Must Live was a slight, bubbly comedy drama with a London
night-club background, a British answer to Hollywood's *Stage Door*,
starring Ginger Rogers and Katharine Hepburn, which had come out
the previous year. Margaret played an upper-class girl determined to
break into show-business who runs away from her exclusive finishing
school and books into a theatrical boarding-house, falsely claiming to
be the daughter of a once-famous Edwardian musical star. Her fellow

boarders are chorus girls and second-rate theatricals, and the film's plot found its humour and dramatic conflict in the interplay between the sheltered, unworldly heroine and the hard-boiled company she keeps.

A Girl Must Live is probably the least regarded of Carol Reed's mature films, made in a dismal year in which he had directed two miscalculations: the Jessie Matthews musical, *Climbing High*, in which Michael Redgrave had followed up *The Lady Vanishes;* and *Penny Paradise*, a film 'so awful it's difficult to believe it wasn't made way back in 1932', according to one critic. Fifty years later it has been re-assessed as a lively period piece, justifying Margaret's own defence of it as 'a good picture . . . it deserved a bigger success'. Certainly, it now has a patina of nostalgic 1930s glamour, unusual for a British production. The art director Vetchinsky, for example, based his designs for the Blue Roof night-club on 'geometrical theorems of ancient Greece – everything in geometrical forms breathing the spirit of Pythagoras'.

In October 1938 *The Lady Vanishes* opened at MGM's flagship cinema, the Empire in Leicester Square. Its reception left no doubt that Alfred Hitchcock – by now in Hollywood – had become Britain's most brilliant director. The opening couldn't have been better timed to catch the public mood. Superficially, at least, there was an air of optimism in the land. Revived confidence in the film industry was reflected in the lavish new picture palaces opening weekly up and down the country, and in the same opening week Warner launched their West End flagship cinema next door to the Empire, with Errol Flynn in *The Adventures of Robin Hood*.

As for *The Lady Vanishes*, its breezy, understated, inimitably British sense of humour, the topicality of its Balkan politics, skulduggery and menacing secret police, its tongue-in-cheek spirit of British integrity trouncing the dark forces of European-style tyranny, all these facets seemed a reassurance that the recent threat of war had been reduced to a proper insignificance.

Margaret and Rupert, like everyone else, had taken the threat, while it lasted, seriously enough. During their holiday trip they discussed the likely horrors to come if there was war and on an impulse decided to find a country retreat they could use as a bolt-hole if London was attacked.

They found the 'inexpensive bungalow' Rupert had in mind at the end of a dirt track in the straggling, nondescript village of St Leonards between Ringwood and Bournemouth in Hampshire. Inexpensive it certainly was – Margaret paid no more than £150 for it – but to describe it as a bungalow was something of an overstatement.

Older villagers remember 'Delcott' as 'little more than a hut', built of asbestos with a corrugated iron roof. These were common enough building materials in that particular area between the two world wars, but it was hardly the type of house the locals expected a well-known film star to be interested in. The country track has long since been adopted, paved and dignified with the name of Braeside Road. Nowadays it is a peaceful suburban avenue of detached houses and genuine bungalows, one of them still bearing the name Delcott: a desirable residence in Spanish hacienda style, standing amid neat lawns and flowerbeds, betraying no sign of its origins.

Margaret spoke of her new property as being 'nice as a country hide-out for weekends. I couldn't believe we would ever need to live in it – there wouldn't be a war.' Weekend hide-out or not, it was a bizarre setting for Britain's most popular screen star – and any lingering doubts Margaret, or the rest of her family, may have had that she was indeed a star, had now to be dispelled.

One day, on the set of *A Girl Must Live*, she got a summons to Ted Black's office. He told her to start packing. She was going to Hollywood.

The manner of the telling said much about the practices under which contract artists, stars no less than bit players, worked in those times. There was no consultation. There were no negotiations, no dispute procedures. Whatever images of glamour and standing the fans may have had of their idols, they were employees, a work force with hardly more leverage or freedom of choice than factory workers. They observed the company rules and did their job.

Margaret's first reaction to the news was excitement. Film-struck all her life, she had retained a true fan's dream of Hollywood and its stars. She was going to work for Twentieth Century-Fox. Who, in her dizzying first thoughts, was to be her leading man? Tyrone Power? Don Ameche? Black's next words shattered such fantasies. True, she would be working with the studio's No. 1 star, its top money-making name – Shirley Temple. And as for her romantic interest, it was to be Randolph Scott, a second-rank player whose name was only just beginning to register with the public, including Margaret.

Her spirits slumped. Intuition warned her that she would be second-rank too, at best. Any film featuring the world's favourite child star was going to be an exclusively Shirley Temple affair, the rest of its cast mere window-dressing, serving time to show off Miss Temple to best advantage. And while Margaret, as anyone then writing about her took pains to emphasise, was devoid of airs and graces or star complexes, she did have a shrewd awareness of her own value. Then and there, for the first time in her career, she showed anger.

'I threw my first temperament. I rose to my feet, stamped my foot and said nobody should be sending me to Hollywood to be the stooge of a child prodigy.'

It crossed her mind to walk out, out of Ted Black's office and out of her Gainsborough contract, but she knew Black held all the cards. Contracts were body-and-soul commitments and hers was no different from any other contract artist's in binding her to Gainsborough's star exchange arrangement with Fox. If she reneged on it, her future could be bleak.

Had she known the studio politics behind the film she was being assigned to, Margaret's tantrum might have been even more violent. Shirley Temple, now approaching her eleventh birthday, was beginning to slip at the box office, her infant charm showing signs of wearing thin as she neared the dreaded 'awkward age' of child stars. MGM had asked to borrow her from Fox for the role of Dorothy in *The Wizard of Oz* but Darryl F. Zanuck, Fox's production head, had churlishly refused. His riposte, *Susannah of the Mounties*, was to be rushed into preparation as a counterblast; Shirley Temple versus Judy Garland.

As Christmas of 1938 approached, a fan magazine ran a full-page picture of Margaret pensively decorating a Christmas tree. There was more than the prospect of playing a supporting role to a fading child star to induce a sober mood. This was the first Christmas she and Rupert had spent together, and not only was it a wrenching break with family tradition, her mother no longer sharing it, but she faced an imminent, prolonged separation from Rupert.

It had been agreed that she could take a companion with her to the United States, but it couldn't be Rupert: he wouldn't be able to get an extended leave of absence from his job. Margaret Evelyn, now 55, felt too set in her ways to be uprooted to another continent and in any case Margaret wasn't going to encourage her to make the sacrifice. The choice finally fell on Rupert's nineteen-year-old sister Betty, a quiet, dependable young woman with whom Margaret got on well.

On the public side, Ted Black emphasised the importance of making the right impact on the American press – a frighteningly more outspoken, difficult-to-please breed than the malleable British variety Margaret was accustomed to dealing with – and on Hollywood itself. She shopped for a 'trousseau' and spent a small fortune on glamorising herself with day and cocktail dresses, evening gowns, a 200-guinea sable jacket, a £150 full-length mink, an £80 ocelot coat; the furs alone cost the equivalent of £11,000 in 1980s money.

Nothing was left to chance in making sure that Margaret was given star treatment. In the weeks after Christmas *Daily Sketch* photographers, by arrangement with the studio, trailed her for three days, recording the everyday life of a star preparing for Hollywood. Even Rupert was pressured to join in, being photographed having a 'last lunch' with his wife, though showing his distaste by insisting on keeping his back to the camera. The experience didn't improve his attitude to what he regarded as the circus of film publicity considered indispensable to his wife's career.

Passage was booked on the French Line's *Ile de France*, the most elegant liner on the Atlantic route, but from the moment Margaret went aboard at Southampton on the afternoon of 11 January 1939 and posed for photographers in her stateroom, surrounded by all the trappings of a film star in transit, the trip was ill-starred. Margaret's old travel allergy returned and she spent the five-day voyage battling with sea-sickness. On the second day at sea news was received that the greatest talent-hunt in Hollywood history was over: the role of Scarlett O'Hara had gone to a little-known English actress, Vivien Leigh. As the liner neared New York one of her furs went missing, believed stolen; it was never recovered.

In New York Fox had booked her into the stately St Moritz Hotel overlooking Central Park, 'a series of terraces like a picturesque cliff amidst towering trees and soaring skyscrapers', according to its 1939 brochure. There was little time for sight-seeing; her 24 hours in New York had been packed with interviews.

Fired by Vivien Leigh mania, the press scented good copy in this latest arrival from London. *The Lady Vanishes* had opened at New York's Globe cinema three weeks before to rhapsodic reviews.

'If it were not so brilliant a melodrama, we should class it as a brilliant comedy,' the all-powerful Frank Nugent of the *New York Times* had written. 'Seeing it imposes a double, a blessedly double,

90

strain: when your sides are not aching from laughter your brain is throbbing in its attempts to outguess the director.'

MGM may have had the rights to the movie but Fox had the star and meant to milk the film's success for its own publicity ends. Next morning Margaret dutifully reported to the Fox offices three blocks from her hotel on West 56th Street, resplendent in the ocelot coat and a muff and pillbox hat in beaver fur; every inch a star. All the same, the real Margaret peeked through the facade: as the photographers readied themselves, a stenographer whispered a warning that her stockings were wrinkled.

With no experience of handling a general press call, and with flippant, often childish questions being pitched at her, she began to bridle and feel at sea with these hard-bitten, seen-it-all-before newshounds. Another session followed after lunch in her hotel suite. One photographer wanted her to slip into a negligée. Testily, she refused, adding that in any case she didn't own one. The cameraman wasn't pleased. He perched her instead on a radiator, displaying her legs, and when the heat began to get uncomfortable she jumped off before he had finished shooting.

One reporter asked her if her hair-style was copied from Brenda Frazier. Who, she inquired innocently, was Brenda Frazier? Unknowingly she had offended American sensibilities in not knowing the identity of New York's reigning debutante, currently a front-page face throughout the country. Such ignorance was not to be forgiven easily. They baited her about travelling West and being apprehensive about Red Indians. In short, she was set up as Uncle Sam's notion of a British Aunt Sally. Exhausted, she was driven to Grand Central Station and ushered aboard the Twentieth Century Limited, with an orchid on every restaurant-car table, for Chicago and points west, but the New York papers, when they caught up with her, added to her depression. She had been typed as a typical British snob; worse, a naïve, condescending snob, and a lightweight. In a profile piece across five columns, the *World Telegram* mocked her unmercifully. Not even her English accent was spared in its headline: 'Study of a British Glamour Gal in a fit of Loffter, Learning About Ameriker and Its Red Indians'. One section of the article summed up the scoffing impression it worked hard to convey:

' "Are you married?" we asked.

' "Yes."

' "What does your husband do?"

' "Steel."

' "What does he steal?"

'She just loffed and loffed. "Ha ha ha ha ha ha ha. How rilly, rilly funny!" '

Fox gritted its teeth. Zanuck's anger, however, was mainly directed at Margaret for revealing that she was married.

Back in London Margaret had been assured that her Hollywood stay would not be longer than six weeks. Long as that had seemed then, the weeks now yawned ahead of her like an eternity.

She and Betty had been booked into a bungalow at the famous Garden of Allah complex, once a byword for smart, raffish film-star living but now no longer fashionable and showing signs of encroaching seediness. Margaret, though, found it still had charm. She plunged immediately into preparations for *Susannah of the Mounties* – camera tests, hair styling, picture sessions – and immediately she found herself in conflict with the studio powers. Zanuck, determined to give her the routine Hollywood glamorisation treatment, wanted her hair dyed blonde. She refused. They experimented with a blonde wig. The effect was disastrous.

'They just had to put up with me as I am,' she reported later. But, in fact, they didn't. The studio portraits released of her show a glossier, more sophisticated Margaret Lockwood than any taken before or afterwards. Fox got its way with lighting, make-up, posing and enamelled, screen-goddess expressions.

Working on *Susannah of the Mounties* would always remain among her unhappiest memories. True, her own negative approach to it wasn't helpful but Fox was far from blameless. Uncertain how to handle Margaret, the studio quickly lapsed into indifference. Off the set, she was neglected and left to her own devices. No attempt was made to introduce her to the social scene. She couldn't even look to her fellow stars for company or an entrée into the social life of the film capital.

Shirley Temple, she found, was 'a sweet child and amazingly clever. I was impressed with her as an artist rather than as a child prodigy.' But she didn't really get to know her. Guarded like the crown jewel she was in the Fox empire, the moment a scene was in the can Shirley would be whisked away for lessons in the red and white luxury caravan which served as her schoolroom or to the lavish bungalow that was her exclusive home on the lot.

Randolph Scott, as soon as the working day was over, rushed away to the Santa Monica home he shared with Cary Grant. Consequently, Margaret spent all her free time with Betty, going to a movie, playing board games in their bungalow or sunning herself beside the pool.

The one big outing Fox did lay on for her was to attend the Academy Award ceremony a month after her arrival. Richard Greene, her future co-star in *The Blue Lagoon*, was designated her escort and he wasn't pleased. His current romance with Arleen Whelan, a Fox starlet, had already run into trouble as a result of the studio's publicity schemings, concocting a fantasy romance between him and the Norwegian skating star Sonja Henie, thus guaranteeing valuable column inches for the film they were making together, *Lucky Star*. Miss Whelan had not been pleased then and Greene forsaw similar problems if photographs appeared of him with this new girl from 'home' – a married one, at that.

The pictures duly appeared, of Margaret arriving at the Biltmore Hotel on his arm, but Margaret herself wasn't worried. That evening of 23 February 1939 was one she was determined to enjoy, shoulder to shoulder with some of the legends and idols who had inspired her own career. She watched, fascinated, as Bette Davis swept in with an entourage of eight men, one of them her current lover, the director William Wyler, whose ex-wife Margaret Sullavan was one of Davis's rivals for the Best Actress award. This, not playing games with Betty at the Garden of Allah, was the real Hollywood.

Fox, with only a handful of minor nominations that year, had been relegated to fringe tables at the banquet. When the presentations began, Margaret, feeling little obligation to her out-of-humour escort, picked up her chair and carried it down to the front for a better view, a breach of etiquette which wouldn't improve her employers' already jaundiced opinion of her. Unconcerned, she revelled in the parade of stars: Bette Davis duly receiving her Oscar for *Jezebel;* Spencer Tracy his for *Boy's Town;* Deanna Durbin getting a special award; Tyrone Power announcing winning names; Shirley Temple presenting Walt Disney with his trophy for *Snow White and the Seven Dwarfs* – one regulation-size Oscar and seven smaller ones in descending order.

A few days later Richard Greene redeemed himself by putting his car at Margaret's disposal, which made life a little more comfortable, but *Susannah of the Mounties* took six weeks to shoot – 'and I ticked each one off the calendar, looking forward to going home'.

She had reckoned without Darryl F. Zanuck. It was Zanuck's rule to view every frame of a finished production before giving his approval to a final print. Everyone involved was expected to stand by for possible retakes until he was satisfied the film was ready for release, a practice which often left people kicking their heels around the studio for weeks while he laboriously worked his way through a log-jam of newly completed films waiting for his clearance.

Margaret, increasingly frustrated and miserable, was likewise ordered to hang around. Hollywood, she had decided, was 'the most dead-alive place on earth, like a seaside resort out of season', and in desperation she demanded and got a personal interview with Zanuck, pleading to be released. He reminded her of his house rules and showed her the door, but at least she wrung one small concession out of him – a trip to New York to pass the time. She was banking on his clearance for *Susannah* coming through while she was there, on the spot to catch the first available ship back home. Any ambitions she had had for a Hollywood future had evaporated; she felt ill-used and out of her depth there.

New York restored some of her morale. On Broadway she went to see Fredric March and his wife Florence Eldridge in *The American Way*, a *Cavalcade*-style patriotic pageant – 'it was awful' – and, more memorably, Katharine Hepburn in *The Philadelphia Story*. Hepburn's performance took her breath away and left a life-long impression. 'I was completely and absolutely spellbound by this woman. She was like a flame.' At the end of her few days in New York, there was still no word from Zanuck, so, dejectedly, she waved Betty off on a sailing home and herself boarded the Twentieth Century Limited for the long trip back to the West Coast. She was still waiting to hear from Zanuck when a phone call from a complete stranger changed both her mind and her plans.

The director Frank Lloyd had recently seen *Bank Holiday* and been impressed by her performance. Learning she was filming at Fox, he'd gone to some trouble to track her down. He was about to start a new film for Paramount but still hadn't found his leading lady. The chance discovery that Margaret was in town and available was the answer to his problem: a meeting was arranged, a contract offered.

Lloyd, born in Glasgow, had emigrated to the United States in 1913 and started in films as an actor the following year. He had soon turned to directing and in 1933 had made the screen version of *Cavalcade*. His greatest success had come two years later with *Mutiny on the Bounty*. His new film, *Rulers of the Sea*, was another seafaring yarn, this time about the dawn of the steamship era, charting the planning, construction and eventful maiden voyage of the first steamship built in the Clydeside yards. Margaret's role would be that of the captain's daughter.

Lloyd listened sympathetically at their first meeting to Margaret's tale of Hollywood woe and decided to open some doors to her. Joan Bennett, more than anyone else, helped to revise Margaret's perception of Hollywood. 'She was very kind to me and we became good friends.' Miss Bennett's memory is of 'a lovely young lady' who, at the parties she now began to frequent, caused amusement and some amazement by refusing alcohol and drinking only lemonade.

When the unit sailed out to Catalina Island for shipboard scenes Margaret was violently ill and her takes had to be scrapped and re-shot against back projection. 'I'd told them I was the world's worst sailor but they thought I was joking. I kept rushing to the rail to be ill over the side. Finally they had to send me ashore.' Even so, it was turning out a much happier production than *Susannah of the Mounties*. She found herself among old friends: Will Fyffe, her *Owd Bob* co-star of the previous year, had been brought out to play her father again and Douglas Fairbanks Jr was her love interest.

Another unexpected phone call, crackling over long distance, added to her new-found cheerfulness: Rupert was on the line with the news that he'd be coming over to join her for her final weeks in Hollywood. The thought of being reunited with Rupert should have eased her mind, but now she was no longer so sure that they would be final or that she any longer wished them to be – Paramount was showing more interest in her than Fox. There was talk of other films to follow. Her ideas of a Hollywood-based future began to revive.

Rupert, when he arrived, startled her by announcing that he'd quit his job in order to be with her but he seemed confident that he could arrange to stay in America and take over one of his firm's agencies there. But any decisions were shadowed by international events. American newspapers were more open than Britain's in their forecasts of an impending war in Europe and Margaret was thrown into more indecision by Rupert's disclosure that he had joined the part-time Territorial Army; she feared he could face call-up if war was declared.

A letter from home brought Carol Reed suddenly back into Margaret's life. He wrote telling her of his next project and unconditionally offered her the female lead. Yet she stalled. On the one hand, the dazzling, if unclear, prospects of a Hollywood career; on the other, the certainty of a prestigious film with Carol. Should she risk abandoning the possibilities of Hollywood so soon after they had started to emerge? Should she again place herself in the hands of a trusted director? – she felt safe with Carol, she knew he wouldn't be wasting her time or his if the part wasn't worthwhile. And what of Rupert?

ᴀN OUTBREAK OF HOSTILITIES

With *The Stars Look Down* Carol had taken on his most ambitious subject to date, one he was sure would earn him a place among the front rank of British directors, and Margaret found herself faced with the first really serious crisis of decision in her career.

A. J. Cronin's novel of the Northumberland coalfield and the determination of a miner's educated son to campaign for reform and improved conditions in the industry was still a best-seller three years after publication. Margaret hadn't read the book and now combed the Los Angeles bookshops for a copy without success.

Carol cabled her again for a decision: pre-production was so advanced that Michael Redgrave, already signed for the main role, was on location in Cumberland filming early sequences. Margaret wired her mother, asking her to read the book and send a report on it as soon as possible. Back, in due course, came the reply. Margaret Evelyn couldn't see which of two likely parts Margaret was being asked to play. The only women of any consequence in the story were 'a thoroughly sordid prostitute called Jenny and a nurse apparently dragged in for romance'.

Jenny was the role Carol wanted Margaret for but it was beyond Margaret Evelyn's comprehension that her daughter might be under consideration for the part of a 'prostitute'. Finally it was not so much Carol's persistence as the threat of war, now very real, that decided Margaret to head for home. Knowing that Paramount were taking an option on her services for two and possibly four more movies, Margaret now accepted that she would go back to England in the interim. She and Rupert booked a passage on the *Queen Mary*, but 'I'll be back soon,' she assured a columnist in her final Hollywood interview. The slinky portrait that accompanied the article showed how 'Hollywood' she had been made to look, more Joan Crawford than a demure little actress from the London suburbs. So she bade Hollywood fare-well, the thought that she'd never again set foot there remote from her mind.

Just before leaving she received the script for *The Stars Look Down* with a letter from Carol urging her that the Jenny role was 'too good to be missed'. Gainsborough, he mentioned, didn't seem too keen on her taking it. She must persuade them to let her.

There was one last overnight stay in New York. *Susannah of the Mounties* had opened that week at the Roxy to tepid reviews and she gave it a wide berth. One columnist reported: 'Beauteous Margaret Lockwood just skipped off to England. She likes Hollywood, we gather, but she also likes her husband of a little more than a year. She says marriage by such remote control doesn't appeal to her even a little bit, so in future she will divide her time better – six months here and six months with her husband.' Rupert couldn't have read about this supposed arrangement even had he chosen to do so, since at the moment it appeared in print he was lying senseless in their hotel room. He'd slipped in the bath, knocked himself out and was unconscious for two hours. Little the worse, he recovered in time to take Margaret out on the town for a last look at New York. Once aboard the *Queen Mary*, she settled down to read the script. Very soon she was flinging it aside in horror.

Jenny was a cheap, scheming, go-getting hussy who trapped the idealistic hero into marriage to better herself, cheated on him with a former lover and came close to ruining him. Worse, she had an illegitimate baby. The character was alien to any Margaret had played before and was totally inimical to her image. 'What can Carol be thinking of?' she raged.

She felt badly let down and the voyage was made even more unen-durable than she'd expected by her disappointment. She was adamant she wasn't going to play the part, but Carol had craftily pre-empted her. In London, the day after the *Queen Mary* had sailed out of New York harbour, newspapers announced that Margaret would be joining Michael Redgrave in the cast. The homecoming at Southampton on 26 June was not the happy release she'd been anticipating for so many weeks. Nor was England, after a five months' absence, reassuring.

Crisis was palpable in the air. War seemed inevitable. On the day she came ashore *The Times* carried a report of a speech by Winston Churchill to his Woodford constituents: 'Ninety-nine out of every hundred square miles of these islands will be practically immune from air attack . . . science will enable our Air Force to levy a heavy toll.' Despite that, the nation was taking no chances. In London Margaret and Rupert found trenches and air-raid shelters being dug in the squares and parks; sandbags being filled and stockpiled. Every household had received a government leaflet advising on air-raid precautions. The people were squaring up for a fight.

Margaret wasted no time in letting Ted Black know her feelings about playing Jenny and found, to her relief, that his views matched her own. He insisted to Carol that if Margaret were to play it, the role must be re-written to make Jenny 'a nicer type of woman'. That, Carol pointed out patiently, would ruin the story. A battle of wills was developing into a major issue of studio policy.

The film was being produced by an independent company, Grafton Films, whose managing director, Isadore Goldsmith, had made a deal with Gaumont-British for Carol, Michael Redgrave and Margaret to be loaned out as a package. 'At one time', Carol recalled, 'there seemed no solution but to drop Margaret from the cast. But this, too, was difficult because we had been sold as a team of three and Grafton demanded that we should stay so.'

For all his outward show of confidence that he would win Margaret over, Carol had been careful to lay a contingency plan in the event of his being overruled. An actress called Phyllis Calvert had recently made a tentative screen debut in a quickie, *Two Days to Live*. The film had gone virtually unnoticed but Carol had spotted Calvert and noted possibilities, keeping her in mind as an emergency option. All the same, the role was tailored for a star name and Margaret's was the one he wanted: 'I had been convinced all along that Margaret was the actress for the part and I remained adamant on this point.'

Quietly, he instituted a campaign to convince her. At their first meeting she told him flatly that she didn't want the part. 'It's downright sordid,' she said, using Margaret Evelyn's adjective. 'If it isn't handled with utmost delicacy, it will kill me dead,' and to drive her point home she delivered what she thought was her *coup de grâce* – the shock effect on the public of sweet, wholesome Margaret Lockwood as a character who has a child out of wedlock.

Carol trumped her. 'Nonsense. It's a terrific part, the sort that makes a Dietrich or a Davis. And, in any case, the baby has been deleted by the censor.' She was partly mollified. The professional in her, always responsive to Carol's power of judgement, was certainly

99

interested in the challenge of attempting an out-and-out bad lot, the kind of role the British cinema rarely offered, but it was 'image' that worried her.

'Repeated rows followed and I was told I must retain Margaret and alter the script accordingly. These discussions went on right up to the start of shooting and we began on some rather harmless scenes, with more or less an understanding that some re-writing would be done later to tone down other parts of the story.' Carol was, in fact, playing for time, convinced that once Margaret started work and began to get under the skin of the character, no re-writes would be necessary.

There is a legend that he finally cleared the biggest hurdle, that of winning Ted Black over, with a consummate piece of acting all his own.

One evening, according to the story, he hung around the route he knew Black would walk after leaving his office. Carol brushed past, apparently unseeing and looking as though he were in the last extremity of dejection. Black hurried after him, insisting on buying him a coffee and trying to coax the reason for his depression out of him. Finally, allowing himself to be persuaded, Carol said: 'It's only that you've messed up my picture. I don't know what to do.'

'You mean you're *that* upset about it? It means *that* much to you?' Black is alleged to have replied.

'Never mind,' Carol muttered, gazing forlornly into his coffee cup. 'It doesn't matter. Don't let's talk about it.'

The ruse worked. The generous-hearted Black walked Carol back home, urging him to get some sleep and adding: 'Get back on the floor in the morning and make a good picture. That's all you have to worry about.'

A few days after shooting began at Twickenham studios Ted Black and Maurice Ostrer hosted a 'welcome home' party for Margaret at the Savoy Hotel. Top executives from Gaumont-British, Twentieth Century-Fox and Paramount mingled with assorted celebrities of stage, screen and Fleet Street to pay their tributes. It was a diamond-studded declaration of her star status, one of the last celebrations of film-world glamour before Britain was engulfed in darkness and austerity. As she was leaving, her head resolutely unturned, Margaret remarked to Gainsborough publicity man Leslie Frewin: 'It was nice but phoney. I'd like to believe that all those people who said I had a great future really meant it.'

100

For the first few days of shooting Margaret was clearly ill at ease. Jenny was an alien character to her. She was having to draw on intellectual and emotional reserves she had never put to the test to appear cheap, shrewish and opportunistic. She never did come wholly to terms with the role. Viewed now, her performance, though a strong one, is revealing in its hints of awkwardness and uncertainty, but Carol was more than satisfied. And his hunch paid off. Once she'd survived the breaking-in sequences Margaret began to enjoy playing Jenny. A few days into shooting she took Carol on one side and admitted she'd been mistaken to doubt him. It would be wrong for the picture and for herself, she agreed, to re-write anything. 'I was most impressed by her honesty and strength of character in making this admission,' Carol wrote subsequently. 'There was something really big about it that I admired immensely.'

Delays – not all of them caused by the debate over Margaret's role – had added £10,000 to the budget, bringing it up to £100,000, an unusually high outlay for a British production of that period. More worrying, however, was the situation in Europe. War with Germany became daily more imminent and the fear of immediate air attack would close cinemas and inhibit film production, if it did not stop it altogether. Every day of shooting on *The Stars Look Down* was counted a bonus as the political situation worsened, with Carol and Isadore Goldsmith increasingly worried that war would break out before the film was finished and force them to abandon it.

On Friday, 1 September 1939 Margaret was in make-up being readied for her last take on the film when news came over the radio that German troops had invaded Poland. Next day production was completed and less than 24 hours later Britain was at war with Germany. By a hair's breadth *The Stars Look Down* was in the can with the distinction of being the last film finished in peace-time Britain.

On the day Poland was invaded *Film Weekly* had carried a full-page interview with Margaret by its chief columnist J. Danvers Williams. 'There was a time when I didn't like Margaret Lockwood at all,' he wrote. 'I thought her just another insipid leading lady doomed to appear in a series of sweet-heroine roles and then fade out. Having seen the rushes of her latest picture *The Stars Look Down* I am convinced that she will very soon follow Merle Oberon and Vivien Leigh right into the front rank of stars.'

He quoted Margaret as saying: 'Ever since I first started making pictures I have been fighting against the tendency of British studios

to make their actresses nothing more than characterless ornaments.'
More than ever had the wisdom of Carol Reed and her own ability
to realise that wisdom stood her in good stead.

The industry's first response to war was an almost wholesale shut-
down. Studios promptly gave staff a week's notice and closed, though
some retained a skeleton crew to keep themselves operational until
the situation had clarified. Cinemas closed too.

Like millions in every walk of civilian life Margaret was confused
and uncertain what her role in the conflict would be. Film production,
it seemed obvious, couldn't continue while the nation was fighting for
survival. Realising that she would be eligible for drafting into war
work, she decided to volunteer as an ambulance driver but Ted Black,
when she managed to contact him, while admitting he was as much
in the dark as everyone else about the future, urged her not to
volunteer for anything yet awhile. There was no work in prospect for
her, that much was certain. *The Blue Lagoon* had yet again been
abandoned.

The war at any rate brought a solution to one pressing problem.
Rupert's impulsive decision to resign his job, which Margaret considered foolish, had left him unemployed and her increasingly anxious
about him and the effect his idleness might have on their marriage.
She was too tactful to make an issue of it but it was obvious that
being the husband of a star had done nothing to reconcile him to her
career and she was sensitive of his pride and feelings.

There were constant small signs of resentment. Rupert still disapproved of her wearing make-up, and now she was expected to wear
it, skilfully applied, whenever she stepped outside her own front door.
She had long ago learned not to take him to see any of her films.
Watching her on the screen, larger than life, disembodied, a stranger,
embarrassed him, and a love scene would drive him, crouching, to
the floor of the cinema. These larger, perhaps understandable, dislikes
aside, she was beginning to notice that his reaction to her fame, as
opposed to her profession, was to make petty personal criticisms of
her appearance, her deportment, her habits. Until now she hadn't
attached any special significance to his words; she could be critical
herself and took the view that this was the 'rough' of marriage. As
far as she was concerned there was more than enough 'smooth' to
compensate for it but she was relieved, all the same, that the war now
took the problem of finding something for Rupert to do out of their
hands. As a 25-year-old part-time soldier he could expect to be called

up soon. She didn't relish the prospect but, like millions of wives, she was resigned to it.

A Girl Must Live had just been released, a success with the critics whose favourite adjective for it was 'saucy'. Their bouquets tended to be concentrated on the flamboyant performances of Lilli Palmer and Renee Houston, and Margaret's was generally taken for granted. 'Any nice girl must necessarily look pallid and prim in such amusingly tough and colourful company,' the *Daily Express* thought. The film was deemed another step up the ladder for Carol Reed but Margaret could be forgiven for thinking that her screen personality, no less than her career, seemed becalmed – and for thanking her lucky stars that she'd been coerced into making *The Stars Look Down*, due for release the following spring.

Fortunately it wasn't long before Ted Black sent word that the studios were cranking up again; she could stand by for a call. In June the trade press had announced that Twentieth Century-Fox had acquired an original screenplay called *Report on a Fugitive*. Michael Redgrave had been signed to star, Carol Reed to direct, and now it was being rushed into production, the first film to start shooting since the outbreak of war and the first British film to deal openly with the Nazi threat. By December, when filming began, the title had been changed to *Gestapo* and the script had undergone considerable revision. Carol had been unhappy with the original draft, written as a straightforward espionage thriller. As soon as the studios received the go-ahead to resume production, he brought in Frank Launder and Sidney Gilliat to lighten the story. The title was changed once more to become *Night Train to Munich*.

Margaret's role cast her as Anna, the daughter of a Czech scientist who is a prime target of the Nazis when they march into Prague. When he escapes into hiding and Anna is caught and sent to a concentration camp, she is cynically set up as a decoy to lead the Nazis to him. An inmate befriends her and helps her to escape but he is a plant. She's tracked down by an apparently high-ranking Nazi, in reality a British agent also desperate to get to the scientist through her, so that he can be smuggled out to Britain.

Michael Redgrave had had to drop out and Rex Harrison took over the role of the agent; that of the treacherous inmate went to an Austrian actor, Paul von Hernried, who had recently made an impact on the London stage playing Prince Albert in *Victoria Regina*. As soon as the film was finished he made his way to America, just avoiding the government's round-up and internment of German and Austrian aliens and ended up in Hollywood as Paul Henreid. Basil Radford and Naunton Wayne infused some comedy with their characters Charters and Caldicott, amid an exciting display of the virtues of British *sang froid* and fair play vanquishing the powers of tyranny. One of the film's minor distinctions was the first portrayal on the screen of Hitler as a non-comic figure. This dubious chore fell to a character actor called Billy Russell, whose likeness to the Führer tended to bring him unwelcome attention in pubs and public places.

War cast a strange mood of unreality over studio conditions. More than two-thirds of the technical staff had diverted into the Armed Forces or factory work and shooting had to finish by dusk to comply with black-out regulations. Paul von Hernried, technically an enemy alien, was 'doing his bit' as a volunteer air-raid warden in the Hampstead district where he lived. Between takes he sat quietly studying his ARP manual.

The production wrapped in January 1940 and the Lockwood-Reed team moved straight on to their next assignment, *The Girl in the News*. It was their seventh collaboration since *Midshipman Easy* and they had come to regard themselves as an indissoluble partnership. Though neither realised it, *The Girl in the News* was destined to be their last joint venture.

Carol by now had an unshakeable faith in Margaret and she in him. After the war, acknowledged as one of the great directors on both sides of the Atlantic, he could still attest: 'I consider Margaret Lockwood the most efficient and the most versatile actress I have ever worked with. She is able to put up a very good performance as, say, a chorus girl in one film on a Saturday and then be equally good on the Monday morning as a woman accused of murder.' And he added (this in 1948): 'I should like very much to direct another picture with her.' For her part, Margaret owed more to Carol Reed than to any other director or producer she ever worked with. It was he who discerned and cultivated the element of quiet, still authority in her, who overcame the shyness that could so easily have stunted her screen personality and who encouraged her to take risks and act against type – not to mention against her better judgement.

The Girl in the News, however, wasn't among their best collaborations; competent enough, but a routine melodrama. Again Margaret's role was passive, as Ann Graham, a nurse whose patient's suicide throws suspicion on her. Tried and acquitted of murder, she is unwittingly drawn into an elaborate plot to incriminate her a second time when her next employer is deliberately poisoned by his wife and her lover. The plot was contrived and underwritten but Margaret played her part in it with intelligence, relying more than in any previous role on facial expression to communicate her suppressed emotions. The technique called for lingering close-ups and she'd never been photographed so searchingly or effectively. Her Hollywood experience stood her in good stead. She looked slim, soignée and glamorous, perhaps too much so for a nurse, but there was no escaping the fact that it was another routine role in another routine film.

Carol's next subject was to be H. G. Wells's *Kipps* with Michael Redgrave. He wanted Margaret for the part of Ann Pornick, the servant-girl whom the self-made Kipps rejects in favour of a society woman, a role assigned to Phyllis Calvert. For reasons of her own, Margaret rejected Carol. He promoted Phyllis Calvert to the servant-girl role – a break that would make her a star and, eventually, Margaret's closest rival in the popularity polls – and Calvert's original part went to Diana Wynyard. Carol was disappointed that Margaret had turned him down but there was some consolation to be derived from these casting musical chairs. During production he and Miss Wynyard were quietly married.

Margaret had something quite different in mind. A recent West End comedy hit called *Quiet Wedding* was shortly due to go into production and she'd set her heart on its key role of the sorely-tried bride-to-be.

COMBAT AND THE MAN IN GREY

On the first day of 1940 two million young men aged between 19 and 27 received their call-up papers. Rupert was one of them and he was posted to the Royal Artillery as No. 990256 Private Leon, Rupert William, reporting to the huge base at Kinmel Bay just outside the resort town of Rhyl on the coast of North Wales.

When *The Girl in the News* was completed in the spring Margaret was tired from making two films virtually back-to-back. She had got her wish and the lead role in *Quiet Wedding* but it would not go into production just yet and she decided to take the summer off. It was a glorious summer that seemed like a last story-book echo of a gentle, peaceful England, while across the Channel the war relentlessly moved closer. Dunkirk . . . the fall of Paris . . . The Luftwaffe was about to begin its offensive against British military targets as a preliminary to invasion. Southern England was suddenly highly vulnerable to air attack.

In August Margaret drove to Wales to visit Rupert, having hoarded her petrol ration coupons for months so as to manage the 400-mile round trip. Rupert had a 48-hour pass and they booked into a Rhyl hotel. It was there they heard that the first German bombs had fallen on central London.

Thoroughly alarmed, Margaret got through by phone to Margaret Evelyn and found her in a state of high excitement: the Highland Road house, with its panoramic views across the capital, would make an ideal grandstand if the bombing got really spectacular! Upper Norwood, Margaret decided, would be a lot safer than Dolphin Square so when she got back to London she arranged to move back in with her mother, keeping on the flat as a *pied-à-terre*.

In the first week of September work on *Quiet Wedding* began. So did the Blitz and the Battle of Britain. Shepperton Studios, where they were filming, seemed a lucky location, a safe haven on the Thames, fourteen miles from the centre of London. But any illusions

106

of relative safety were quickly dispelled and the film unit found themselves in the front line.

Just across the river at Weybridge on the Surrey bank was a huge Vickers Armstrong aircraft factory producing Spitfires and Wellington bombers, and it was a prime target for daylight raids. Work in the studios was continually interrupted by the air raid sirens and stray bombs falling in the grounds. Eventually the factory was hit and partially put out of commission. Studio space was promptly requisitioned and the unit suddenly found themselves working on the only stage exempt from warplane production.

Studio hands were put to work building dummy aircraft sited in the grounds as decoys. In those early days of the war the depleted art departments of the few studios left operating often doubled as war workers, producing camouflage materials, mock planes, vehicles and guns to fool enemy reconnaissance aircraft. Production chiefs were only too happy to co-operate, not just out of patriotism but also as a strategic war effort to justify continuing film production.

Because of the constant disruptions and the dangers of the nightly raids on London, it was decided to accommodate people at the studios for the duration of the production. Margaret moved into one room in a house in the studio grounds and when the bombing of London intensified she persuaded Margaret Evelyn to join her there, sharing the room. Her 24th birthday, on 15 September, coincided with the decisive day of the Battle of Britain, the day the Luftwaffe was determined to deal the *coup de grâce* to the Few of the RAF. Wave after wave of German bombers attacked London and dog-fights raged all day over south-east England.

With a few hours free during the day Margaret offered to drive her mother over to Upper Norwood to check on the house and enjoy a simple birthday tea, but before they got halfway the ferocity of the bombing forced them to take shelter. One of the casualties that day was the Dolphin Square building. Margaret had already arranged for her belongings to be put into storage but the empty flat was wrecked. That decided her. Margaret Evelyn must not return to Highland Road while the bombing continued. She should move to Delcott and live out the Blitz in the peace and safety of Hampshire. In fact, Delcott, with its asbestos walls and corrugated iron roof – 'our dear little cottage' as Margaret liked to call it – was to be her mother's home for the rest of her life . . . and the setting for Margaret's most bitter personal drama.

Throughout the spring of 1940 press anticipation of *The Stars Look Down* had been unprecedented. Thousands of column inches had been lavished on interviews, picture spreads and behind-the-camera stories, and the critics were fulsome in their praise when it opened in July at the West End's most glamorous cinema, the Odeon, Leicester Square. Everyone was agreed that *The Stars Look Down* was a landmark film, pioneering a socio-documentary style that was a breakthrough in British cinema and confirming Carol Reed as the industry's most innovative and assured young director. They eulogised Michael Redgrave's performance and some let their praise spill over on Margaret's, too, but by and large the reviews politely noted her contribution without examining it too closely.

Impressions were perhaps coloured by her two Hollywood films, now on release. In the view of a *Picturegoer* writer, they 'brought out all the old faults in Miss Lockwood which had faded in her recent British films. She is stilted again; she looks ill at ease.' *Night Train to Munich*, though it was well received critically and at the box office, did little more for her than shunt her along the same tracks as *The Lady Vanishes*. *The Girl in the News* had been undemanding, and she was the familiar passive Margaret Lockwood in *Quiet Wedding* as the tranquil eye of pre-wedding family storms. So in spite of the prestige of starring in what was generally acclaimed the best British film of 1940 – for some commentators the best British film ever – Margaret began to feel that her career had reached a plateau with no clear direction, no challenge. The same week that *Stars* opened, *The Times* reported 'A new actress, Miss Ingrid Bergman, appears with Mr Leslie Howard at the Gaumont,' (in *Escape to Happiness*).

As 1940 drew to a close negotiations were in hand for her to turn further A. J. Cronin pages as the tragic heroine of *Hatter's Castle* – Isadore Goldsmith was keen to cash in on the success of *The Stars Look Down*. Robert Newton would play the story's tyrannical father and a rising actor of unusual intensity was being considered for Margaret's romantic interest. His name was James Mason.

Margaret was interested but production wouldn't be starting for some months so she arranged to join Rupert in North Wales, this time for a prolonged visit. Speculative building had ribboned the coast roads outside Rhyl with neat bungalow developments and Rupert managed to take a short lease on one of them at Kinmel, a few yards from the camp gates.

For the first time in her life Margaret assumed the role of a full-time housewife. All her adult life she'd been spared the tedium of housework and now she found that 'struggling to cook a decent meal, difficult enough for the expert housewife on rationing, was a perfect nightmare to me'. But she threw herself into the part, if with more amateur enthusiasm than skill, acquiring a bicycle for shopping expeditions into the town a couple of miles away. At first she found these an embarrassment – she was frequently recognised and would stand in food queues signing autographs – but the novelty soon wore off and once the sight of Margaret Lockwood cycling along the street became commonplace, the locals stopped bothering her. At one point Rupert had to stay in the camp hospital with a severe bout of 'flu. Margaret's twice-daily visits to him were even more of a tonic for the other patients in the ward, though they failed at first to realise that it was Britain's top film actress who was cheering them up in this far-flung corner of Wales. Rupert wasn't anxious to tell them who she was.

Those months, far removed from the threat of bombs, with nothing worse than the coastal defences along the wide sandy beaches, the restrictions of rationing and Rupert's uniform to remind her of the war, were a period of contentment. She came closer then to living a natural, anonymous life than at any other time. Occasionally she would travel to London for discussions with Herbert on *Hatter's Castle*. The starting date was continually being put back. There were nightmare journeys on overcrowded trains and endless delays and diversions. The glimpses she caught of the battered, bomb-weary capital sent her hurrying gratefully back to North Wales. Postponements dragged on into 1941 and with each one her prospects of being free to play the role receded further. With the new year a few weeks old and still no definite production date fixed, she finally told Herbert she would have to pull out – she was pregnant. The part went to Deborah Kerr.

The baby was expected at the end of August so, knowing she would want to nurse it herself, Margaret decided to take the rest of the year off.

It was a significant time for her to go into even temporary retirement. As the foremost screen actress of her generation, challenged only by Valerie Hobson, she had had the field to herself. Now others were beginning to stake their claims. Phyllis Calvert with *Kipps;* Deborah Kerr, who had made a big impression in *Love on the Dole* and, with *Hatter's Castle*, was certain to achieve stardom; the lovely

Sally Gray, who had been beavering away in secondary roles since 1930, was about to move into the spotlight with *Dangerous Moonlight;* and another long-serving blonde, Ann Todd, came to the fore in *Ships with Wings*. It was the year, too, when Patricia Roc was first spotted as a likely leading lady for the future.

More worryingly, Margaret sensed a change in Rupert. He had failed to win a commission and was now a lance-bombardier. His reaction to the news that he was to be a father wasn't the delight she'd expected. Margaret Evelyn, on the other hand, was thrilled and the bond between the two women strengthened.

Delcott was now the family's only established home and Margaret settled in with her mother. With only two bedrooms, it was cramped but she was perfectly content, easing herself into a therapeutic regime of rural living under Margaret Evelyn's only-too-welcoming care, strolling down to the village store, voraciously reading books from the mobile library that served the village and, under her mother's tutelage, learning to knit. She never doubted the baby would be a boy. Layettes in blue poured from her needles.

There was just one problem: as long as Margaret was at Delcott Rupert couldn't visit her. He was willing to but Margaret Evelyn, despite her pleasure in the prospect of a grandchild, wouldn't remain under the same roof with him. There was nowhere else she could go except into an hotel and the last person she would consider inconveniencing herself for was the son-in-law she despised. Margaret made no attempt to force the issue. When Rupert got leave, he would check into a small hotel in Bournemouth and Margaret would make the ten-mile journey to be with him.

Her first serious qualm over the state of their marriage came when they met up in Oxford for the wedding of one of his sisters. Margaret, proud of her knitting prowess, had taken samples of it to show him, to be met with indifference.

'I suppose I had thought Rupert's excitement and interest would match my own,' she wrote. 'Perhaps I expected too much of him.' But it wasn't just indifference towards the baby; his manner towards her had become aloof and disinterested. 'This puzzled and bewildered me and left me more lastingly hurt than I realised even at the time.' She tried to shrug it off. It was a common enough syndrome for husbands to resent the idea of a first-born intruding and disrupting the established pattern of a marital relationship. And Rupert could not be expected to enjoy coming a poor second-best to Margaret

Evelyn. Margaret told herself she was being over-sensitive because of her condition. But the doubts persisted. She forced herself to face the fact that their marriage hardly had a conventional pattern to disrupt. The strains increased.

She had been warned that a Caesarian delivery would be necessary. She and Rupert, both convinced a son was on his way, had agreed on Timothy for his name. Now she added Julius. In mid-August she moved into a private nursing home in West Cliff Road, Bournemouth, and suddenly she had a premonition that the baby might be a girl. Frantically she sent out for pink wool and started knitting afresh.

Rupert got compassionate leave. They went into Bournemouth a few evenings before her confinement to see a summer show, Arthur Askey at the Pavilion. Margaret, trying to forget her anxieties for a couple of hours and doing her best to make her ungainly body comfortable, found Rupert morose, prickly and inattentive to her. Suddenly he snapped at her: 'Sit up and don't slump like that. It doesn't look nice.'

The old Rupert of the tea party all those years ago, the same thoughtless, unreasoning reproof, as though she were still a child. She felt humiliated and deeply hurt. For so long she had made light of his petty criticisms of her smoking and make-up, of his distaste for her career and fame. But this rebuke in what should have been one of the happiest, most exciting hours of their life together seemed a cruel confirmation of the suspicions she'd been suppressing.

Margaret was delivered of a daughter on 23 August 1941. Her eleventh-hour premonition had been right. They hadn't even considered names for a girl so Margaret chose them herself . . . Margaret Julia. Before long Margaret Evelyn would coin a nickname for the baby; to the family, and eventually to the public, she'd be known as Toots. For the time being, there were more important considerations. Margaret had confided the sensitive family situation to the matron of the nursing home. Two rooms had been made available for the waiting relatives, one for the father, another for the grandmother. Briefly, for the first time, her husband and mother came together as in-laws at Margaret's bedside for their first glimpse of the baby in what Margared called 'an armed truce.' Then they went their separate ways.

Quiet Wedding, 'the first Blitzkrieg film' according to its publicity, pleased everybody, critic and customer alike. It appeared at just the right moment to take people's minds off the depredations of war and remind them of the gentler values they were fighting for. There were even rumours that a sequel was being prepared to be called *Quiet Christening* – apt timing for Margaret, but nothing came of it and she was left undisturbed to enjoy her latest role.

A reporter, anxious for a description of the star baby, was told: 'She resembles her grandmother very much, even to the dimples.' Nothing could have been more calculated to delight Margaret Evelyn. No visible reminders of Rupert! And after all the friction of the past four years, she'd got her daughter back, all to herself again . . . and a granddaughter into the bargain. Three generations of Margarets under the same roof. The tiny house was even more cramped and Rupert could hardly be expected to stay in a hotel every time he got leave and came down to see his wife and daughter. Unpredictable as ever, Margaret Evelyn now took herself off to London each time until he returned to camp.

This delicate situation was resolved when Margaret, planning ahead for the time when she would go back to work, hired a nurse. There was obviously no room for her to live in at Delcott so a nearby house was rented, an arrangement which worked surprisingly well. Margaret Evelyn was close enough to drop in whenever she liked but could keep to herself whenever Rupert came.

Margaret began to think she had been over-sensitive in her earlier doubts. On his visits he fussed proudly over his daughter and seemed to be accepting fatherhood far more enthusiastically than she'd dared hope. He did not adapt quite so readily, though, to the idea of her going back to work. The six months she had allowed herself following the birth were nearly over and all that time she had been reading scripts. 'It never occurred to me to give up work and I was looking forward to resuming.' She was, in any case, the family's principal source of income.

In March 1942, when Margaret reported back to the studio, she found there had been changes.

Gaumont-British, Gainsborough's parent company, had, a few months earlier, been absorbed into the growing film empire of J. Arthur Rank. Heir to a flour-mill fortune, and a devout Methodist, Joseph Arthur Rank had first become interested in film production in the early 1930s. His initial ambition for it was a missionary one, seeing the screen as a powerful channel for propagating his own religious ideals. The first film he was involved with, in 1936, had been a commercial flop but the experience taught him a lesson that would become the cornerstone of his future monopoly . . . you needed to control the outlet as well as the product.

In text-book style he then proceeded to expand production resources by taking over white-elephant studios which came cheap during the mid-1930s slump, and acquired a controlling interest in the 306-cinema Odeon chain. He had bought out MGM's stake in Gaumont-British and made a new deal with the company's other Hollywood partner, Twentieth Century-Fox, which opened up access for him to 300 more cinemas. With a wartime boom in production and cinema attendances about to explode, he was poised to become the colossus of the industry. Late in 1941, when Isidore Ostrer retired as chairman of Gaumont-British/Gainsborough, Rank, who had added Korda's old Denham Studios and the newly built Elstree Studios to his conglomerate, took over personal control of the company with Maurice Ostrer as his second-in-command.

Margaret was in good shape for her return, slimmer even than before her pregnancy. Welcoming her back, old colleagues detected a softer look and a more accessible warmth. In turn, she noticed small shifts of emphasis in the way the studios were being run, now that Rank had control of them. Rank had increased Maurice Ostrer's power at Ted Black's expense and there were signs of a conflict of interest between these two main executives.

Her return film was *Alibi*, playing a Paris night club hostess who unwittingly provides a murderer with an alibi and places her own life in danger while falling in love with one of the detectives on the case. It had been a French film a few years before and a British version had first been announced back in the summer of 1939 as a vehicle for the Lockwood-Redgrave team, with Erich von Stroheim repeating his role in the original as the murderer. Redgrave was now serving with the Royal Navy, and von Stroheim was in Hollywood. Hugh Sinclair and Raymond Lovell, somewhat less charismatic names, stepped in for them, and the detective part went to James Mason.

'Immediately we started acting together I realised we were a well-balanced team,' Margaret later said of him. Privately she found him 'dour and uncommunicative' though for public consumption she would tell an interviewer: 'He had the reputation and appearance of being a taciturn man.' Mason's bad humour was partly due to a running battle he was conducting with the producers over his billing. Hugh

Sinclair was officially Margaret's co-star, with Raymond Lovell billed third. Mason's name was to be below the title but he was insisting on co-star status. A compromise brought him up to No. 3, displacing Lovell, but his reputation for challenging the studio establishment was firmly established.

During production, *Picturegoer*, the most widely read British fan magazine, celebrated Margaret's return to work with a full-page article which seemed to echo some of her own concerns. Headed 'Margaret Lockwood's Future', it contrasted the 'nice' girl-next-door roles on which she'd ridden to stardom with her one excursion into 'bad girl' territory as Jenny Sunley.

'When she appeared as the bitter, shrewish wife of *The Stars Look Down*, the critics hurried to acclaim her performance, while fans all over the country wrote indignant letters both to the star and to the producers. "We do not like this Margaret," they wrote.' Then came the leading question: 'Which is to be the Margaret of the future?' Did *Picturegoer* know something Margaret didn't?

Soon afterwards she was summoned to Maurice Ostrer's office and told what her next subject was to be. He'd acquired the film rights to a best-seller, *The Man in Grey* by Lady Eleanor Smith, her latest in a canon of florid romances, several of which had already been filmed.

Margaret went away to read the book. She was excited. The story had all the hallmarks of screen success . . . high romance against a colourful Regency setting, strong characters, dramatic situations. There were two female roles of equal importance; Clarissa, wife of the enigmatic Marquis of Rohan, the most beautiful woman in Regency London, and Hesther, dark and foreboding, the school-friend she takes under her wing who stops at nothing, including Clarissa's murder, to get what she wants. There was no doubt in Margaret's mind which part she would be playing. Clarissa was perfect for her.

Ostrer, when she reported back to him, had other ideas. He wanted Phyllis Calvert for Clarissa. Margaret would be playing Hesther.

She was appalled. It was *The Stars Look Down* and the Jenny battle all over again, but this time there was a further complication. Phyllis Calvert had set her sights on the Hesther part.

Margaret's image consciousness was a strait-jacket. It simply wasn't in her nature to take risks in her professional life and the letters she'd received from indignant fans after *The Stars Look Down* had strengthened her conviction that her instincts were the right ones. Over a three-hour dinner the director-designate, Leslie Arliss, argued

'What can Carol be thinking of?': Margaret directed by Carol Reed in her first unsympathetic role as the hussy in *The Stars Look Down* with Emlyn Williams and Michael Redgrave, 1939.

Between takes on the set of *Night Train to Munich* with
Rex Harrison and Paul Henreid, 1940.

Margaret with Margaretta Scott in *The Girl in the News*, 1940.

With Barry K. Barnes and Roger Livesey in the same film.

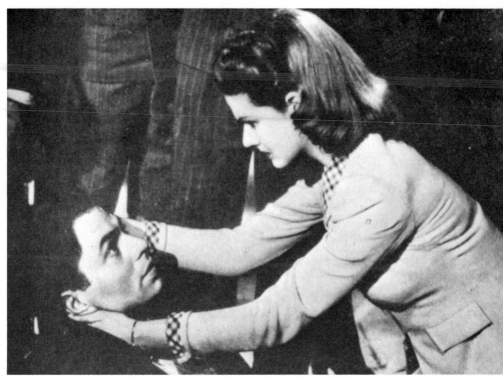

First encounter with James Mason in *Alibi*, 1942.

The making of legend: Mason and Lockwood in *The Man in Grey*, 1943.

Michael Wilding had his first important role in *Dear Octopus*, 1943.

The tear-jerking *Love Story* with Stewart Granger, 1944.

Above and right: The Wicked Lady – bawdy… salacious… an outrage… until it received a royal seal of approval.

An unforgettable duo, creating a legend in British cinema.

his case for casting her against type just as Carol Reed had done. Hesther, she protested, was a very different proposition from Jenny; wicked through and through, a murderess. 'I can't do it,' she said. But just as she was no risk-taker, neither was she by nature a rebel. Finally she accepted the inevitable with the same misgivings she had felt over the Jenny role.

The part of the Marquis of Rohan, known as the Man in Grey, had first been offered to Eric Portman, who had turned it down. Robert Donat wasn't interested, either. Third choice was James Mason. When filming got under way at Shepherd's Bush studios in October 1942 there was still one principal role left to cast, that of the dashing young Rokeby, an old flame of Hesther's who falls in love with Clarissa. There were several contenders, all of whom were tested in a scene with Margaret. There was no question in her mind which of them deserved it; a dark, handsome, ebullient fellow called Stewart Granger.

Thus the quartet of stars who would dominate British films for the next four years was assembled. But the significance of *The Man in Grey* went beyond launching a stable of home-cultivated stars who would rival Hollywood's greatest in box-office appeal. It signalled a change of direction which Rank's takeover had instigated by vesting greater powers of decision-making with Ostrer, and the first hints now appeared of a split in Gainsborough's hierarchy that was to have a profound influence on production policies.

As executive producer of the film, Maurice Ostrer had been content to leave the detail of production to Ted Black, his No. 2, but *The Man in Grey* was, in Black's view, Ostrer's project and one that didn't have his own whole-hearted favour. Black was simultaneously producing *Millions Like Us*, a documentary-style tribute to the new workforce of women in Britain's munitions factories. The neo-realism of its treatment of ordinary people and their conditions was in direct line from *The Stars Look Down* and *Bank Holiday*. This, more than romantic tosh, was the kind of material he wanted to make. Ostrer, on the other hand, was convinced that film-goers were tiring of war themes and were ready for some escapism. He was sparing with money, though not with effort, to ensure that *The Man in Grey* would make audiences forget the realities outside the cinema for a couple of hours.

The picture was budgeted at £90,000, an average Gainsborough outlay at that period, but in the context of rising wartime costs a fairly stringent investment compared with pre-war production. The final cost came to £105,000, an indication of how rigorously the budget was adhered to. The original art director had designed elaborate sets. These were jettisoned, along with their designer, before filming started. Art direction was trimmed to basics, but basics that had to be compensatingly rich in detail. Location shooting was vetoed. Even historical accuracy and authenticity, if they entailed extra expenditure, were sacrificed to economy. This sort of restriction presented technicians and artistes with a challenge, a test of how the studio could create a film that could look and 'feel' expensive on a shoestring.

Work didn't always run smoothly. In return for the Rohan role, James Mason had allowed himself, against his better judgement, to be signed to a contract which gave Gainsborough an option on his services for another five films. He already had a reputation for bucking the system, making no secret of his antipathy for studio politics and politicians, but his position at Gainsborough was particularly delicate. A year before, he had married Pamela Kellino, daughter of Isidore Ostrer, niece of Maurice. For a man of such independent principles it was a sensitive situation to find himself in. And he'd developed a fine contempt for the director, Leslie Arliss, with whom he had worked the year before on *The Night Has Eyes*.

Mason realised that *The Man in Grey* had commercial possibilities, might even be his springboard to stardom, but he couldn't bring himself to co-operate amicably with Arliss. One minor argument between them led to him hitting the director. In his autobiography he recalled: 'Angered by my own inability to cope, I wallowed in a stupidly black mood throughout and since my own imagination had contributed nothing to the Lord Rohan who appeared on the screen, I have to conclude that only my permanent aggravation gave the character colour and made it some sort of memorable thing.'

Initially Margaret was preoccupied with the same anxieties she'd wrestled with over the Jenny Sunley role. They resolved themselves in the same way. After a few days she began to 'feel' the part and enjoy it. Stewart Granger, the 'new boy', was inevitably something of an outsider and compensated by being the life and soul of the unit, but the combination of a boisterous self-assurance, a certain degree of nervousness over handling a part he realised could make him a star, and a short fuse, didn't always endear him to his colleagues, nor did it ease his own tensions to be appearing nightly in the West End as Maxim de Winter in the stage version of *Rebecca*.

'He kept us all laughing,' Margaret recalled. But sometimes Granger's barrack-room language caused offence. Unlike Mason, a conscientious objector, he had been in the army but had recently been invalided out. On one occasion, knowing time was running short for him to get to the theatre, he kept fluffing his lines and fired off a fusillade of expletives at everyone in earshot. Margaret, along with others on the set, was not amused.

'He had what seemed to be an enormous inferiority complex which came out sometimes in a flow of bad language and at other times in round abuse of everybody, because *he* hadn't done his piece as well as he wanted.' His colleagues decided to send a letter to his agent, asking that he should 'cloak his feelings a little more ably'.

When all these little local difficulties had been ironed out, *The Man in Grey* became a relaxed production. On the set there was a quiet confidence that something 'different' was coming together.

'I got on fine with Margaret Lockwood, who, although having patrician beauty, also had the raucous laugh of a truck-driver, an endearing combination,' Granger wrote in his autobiography. One scene, in which he had to slap her face, needed several re-takes and with each one her expression became more stricken. Full of remorse, he tried to comfort her. 'You silly twit,' she reprimanded. 'Stop being such a gentleman and finish the bloody scene.'

Rupert had been posted overseas. Just before he sailed Margaret joined him for a week at York, where he was then stationed. Each was aware that the rift between them was widening. Whenever they were together they seemed to argue and quarrel. Her world wasn't one he wanted any part of and his was one from which a wife was excluded. Margaret had re-established a London base at Dolphin Square, leasing a tiny two-roomed flat for the working week and returning to Hampshire and Toots at the weekend. She was now maintaining three homes.

After a quiet Christmas in Hampshire she learned that her first film of 1943 was to be *Dear Octopus*, a West End stage hit by Dodie Smith in 1938. She didn't care for the script. An archetypal comedy/drama of middle-class family disruptions and discords, it seemed to plough the same furrows as *Quiet Wedding* and her role as the mother's companion/secretary who falls in love with the son of the house, played by Michael Wilding, struck her as particularly dull. Once again there were pre-production arguments. Her character was built up but

117

she went to work on it grudgingly. She still regarded the film as 'a step backwards' but worse followed.

The script of *Give Us The Moon* seemed to promise a change of direction and pace, a comedy based on the witty novel *The Elephant is White* by Caryl Brahms and S. J. Simon, whose books had won them a high reputation for crisp, sardonic humour. Set in the future, three years after the war had ended, it revolved round a group of Russian emigrés in London dedicated to the principle of making a living without working.

Margaret looked forward to playing a countess at whose restaurant the group meets to part well-heeled clients from their money, but the script failed dismally to translate to the screen. The film was a flop, notable only for the debut of fourteen-year-old Jean Simmons playing Margaret's sister.

Maurice Ostrer had consolidated his power-base with Rank. Black's *Millions Like Us* had been a success artistically and at the box office, and he had followed it with *Two Thousand Women* – another hit – about British civilian women captured and interned by the Nazis in France, and he was now preparing *Waterloo Road*, a hard-hitting drama dealing with a sensitive topic, the infidelity of a soldier's wife who takes up with a black marketeer. Ostrer particularly disliked this subject, which he felt was taking Black's line in naturalism too far from his own 'escapist' policy, and he was determined to end the association.

The Man in Grey was unveiled in August 1943. Such was Ostrer's faith in it that he opened it simultaneously in two West End cinemas, unprecedented for a British film, but its critical reception was muted, except for one influential review. The perspicacious C. A. Lejeune in *The Observer* welcomed it as a film which 'tells a story with every chance of interesting you as much as a good novel'. Hers was a lone voice, too, in singling out Stewart Granger as a future star. 'As a star performer he is still quite brilliantly bad. I don't know any British actor I would sooner sign as a prospect.'

Ostrer could afford to ignore the critics. Film-goers, relishing a gamey new flavour in British movies, flocked to it. Never had a British film peddled sex and sensation so boldly. 'Spectacle and sex, a dash of sadism, near-the-knuckle lines and an end where virtue is rewarded,' as the London *Evening Standard* perceived it, was the formula, more stumbled on than arrived at, which would make Gainsborough the dominant studio for the next six years.

As a director, Leslie Arliss lacked imagination and there was a crudeness in his style as apparent then as it is today. His gift was for telling a story, keeping it on the move and holding attention. He believed in emotionalism. British films and players, he once declared, 'are afraid of genuine emotion on the screen and this is the reason for the supremacy of the Americans in human drama'. It was his self-appointed mission to redress the balance. His instincts were quickly proved right. In London and on release the film broke box-office records and the public's reaction to its stars was phenomenal.

Margaret's fan mail soared. People thrilled to this wicked new Lockwood as they had not to the mere bitchiness of her character in *The Stars Look Down*. This was a very different Margaret; scheming and steely, more flamboyant and authoritative than anyone had ever thought her capable of being. Above all, a glamorous Lockwood. In one role, with one leap, she'd acquired star quality to rival that of any Hollywood goddess. Gratified as she was, she didn't altogether welcome this new, slightly discomforting status. She had never sought stardom except as a platform for roles that would stretch and test her as an actress, despite her nervousness about taking them on, and she was shrewd enough to guess that Ostrer, now that he'd sunk a shaft in a potential gold-mine, was going to be more interested in box-office returns than in great acting. What she did not guess was that he would use the huge success of *The Man in Grey* as an excuse to lever Ted Black out of the company he had served so well for the past decade. Black quietly quit and joined Alexander Korda, for whom *Waterloo Road* proved yet another hit.

For Margaret it was a personal loss. Ted Black, with Herbert de Leon, had been one of the two indispensable props of her professional life, always there to be trusted and turned to for advice and support. In a sense she had looked on both men as surrogate fathers in the absence of her own, and while she respected Maurice Ostrer, she never developed the same rapport with him that she'd known with Black.

Predictably, Ostrer mixed the same chemicals for her next film. Arliss and Margaret were re-teamed for her third picture of 1943, *Love Story*, in which she played a concert pianist who, learning she has a heart condition and only a year to live, retreats to Cornwall where she falls in love with an RAF pilot who is going blind, played by Stewart Granger. Her other co-star was Patricia Roc as the flier's childhood sweetheart, whose possessive jealousy threatens to wreck the romance.

In line with the fashion of the time, when the cinema had discovered that classical music and musicians provided romantic themes with a strong emotional undertow, the heroine was composing a piano concerto. Specially written for the film, Hubert Bath's 'Cornish Rhapsody' swept the nation, rivalling the 'Warsaw Concerto' in popularity. No pianist herself, Margaret installed a piano in the tiny Dolphin Square flat, driving her neighbours to distraction with her practising under the guidance of Harriet Cohen, who dubbed the piece on the soundtrack.

Love Story was the first of three films in which Margaret and Patricia Roc played rivals in love. In each of them one was required to slap the other's face. Working with Margaret, Miss Roc recalls, was a joy. 'She had a tremendous personality, possibly at times reserved but never boring. She was always alert, never late on the set and always word perfect. And such a sense of humour, with a most marvellous laugh that started in the stomach and rang round the studio.'

When they came to the face-slapping scene, 'I didn't pull my punches but then neither did she. In my autograph book, which I carefully kept for each film I made, she wrote in January 1944: "*Love Story* is the first picture we have made together and I have to sock you on the jaw, not once but twice – here's hoping that in our next we can be friends, not enemies." '

There was a buoyant spirit at Gainsborough now. By the end of 1943 the success of *The Man in Grey* had given Ostrer and Harold Huth and R. J. Minney, the two joint producers he had picked to replace Ted Black, an open-ended licence for all-out escapist material. James Mason, Phyllis Calvert and Stewart Granger had just completed *Fanny by Gaslight*. Going into production were *Madonna of the Seven Moons* (Calvert and Granger) and *They Were Sisters* (Mason and Calvert). These were to be the bedrock of the reputation Gainsborough would carry into posterity, all offering the studio trademark of rampant melodrama, sex, sadism and unfettered emotions, topped off with fancy-dress costume and elaborate art work.

The stars were given little rest, with the production line, Margaret said in after-years, like a treadmill, 'going straight out of one picture into the next. It was just like being a machine. You didn't query anything. You just did as you were told and got on with it. You have to remember we were being well paid for those days and you didn't look a gift horse in the mouth.'

KEITH AND THE WICKED LADY

In the New Year of 1944 the studio game of musical canvas chairs brought Lockwood and Mason back together for *A Place of One's Own*.

This was something of a departure from the formula; a gentle film from a story by Sir Osbert Sitwell about a young woman companion to an elderly couple who is possessed by the ghost of a girl murdered in the house 40 years before. The film was restrained and tasteful, with superb designs by the brilliant artist Rex Whistler, completed just months before his death in the Normandy landings. Margaret's performance was the most subtle and delicately shaded she had given since *Bank Holiday* and once again she was beautifully photographed. Yet despite being one of the few Gainsborough pictures to find favour with the critics, it failed at the box office. The fans felt their expectations of the Lockwood-Mason teaming had been betrayed; an almost unrecognisable Mason, cast as the elderly husband, was kindly and ineffectual. It had been a brave inspiration but a misguided one. The romantic interest for Margaret was Dennis Price, playing a young doctor who exorcises the ghost that possesses her. It was only his second film, the first of four he would make with her to rank, alongside Mason, as her most consistent co-star.

On a personal level life for Margaret had become moribund. She was lonely, yet the pressures of almost non-stop filming left her with little time or energy for socialising. Her usual routine on getting home late from the studio was to eat a solitary dinner in the restaurant at Dolphin Square and be in bed by 10.30 p.m. Each weekend she would travel down to Hampshire, and the solace of Toots.

For some time Margaret Evelyn had been pointing out the unnecessary expense of running three homes. Surely it made more sense to get rid of the rented house and the nurse and let Toots stay with her at Delcott. Or, as Margaret interpreted the reasoning: 'Surely you

121

can let your little daughter stay with her own granny?' Whatever the personal arguments, Margaret Evelyn could rarely be faulted on practicalities and she made a good case. Margaret agreed.

Her estrangement from Rupert seemed more marked than ever. They hadn't seen each other for more than two years. Their letters were getting fewer and with each one there seemed to be less to say. Rupert, now transferred to the Intelligence Corps, was wrapped up in his work, Margaret, as ever, in hers. Never having shared much common ground, they might now be inhabiting separate planets.

That summer Britain's premier film award, the *Picturegoer* Gold Medal poll of readers, gave Margaret second place after Greer Garson among the nation's favourite screen actresses. She polled more than sixteen per cent of the votes, well ahead of Ingrid Bergman in third place and far outdistancing her nearest British challenger, Rosamund John. So now it was official. She was everyone's favourite British screen actress. Confirmation came three months later in October with the release of *Love Story*. The critics predictably scorned it and just as predictably the film-going public turned it into another Ostrer gold seam. In only twelve weeks it took £200,000 at the box office, making it, after *Fanny by Gaslight*, the second most profitable British film of the war years. The title was prophetic for Margaret. Even as the fans were shedding their tears over her ill-omened screen romance, she found herself falling unexpectedly, intensely, in love.

Long after the affair was over Margaret went to elaborate lengths to keep her lover's identity a secret, protecting his privacy as closely as she protected her own. In her autobiography, published ten years later, she called him Bill, an army officer. His real name was Keith Dobson and he was in the RAF.

His mother had a flat in Dolphin Square. One evening in the restaurant there, just about to start her meal, Margaret was asked by the head waiter if she would mind sharing her table with another resident, a Mrs Dobson. They took to dining together occasionally and struck up an acquaintance. The older woman told her about her two sons in the services, perhaps naturally dwelling more on Keith who was stationed near London and got home frequently. Her life wasn't exactly lonely but his visits meant a lot. He was pleasantly intrigued to find that his mother had become friends with a famous film star. Next time he came home, she asked tentatively, would Margaret mind dropping in for a coffee and meeting him?

Shades of Mrs Leigh Bennett. Margaret had come to appreciate her occasional quiet chats with Mrs Dobson at the end of a hard day, when she could be herself rather than the on-duty film star. Separated from Toots and her own mother during the working week, her social life limited to the set or studio-ordained functions, the realisation of how much she missed the undemanding pleasures of woman-to-woman conversation proved sometimes harder to withstand than the absence of child or husband. So in due course she rang Mrs Dobson's doorbell and found herself being introduced to 'a rather attractive young officer with a mobile face, nice eyes and straight, carefully-brushed hair'. The reddish-brown hair was receding slightly at the temples. He was just comfortably taller than her own five feet five inches, his features clean-cut, the mouth a little small, perhaps, but the jaw strong and well-shaped. A quick, observant, almost professional assessment.

It was not, she later claimed, love at first sight, but she was attracted to him at once, amused that he should seem so impressed to be drinking coffee with Margaret Lockwood in his mother's home – 'though he went to some pains to disguise this' – and warmed by his sense of humour. She laughed a lot that evening and left feeling refreshingly relaxed. Afterwards, she acknowledged to herself that it was the first time for a long while that she had been aware of enjoying herself in the company of others. When Mrs Dobson issued another invitation a week or so later, she was more than ready to accept. Gradually she began to realise that she couldn't wait for the day's filming to be over whenever she was due to meet Keith.

The film she was working on now was *I'll Be Your Sweetheart*! Her first musical, a cheerful, enjoyable assignment, it set off her new-found happiness perfectly. Keith's infectious enthusiasms and the uncomplicated delight he seemed to take in her fame acted like a tonic on her. She felt appreciated.

One evening, looking every inch a filmstar, she slipped away from a formal function to join him and he saw her for the first time at her elegant best. Overawed, he told her: 'You are beautiful. I wish I could take you out looking like that.' Glorying in the glamour of her appearance and calling, Keith unconsciously brushed a dormant nerve Rupert had never been willing or able to touch.

They went to a night club. Keith was astonished when she told him it was the first time she'd ever been in one. From that night they plunged into a round of night clubs, parties and first nights, a social scene that was totally new to her.

'I could never remember hurrying home so eagerly to get into a dance frock, to dress my hair in a different style nearly every night, to look anxiously in the mirror . . .' Suddenly a new Margaret Lockwood emerged, conscious of her appearance, fastidious over her clothes, eager to please a man . . . This was love as she'd never known it with Rupert, drifting, as they had, out of a first teenage infatuation into a marriage that both had accepted as inevitable because neither of them, playing the star-crossed lovers, knew any different.

Margaret has often cited *I'll Be Your Sweetheart* as one of her favourite films, careful to plant the impression that it was a happy production with a happy result. But the memories it recalls for her are intensely private ones, the weeks she spent working on it perhaps the happiest, most carefree of her life.

Modelled on the popular period musicals which Hollywood was mass-producing at that time, it gave Margaret a song-and-dance role as Edie Story, queen of the music halls in 1900 when song-writers and publishers were waging a war against sheet-music pirates which eventually led to the introduction of copyright laws. It was a fair copy of the Hollywood prototype, with good production, a lively storyline, plenty of old song favourites and Margaret Lockwood in tights, revealing a trim leg for the first time. All it lacked was Technicolor . . . and her own singing voice.

She'd begged Maurice Ostrer to let her do the musical numbers herself, reminding him that she'd started out as a song-and-dance girl, but he'd refused. The fans, he reasoned, wouldn't believe it was her anyway (the same argument would be given Bette Davis the following year when she wanted to play a Beethoven sonata herself in *Deception*!) So Maudie Edwards, a music hall artiste with a small part in the film, was designated to dub the songs. The cast also included Vic Oliver and Peter Graves, both of whom had appeared in *Give Us the Moon*. Lord Graves – he later inherited his family's eighteenth-century barony – remembered how everybody on the set commented on Margaret's high spirits and good humour – 'though she was never easy to know'.

By the end of 1944 it was an open secret that Margaret and Keith had become something more than 'just good friends'. People in the know were beginning to accept them as a couple, at premières and parties, in restaurants and clubs. Margaret was understandably more guarded about confiding in Margaret Evelyn who, at a safe remove down in Hampshire, was not in a position to monitor her comings and goings, yet she made little attempt to cover her tracks or hide the liaison in public. When photographers caught them together on the town she merely declined to name her 'mystery' escort.

Herbert was worried. There had never been a breath of scandal in Margaret's private life . . . but nor had she ever been as vulnerable to a suggestion of it than she was now. He reminded her that she was the wife of a soldier serving overseas, the mother of a young child who still hadn't properly known her father. The Allied armies were battling their way into Germany, victory was finally in sight, the troops would soon be coming home . . . many to unfaithful wives and sweethearts.

Of course Margaret Evelyn found out before long. It was like a flashback across ten years to the scenes over Rupert.

'You're a married woman and you're making a fool of yourself!'

Margaret didn't seem to care any more. She ignored her mother and disregarded Herbert. She was in love with a recklessness that seemed almost youthfully defiant.

A fan in the crowd, watching celebrities arriving for the première of Olivier's *Henry V* that November, suddenly spotted the most famous film face of them all skirting round the crush in the Haymarket: Margaret Lockwood, on the arm of a fair-haired young man, hurried past unnoticed. Curious, the fan broke away and followed them to another cinema nearby where, the night before, a new Hollywood musical had opened starring the latest crooning sensation, Frank Sinatra. While Keith bought tickets for *Step Lively*, Margaret disappeared into the ladies' room. The fan waited with pencil and paper. She was a little brusque when he confronted her, but she signed.

The Olivier première that night was the most glamorous event West Enders had seen since the start of the war, an augury that the hard times were ending and life was edging back to normality. Margaret would soon be starting her own next picture, which promised to be fun. Life was already better, happier than she'd ever known it.

Towards the end of 1944 Leslie Arliss had read a newly published novel recommended to him by Lady Eleanor Smith, author of *The Man in Grey*. He'd been playing around for some time with an idea of making a film about 'a woman so wicked that Scarlett O'Hara would look like a puritan beside her', and as he closed the book he knew he'd found her.

Immediately contacting the publishers to inquire about buying the screen rights, Arliss discovered that he'd been pre-empted by Maurice Ostrer – Gainsborough already held the option to film Magdalen King-Hall's *Life and Death of the Wicked Lady Skelton* and there was no doubt in either man's mind about who should play the fascinating Barbara.

Margaret read the book and was excited. No misgivings this time about portraying an evil woman, and unquestionably the raffish Lady Skelton would be the most ruthless, amoral character any British film had ever dared present. It was a role in a thousand, offering more scope for characterisation than any part she'd ever played.

Barbara, a bewitching but penniless beauty of Charles II's reign began by stealing and marrying her best friend's fiancé; progressed to highway robbery in male disguise; encompassed partnership and a passionate affair with a notorious highwayman; coolly shot dead one of her husband's tenants guarding a gold shipment; cold-bloodedly poisoned the faithful old family retainer who discovered her secret; plotted, steely eyed and iron-hearted, her husband's murder; and, to square the circle of infamy, seduced her best friend's new fiancé. A star vehicle indeed!

Stewart Granger was first choice to play the highwayman but turned it down. A reluctant James Mason came to the film, admitting later, with eloquent understatement 'The part I played in it was rather small . . .' The 'nice girl' role of the long-suffering best friend went to Patricia Roc and Griffith Jones played the hapless husband, Sir Ralph Skelton. Leslie Arliss, of course, was to direct, a prospect Mason didn't relish, though, after *The Man in Grey* and *Love Story*, at least Margaret felt comfortable with him.

The six months shooting schedule took up most of the spring and early summer of 1945 and everybody connected with the film remembered afterwards how much they had enjoyed it.

Margaret, faced with riding a horse for the first time, mastered the technique in just four days, refusing the services of a stuntwoman for the scene in which the scheming Barbara goads her horse to gallop out of control so that she can take a fall and complete her systematic seduction of Sir Ralph. She did, however, agree to be replaced for the actual tumble. Everyone on the set remarked on her high spirits and readiness to laugh, a side of Margaret her colleagues weren't familiar with. 'We did the horseback close-ups on studio rocking horses and jogged about on a wave of giggles,' Griffith Jones recalled, 'and I remember her asking Leslie Arliss to tell her live horse what to do because she hadn't a clue. She was a joy to work with; refreshingly honest and with a great sense of humour.'

The only person not enjoying himself, and making no attempt to disguise it, was Mason, who, Margaret later confided to an interviewer 'stalked off the set after almost every shot muttering "bloody codswallop" '.

To coincide with the film's general release in the autumn of 1945 the studio arranged a personal appearance tour for Margaret of major cities. Following the première of *I'll Be Your Sweetheart* that summer, the public had taken both film and Margaret to their hearts. She was now receiving 25,000 fan letters a month. For a film industry riding a wave of popularity without precedent in Britain, the future seemed limitless. Maurice Ostrer, anticipating an Allied victory at the start of the year, had already announced a £1 million Gainsborough investment for the twelve months ahead in 'screen romance to help fill the void in the hearts of the people'. The autumn tour was part of that plan. It was the first time Margaret had faced the fans *en masse* and the enthusiasm of the crowds wherever she turned out overwhelmed and disturbed her. Starved for nearly six years of the glamour she embodied, they mobbed her, struggling and fighting to touch her. It was a frightening experience. She returned home exhausted but exhilarated, left in no doubt that she was the reigning queen of British cinema.

Her next film was to be *The Magic Bow*, scheduled to go into production in November. It was the story – highly fictionalised and coloured – of the eighteenth-century violinist Paganini . . . another costume melodrama; more sin and sex and low-cut necklines . . . the formula as before with only the names changed. She could already visualise the cleavage, the low-lidded looks, the scheming and tantrums . . . Perhaps it might have worked but when she read the script, for the first time in her career, Margaret, the star without star temperament, felt stirrings of real rebellion. It was a poor script. James Mason, initially cast as the saturnine musician believed by many of his contemporaries to be in league with the devil, had been keen enough to take violin lessons when he first heard of the project. After reading the script he dropped them and told his Uncle Maurice to look for someone else: no longer under contract to Gainsborough, he could afford to be choosy.

'All my imagining had concerned itself strictly with the professional and politico-social history of the man. I should have known they would concentrate on his alleged love life,' he wrote in his memoirs. That love life, according to Gainsborough, was restricted to two women from central casting – the vapid aristocrat who becomes his adoring patron and the passionate spitfire, Bianchi, who flits in and out of his emotions.

Stewart Granger replaced Mason, Phyllis Calvert found herself predictably lined up for the noblewoman and Margaret was to be Bianchi. None of the three was happy, Margaret least of all. Not only was her role stereotyped, it was third ranking after the other two, little more than a walk on (and off) part.

She let it be known that she didn't want to do it. Ostrer's response was to remind her that she was under contract, but he took her point about the size of the role and gave her an assurance that the character would be built up. There were other factors, however. Neither Phyllis Calvert nor Margaret was particularly keen to work with Granger. In an interview years later Miss Calvert recalled:

'After three films we did get rather bored with each other. This was why I wanted to get out of *The Magic Bow*. I remember ringing Granger and saying "Do you think we ought to do it?" and he said "If you're talking about personal feelings, no. But if you're talking about Our Public, yes." '

Margaret's attitude was similar but complicated by a factor the others weren't aware of: she'd been offered an alternative script by an independent producer which promised much greater scope.

She and Phyllis, by now the best of friends, agonised over their dilemma and decided that the most honest and honourable way to resolve it was to petition J. Arthur Rank himself. Without telling anyone they went to the Rank headquarters in Park Lane and were ushered into the magnate's vast office. He was sitting at the head of an onyx table which stretched almost the entire length of the room.

Phyllis Calvert recalled: 'Margaret was very, very timid about it but I wasn't at all. One of us went one way round the table and the other went the other way, and as we got towards him he rose up from his seat and said "I hear you've come to talk about more brass." '

Rank enjoyed a paternalistic role as the head of his 'family' of contract artists and he listened sympathetically to each of his leading ladies in turn. When they left him 'timid' Margaret had won a famous victory, Phyllis a compromise.

Rank not only agreed that Margaret needn't do the film; he released her from her Gainsborough contract, due to expire within a few months, and promised to replace it with one of his own. Phyllis was persuaded to stay with *The Magic Bow*, but for substantially more money, and the Bianchi role went to Jean Kent, a personable new-comer beginning to make headway at Gainsborough as a pocket-size Margaret Lockwood-type.

Margaret saw the advantage she had gained as a small but significant confirmation of principle. In the wider context of her future, it sig-nalled a turning point. She had won a battle and, without realising it, lost a campaign.

It's impossible to say now whether the transfer of contract Rank suggested shifted the course of her career. Other factors had a more direct influence on the films she subsequently made, notably the econ-omic crisis which hit the industry in the immediate post-war period, and changes in audience taste. Other studios under Rank's control were beginning to produce quality movies, films that were original, serious, different, and they were winning respect from the critics, favour from the public. Gainsborough's romance and escapism seemed dated and trivial to Margaret and now she was free to indulge her own instincts and work for an independent producer.

Maurice Ostrer was furious when he found out how Margaret had outflanked him. Rightly or wrongly, he regarded himself as the archi-tect of her standing as No. 1 among British screen actresses and duly expected appreciation, if not gratitude. In his view she had, instead, repaid him with deception by going to Rank behind his back.

Patricia Roc, in Hollywood filming the western *Canyon Passage* with Dana Andrews and Susan Hayward at Universal, had been the first contract player to be sent to Hollywood under Rank's loan-out arrangements with Universal and Twentieth Century-Fox. She received an unusually indiscreet letter from Ostrer, venting his feelings over *The Magic Bow* affair. 'He was angry because Maggie had refused to play in the film. He said that he didn't intend to use her ever again, that he was glad to give up her contract to Arthur Rank and that after her next film he guaranteed she would start to go on the down-grade quickly.'

Vindictiveness of that order from a studio head towards his top box-office star may not have been unknown in Hollywood but in the more gentlemanly British industry it was unprofessional. Phyllis

Calvert, too, had been a party to this perceived act of betrayal, but, by omission, she seemed to have been pardoned.

Ostrer was right in thinking Margaret's next film would prove a backward step (though no more than *The Magic Bow* would have been for her). He was even prophetic, in the longer term, in forecasting that she would go 'on the down-grade'. What he failed to foresee was that the contract transfer was a small warning signal of his own downfall.

The script Margaret had favoured over *The Magic Bow* was *Bedelia*, based on a novel by the American author and screenwriter Vera Caspary, whose *Laura* was one of that year's most stylish Hollywood thrillers. The independent producer John Corfield, had acquired the rights against stiff competition from Hollywood. Neither as story nor novel was it in the same class as *Laura* but the title role at least was a difficult one to resist. Bedelia, having poisoned two husbands for their insurance money, is now working on a third, unaware that the stranger she has recently befriended is an insurance investigator closing in on her. Echoes of Lady Skelton and undertones of another recent acclaimed thriller, *Double Indemnity*.

The lure of the part probably blinded Margaret to the failings of the rest of the script, which was limp and flawed by John Corfield's decision to change the locale of the story from America to Britain. New England became Yorkshire, Colorado was transposed to Monte Carlo. Somehow it all seemed less menacing, more cosy. Nor was Margaret's strong casting carried through in the choice of leading men for her – a bland Ian Hunter as the husband, a worthy but colourless Barry K. Barnes as the insurance representative. As production geared up at Ealing studios, the trade press was gushing that *Bedelia* would be 'the best-dressed British film of the year with all the latest post-war fashions included in the lovely range of clothes being specially designed for Miss Lockwood'. Fine feathers weren't, however, destined to make a fine *Bedelia*.

With nice timing, shooting started three days after *The Magic Bow* went into production. A week earlier, the Fates, with an even nicer sense of mischief, had engineered a frosty encounter between Margaret and Ostrer at the première of *The Wicked Lady* at the Gaumont, Haymarket on 19 November 1945.

For weeks Gainsborough's publicity team had been whipping up anticipation in the cinema trade with teaser display advertisements, and the public had caught a whiff of the excitement. It was to be the first 'full dress' gala première London had enjoyed since the war, in the gracious presence of Queen Mary and with proceeds going to the British Hospital for Mothers and Babies at Woolwich. A society event in a worthy cause, a public parade of celebrities, two of them at private war while preparing for the acclaim that would crown their careers.

The storm broke on the morning of the première. Critics who had already seen previews had alerted their news editors to a story and *The Wicked Lady* invaded the front pages that day to outraged charges of 'bawdy' . . . 'disgraceful' . . . 'salacious'. Queen Mary, the reporters huffed, should not be allowed to see it.

It was not general public knowledge that the 87-year-old Queen Dowager, stiff, stately and a symbol of old-fashioned royal propriety, was in private an avid film fan, the most regular première patron of the royal family and frequently in the habit of commanding a new picture to be screened for her in the cinema at Marlborough House, sometimes inviting its star to join her in watching it. Even so, her advisors were alarmed by the reports that morning on *The Wicked Lady*: the synopsis submitted to them when the première was being arranged had given no indication that there might be anything offensive to royal eyes and ears.

With only hours left before the performance at six o'clock that evening, worried Rank executives received a call from Marlborough House asking for an emergency screening: an equerry would view the film and make a snap decision on whether or not it was suitable. For an hour and three-quarters some of the most powerful men in the film industry paced the floor outside the viewing room, contemplating the humiliation of a monumental royal snub. The equerry emerged, smiled and gave his approval.

Margaret arrived at the Gaumont in an advanced state of nervous tension, trying to conceal it by chatting vivaciously with J. Arthur Rank as they waited to receive the Queen. Sharp-eyed onlookers noticed something slightly different in her appearance – a prominent beauty spot on her left cheekbone. There was a small mole there which had always annoyed her. While making the film she had suddenly had the idea of turning it to advantage by painting mascara over it to suggest a patch or beauty spot fashionable with seventeenth-century ladies of quality. In so doing she unthinkingly created the Margaret Lockwood trade-mark.

'I can't tell you how I felt,' she said later of that night. 'You could have cut the atmosphere with a knife.' Maurice Ostrer, standing in the presentation line a few steps away from her, was even more overwrought. His reputation and credibility were riding on the outcome of this night. He and Margaret acknowledged each other politely but it was Margaret who bore the brunt of the strain. It was *her* contribution to the film that had triggered the controversy . . . the wanton vice of the character she played, unprecedented in a British film; the revealing décolletage of her Restoration wardrobe; above all, the suggestive dialogue and actions between herself and James Mason – 'Oh, just one more,' says Margaret, hefting gold bullion at a stage-coach robbery; to which he replies, 'I've heard you say that in other circumstances.' The most notorious sequence was an erotic – for those days – love scene between them on the bank of a moonlit lake. A rumour has long persisted that the soundtrack at that point was deliberately muffled so that royal ears would not be offended, but Margaret has denied it. 'My seat in the circle was four or five rows behind the royal party on the aisle,' she recalled. 'I could see the journalists who had got tickets, the gossip columnists, never taking their eyes off Queen Mary for a moment. Hoping, of course, she would get up and walk out or give some sign of disapproval.' Everyone connected with the picture in the cinema that evening did in fact sit rigid with dread of the ultimate snub – a royal walk-out – but Queen Mary sat through it, unflinching and immobile.

'At the end, we stood as she left her seat. She came up the steps, that majestic figure, without a word. When she was abreast of me, she stopped. I curtseyed, not daring to look her in the face, and I heard her saying: "That was very good. I enjoyed it very much." '

The moment she left, Margaret was besieged by journalists demanding to know what the Queen had said. The royal 'review' kept *The Wicked Lady* on the front pages all next day – and made the film's fortune.

Within a week it had broken all previous attendance records at the Gaumont. Generally released for Christmas, it shattered every box-office record wherever it showed, probably the only instance in the history of the cinema of a royal endorsement guaranteeing the commercial success of a film.

The critics condemned it, almost to a man, citing its 'salacity', the banality of its script 'to the point of stupidity', the crudeness of the production and the inadequacy of much of the acting. What they failed to appreciate was the energy of its story-telling and a powerful identification for the women in its audiences with the Wicked Lady herself. Margaret had unwittingly touched a chord in the 'new woman' emerging from the disciplines of a long war. This wicked lady was a woman of independence, flouting hidebound convention, flaunting her superiority over men and contempt for them with courage, single-mindedness and feminine wiles. She plotted her own escape from the boredom of domesticity, depended on her own will, not a man's whim, to get what she wanted.

Of all Margaret's roles, many of them showing her to be a better actress, this was the one that made her an immortal of the screen. It isn't one that gives her particular satisfaction – there are others she would prefer to be remembered for – but she has always defended *The Wicked Lady* stoutly if she feels it is under attack.

'It may have been rubbish,' she'd say, 'but we took it seriously, and it showed. That's why it was so successful.' Nearly half a century later the film has established itself as a classic and when it was re-made in 1983 the new generation of critics condemned it anew . . . by referring back to the original with affectionate nostalgia. For Margaret the role and the title were destined to become synonymous with her. From that time on, for the rest of her days, she would never be allowed to forget that she was *The Wicked Lady*.

There was another Restoration beauty spreading scandalised delight on both sides of the Atlantic at that time, a second cousin to the wicked Lady Skelton by the name of Amber St Clair. Kathleen Winsor's *Forever Amber* was the current publishing sensation.

Twentieth Century-Fox held the film rights and was orchestrating a search for an actress – preferably English – to play the title role intended to make that for Scarlett O'Hara seem like a halfhearted game of hunt the thimble. The publicity quest was at its height when *The Wicked Lady*, with all its attendant newsworthiness, was released. Fox's star exchange agreement with Rank could never have seemed more fortuitous than now, with *The Wicked Lady* almost a dry run for the lavish *Amber* project, and the Hollywood studio was keenly interested in a package deal to borrow both Lockwood and Mason.

It was the chance for Margaret to become a fully fledged international star, but she wasn't interested. Her memories of Hollywood still rankled, but there were other, more private considerations. She would be separated from Keith for an indefinite period and she would have to leave Toots at home. She turned the part down. So, it was reported, did Vivien Leigh, and Mason also declined. 'They sent over the script but the part wasn't good enough for me,' he told a reporter. The Amber role was eventually awarded to the relatively unknown Peggy Cummins, but after filming began, she was found to be unsuitable and was replaced by Linda Darnell. Margaret's judgment, for once, had probably served her well: the film failed lamentably to measure up to expectations.

Instead, under her new deal with J. Arthur Rank, she was seconded to another of his production companies, Two Cities, for *Hungry Hill*, based on Daphne du Maurier's recent best seller. This, she considered, really was a move in the right direction, distancing her from Ostrer's 'pulp for the masses' policy at Gainsborough and linking her to a company with a growing reputation for quality film-making. Its roll of prestigious titles included *In Which We Serve*, Olivier's *Henry V*, *The Way to the Stars* and, significantly, Carol Reed's outstanding *The Way Ahead*. Carol, discharged from the army, was now back in harness with the company and working on his first post-war film, *Odd Man Out*, with James Mason. By aligning herself with Two Cities Margaret's chances of being reunited with him in some future project must have seemed a tempting possibility.

The role of Fanny Rosa in *Hungry Hill*, a saga of two powerful feuding Irish families against a background of copper mining in the nineteenth century, required Margaret to age over 40 years from young belle to elderly matriarch.

Margaret's leading man was the talented, tragic Dennis Price, her co-star in *A Place of One's Own*. A tortured man, married but secretly homosexual and well on his way to becoming an alcoholic, he was particularly fond of Margaret and she of him. One day Toots accompanied her to the studio and made her film debut in a tiny scene.

Dermot Walsh, a young Dublin actor newly arrived in London, was given his first big-screen role playing Margaret's grown-up son. She made a strong impression on him.

I remember being totally knocked out by her star status. I mean, she was *the* star at that time. On the set the rest of us would have to find seats for ourselves or fetch our own coffee but Maggie had her own special chair and her coffee was always brought to her. She was treated with great deference. I found her extremely warm and friendly to work with, but she hardly ever mixed with the rest of us once we'd stopped working. She never formed any relationships among the crew that we were aware of.

Just as Margaret, in her early days in the studios, had done with other actors, Walsh studied her closely on the set, learning from her.

My most powerful memory of her is that she was a hundred per cent professional. She never arrived late, she always was word perfect, never fluffed a line, let alone dried. Her camera technique was incredible, the best I ever saw. As good as any Hollywood star's. She seemed to know instinctively the exact angle needed for the camera and lights. I don't ever recall her having to be told. I learned an enormous amount just from watching her. She wouldn't go out of her way to teach you, but she wouldn't try to put you down, either. Her reserve always seemed to be accepted by the people working with her and, as far as I was aware, she was liked. I think the measure of that is that I never heard a joke or a story told at her expense, which is fairly unusual in our business.

Before starting *Hungry Hill* in April 1946, Margaret had taken stock of her own domestic life and decided on some changes. It worried her that she spent so much time apart from Toots, and living in such confined conditions in central London made her realise how much she missed the space and greenery of Hampshire. Her younger brother Lyn, a civilian again after his wartime service and now married, was looking for a home and so Margaret signed over the lease of the Dolphin Square flat to him and found herself a roomier one at Roehampton on the western outskirts of London. At the same time she made over the deeds of Delcott to her mother.

Margaret's new home, in a smart, anonymous block of apartments, was a compromise between town and country. Its windows looked out across the magnificent acres of Richmond Park; three miles away on the other side of the park lay Richmond, her father's birthplace. Unknowingly, she was returning to her family roots. But most importantly, here she could resume being a practising parent, reclaiming her rightful place in her daughter's life and showing the world that she was capable of reconciling the roles of actress, star and mother.

In April 1946 Maurice Ostrer had announced that he was resigning from Gainsborough Pictures, the company he had helped to create eighteen years before. The news was not unexpected but still it sent tremors through the Rank Organisation, proof positive of the disagreement, disenchantment and conflict of ideology that existed between the top executives.

Since the end of the war, J. Arthur Rank had been developing a grand design for expanding his cinema interests into the 'world market', acquiring control of leading cinema circuits and distribution outlets in Canada, South Africa and Australia and negotiating deals in New Zealand. But the main thrust of his ambition was directed at the United States; only there could his films reap the profits he envisaged for investment and production. It followed that British studios – his studios – would need to 'think big', to produce films with wider international appeal to compete with Hollywood's. Until now they had been little more than a cottage industry, catering successfully but with limited return to an exclusively domestic market – Ostrer's specialist market.

As one contemporary trade analyst revealed: 'Ostrer has been far from happy in his present position and more than six months ago he told me that he was against policies that advocated the making of British films for large sums of money.' Another contended that he had 'never concealed his disapproval of many of the decisions taken by the Central Production Facilities [of the Rank Organisation] in its attempts to rationalise the studio end of the Rank companies'. There had been 'stormy Tuesday afternoon sessions with Ostrer vehemently defending his middle-budget box-office winners against criticism'.

Films like *Henry V, I Know Where I'm Going* and *Brief Encounter* pointed the way towards serious, quality film-making, opening the way for fresh talents such as Michael Powell and Emeric Pressburger and David Lean. Perhaps the most significant of them all was a small-scale production, made on a shoestring by an independent producer and 'adopted' by Rank for distribution, which had opened within days of *The Wicked Lady* and to everyone's astonishment was competing with it for box-office records.

The Seventh Veil, starring James Mason, had taken both London and New York by storm, creating an overnight international star of Ann Todd whom French critics hailed as 'a new Garbo'. A year later its producer, Sydney Box, and his co-writer wife Muriel Box won an Academy Award for Best Original Screenplay. It was the first time an Oscar had gone to a film carrying the Rank imprint; it was perhaps

136

not surprising that Maurice Ostrer, resentful and increasingly isolated, cast himself out into the wilderness.

One particular news item that April must have made bitter-sweet reading for him. The *Daily Mail* had recently instituted an annual National Film Award to mark the golden jubilee of cinema in Britain. Though nobody guessed it, in fact an era was ending: of Ostrer, of Gainsborough and of the British film-going public's infatuation with the cinema. *The Wicked Lady* was its apotheosis. But for weeks readers had been voting for their favourite British film, actor and actress in an inaugural poll which covered the entire output of the war years. Five days before Ostrer made his resignation public, the results were announced.

Margaret Lockwood was named the nation's favourite actress with 54,588 votes, 832 ahead of her nearest rival, Phyllis Calvert. The actor's award went to James Mason and the most popular film was *The Way to The Stars* – a Two Cities production. Three of Ostrer's own Gainsborough titles, *The Man in Grey, Madonna of the Seven Moons* and *They Were Sisters* were voted into second, third and fourth places.

On 12 July 1946 Margaret and J. Arthur Rank signed her new seven-year contract in a suitable glare of media attention. Nine days later she stepped out of a studio limousine on to the red carpet outside the Dorchester Hotel for the *Daily Mail* Silver Star presentations. It was London's answer to Oscar night. Huge crowds packed Park Lane, straining and screaming behind police barriers. Margaret turned and waved. Keith stood at her side, no qualms now about discretion and secrecy. She was proud that night to be seen openly in love.

'In the car I held his hand tightly,' she wrote later. 'As the crowds cheered and waved, I felt my eyes stinging as I waved back. Now I could no longer doubt that I had reached the top of the pathway to the stars. The world seemed at my feet. All I wanted now was to be able to marry and then, I thought, I could expect no further measure of happiness.'

She grew into her own individuality for the first time in that heady summer of 1946. All her life she had subjected herself to a stronger authority, a more dominant personality – Margaret Evelyn, Rupert – and relied on the judgements of others – Carol Reed, Ted Black, Herbert de Leon.

'I hadn't really grown up until I was thirty,' she was to write a decade later. 'It had taken me till then to realise that an adult is not only entitled to stand on her own two feet but, indeed, she *must* do that if she is to make a complete and satisfactory life for herself. No one but I knew how intensely I disliked defying anyone, even over the most trivial matters, a dislike which usually compelled me to take the line of least resistance and give in. From childhood I had hated arguments or rows with my mother. I dreaded arguments with Rupert and for years I shrank from raising any objections when I was working.'

The stand she had taken over *The Magic Bow* – her own independent decision – had opened her eyes to her own bargaining power. Now the public had endorsed it with its vote of ultimate confidence. So, even more convincingly, had J. Arthur Rank himself.

She took stock of her life. In September she would be 30. There were decisions to be made, a spring-clean to be faced. The first, overriding priority was to marry Keith. She wanted to be his wife. She wanted to make a proper family home for Toots. She wanted, however regretfully, a divorce.

Rupert was still in the army, serving now with the occupation forces in Germany. The letter she steeled herself to write to him was the most difficult she had ever tried to compose. 'I told him as honestly and as simply as I could that I had fallen in love with someone else.' His reply was noncommittal. He made no mention of divorce, merely told her that he would get some leave as soon as possible. She had to resign herself to the suspense of waiting.

Maurice Ostrer's successor at Gainsborough was Sydney Box, appointed largely on the strength of *The Seventh Veil*. Since making his name with that, he had completed *Daybreak*, again as an independent, and had just started production on another film, an adaptation of Graham Greene's novel *The Man Within*, leasing Gainsborough studio space.

Muriel Box, who, after her divorce from Sydney, married Lord Gardiner, Lord Chancellor in the Labour administration of the late 1960s, estimated that Gainsborough's output in the final troubled phase of Ostrer's management had dwindled to an average of one and a quarter films a year. Box's remit from Rank was to boost production to between ten and twelve pictures a year, each costing no more than £200,000. Taking an initial inventory of his new domain, he was appalled to discover how Ostrer had allowed it to run down.

'A studio such as Gainsborough should have had a reserve of scripts ready to go into production, waiting to be developed or under option,' said Lady Gardiner. 'We inherited just one, and even that hadn't been fully scripted.'

That one was *Jassy*, from a novel by Norah Lofts, and it immediately presented Sydney Box with a problem of principle. Yet another costume melodrama in the tried, tested, over-worked Gainsborough tradition, it was precisely the kind of subject he was determined to steer the studio away from. Lady Gardiner recalled:

'He wanted to leave costume melodrama behind and open up a wider variety of material. But his first priority was to put the studio space to work . . . it was frightfully expensive and wasteful to leave the stages idle. So he had to press ahead with *Jassy* just to buy time for acquiring new scripts.' Box compromised principle by deciding to make *Jassy* the finest of its genre, an elaborate last flourish for the cycle, sumptuously designed and costumed – and the first Gainsborough film ever photographed in colour.

'He also knew he needed a big name for it and the obvious one was Margaret Lockwood,' said Lady Gardiner.

The prospect of returning to Gainsborough and its tired old formula so soon hardly filled Margaret with enthusiasm but when Box explained his problem to her she agreed to do it. Production started in September 1946, a few days after Maurice Ostrer officially relinquished control and bowed out.

The film was Margaret's first in colour, the title role one she could now play blindfold – a village girl with the gift of second sight who schemes her way into marriage with the Regency rakehell who has murdered her father. An even more pressing motive than revenge, though, is to reclaim the estate he won at cards from the father of the young man she really loves.

A well-schooled Gainsborough writing hand had clearly measured the part of the sadistic gambler to James Mason specifications but he was now above such 'codswallop', working on *Odd Man Out* and his own production *The Upturned Glass*. Basil Sydney, who stepped into his boots, was an excellent character actor but not a star. Still, at least he was more amusing to work with.

'He was a giggler,' Margaret recalled. 'It was like being back at school. In some of our most dramatic scenes, we'd crease up laughing and couldn't carry on.'

Patricia Roc was her rival in love – faces were again slapped – and

139

Dermot Walsh graduated from being her son in *Hungry Hill* to her lover, the dispossessed heir.

Before production of *Jassy* got underway, Margaret had been called back to Gainsborough rather sooner than she expected. *The Wicked Lady*, due for release in the United States and carrying J. Arthur Rank's high hopes for the crucial American breakthrough, had been blocked by the Hays Office, the US censoring board, objecting to the expanse of cleavage revealed by Lockwood and Roc, specifically in shots of them riding in a coach. There was, it decreed, too much bouncing flesh for American sensibilities.

Gleefully exploiting the publicity, Rank ordered the offending scenes to be re-shot but it was a tiresome business. Both actresses had to duplicate gestures and expressions, props and accessories had to be reassembled with pinpoint precision, costumes trimmed with decorous frills and ruffles. One dress of Margaret's had to be retrieved from the Ambassadors Theatre where Hermione Gingold was wearing it for a sketch in the revue *Sweetest and Lowest*. The press revelled in mocking American prudery and the publicity gave the film a renewed lease of life at the home box office.

Jassy turned out to be an enjoyable production, sharing laughs with Basil Sydney and working, as Dermot Walsh remembers it, in a happy atmosphere, but Margaret felt surfeited with costume roles and less than happy with the way things seemed to be going. There was a depressing sameness about the roles being offered to her. She was the undisputed star of British cinema but nobody was praising her performances now as they had in *Bank Holiday* or *The Stars Look Down*.

That September the Cannes Film Festival, originally planned for 1940 but pre-empted by the war, was inaugurated and Margaret made her first trip abroad since the Hollywood excursion. She was fêted as Britain's reigning star, but the award of the festival's top prize to *Brief Encounter* only served to accentuate the void in her own career. Ironically, the single British entry for the year of 1946 was *The Magic Bow*. It could so easily have been herself up there on the festival screen for the critics and jury to contrast with Celia Johnson, though the Gainsborough film would have done her little good. According to the *Times* correspondent, it was 'saved from humiliation only by the symphony orchestra under Basil Cameron and violin solos by Menuhin'.

In November the annual Royal Film Performance was also inaugur-

ated with the Powell and Pressburger film *A Matter of Life and Death*.
London had rarely known such a night. Five thousand fans jammed
Leicester Square to see the King and Queen and the stars arriving at
the Empire. The excitement was so great that the royal car was
nearly overturned in the crush. Hollywood had flown in a glamorous
contingent yet Margaret, her hair carefully dressed in the elaborate
coiffure she had worn on the *Jassy* set at Denham that day, proved
to the screaming fans she was the equal of any star Hollywood could
field.

Margaret Evelyn, 'quite excited for once', was at her side, and
holding the hands of mother and grandmother was Toots, now five,
who was to present the bouquet to the Queen. Only Keith was missing,
as a concession to public mores. It was a night to crown Margaret's
crowning year. A few nights later, returning home after a long day at
the studio, she found a letter waiting for her. Rupert was coming
home.

℘ARTING COMPANY

The last time they had seen each other had been more than four years ago, in York, just before Rupert had gone overseas. He hadn't changed a great deal in appearance or, when they settled into conversation, in his attitudes.

'I see you're wearing more make-up now,' he remarked, matter-of-factly.

It was Margaret who had changed. There was a new gloss of success on her, a deeper assurance and an unconscious poise. She knew, from that give-away remark, that Rupert was no more reconciled to her way of life than he had ever been, less so, probably, now that she was the most famous star in Britain. More than ever, they were strangers to each other.

When they finally spoke of the reason for his visit he was sensible and restrained. He was willing to 'try again', he said, for Toots's sake if not their own, but Margaret told him she wanted a divorce: she loved Keith and wanted to marry him.

They were both trying hard to be civilised and conciliatory. Rupert's overriding concern was for Toots's welfare. Before giving her his answer, Rupert wanted to meet Keith, to make his own assessment of the man who had usurped his place in Margaret's life and now stood to act as father to his child.

The two men met and whether in genuine dislike or simply to strike back Rupert told Margaret bluntly that although he accepted that their marriage was over he wouldn't agree to a divorce. He also insisted that Toots's place now was with Margaret, her mother, not with her grandmother.

Margaret's world crumbled as she realised that the options left open to her were fraught with risk. If she decided to live openly with Keith she would risk Rupert demanding custody of Toots and in the constant glare of the publicity surrounding her she would risk scandal that

142

could be incalculably harmful, both personally and professionally. If, on the other hand, she could bring herself to renounce Keith, she would be repudiating her greatest happiness. It was true that she had moved into the spacious flat at Roehampton with the intention of making it a permanent home for herself and Toots with Keith but she had delayed taking Toots away from St Leonards until her marital problems had been resolved. Even setting aside the question of Keith, Margaret knew she would still have to brace herself for a showdown with Margaret Evelyn.

'She had become very possessive over Toots. She liked to choose her clothes, to plan her upbringing; in other words, to replace me as her child. As my father had been abroad all our lives she had had complete control of me and my brother. She never had to "share" us with anyone. First, and against her will, she had "lost" me when I married. Then my brother had married. But in the interim Toots had been born and my mother had transferred all her maternal care to her and had practically sole charge of her.'

Disengaging the child from this delicate arrangement was going to be painful and Margaret dreaded it. Her mother, disregarding the underlying reasons for the change and feeling only her own hurt, took Margaret's decision as an unwarranted slur on her upbringing of Toots and argued that the little girl's best interests lay with her, in a peaceful country life at a safe remove from corrupting influences, from being identified as the daughter of a famous star. Wounding words were exchanged but Margaret was determined to have her way. Indeed, she knew she must have it if Rupert were not to be antagonised.

Eventually a barely satisfactory compromise was reached. Margaret Evelyn would be welcome to stay at Roehampton as long and as often as she pleased. It was like a replay of the scenes over Rupert, mother ejecting man. Margaret knew she would be sacrificing something of her freedom, knew that whenever Margaret Evelyn was staying there would be added strain on her relationship with Keith. Just what would that relationship be now? The stresses caused by Rupert's intervention had brought the question into even sharper focus. Keith was 'an important part of my life; so important that I automatically thought in terms of "we" and never "I" any more.' But more important than her daughter? The question nagged but she evaded it, playing for time, continuing to see Keith and hoping that, given time to consider, Rupert might change his mind.

'At thirty,' she wrote, 'I'd been voted the most popular screen actress in Britain. I held a great career in my hands, I was financially secure and yet I sometimes wondered if I was becoming cynical, even bitter, over the very success I had always wanted and worked for all my life.' She couldn't honestly say she regretted that her marriage was over – 'Rupert and I had outgrown each other' – and she could convince herself that she had made the right decision but her personal life was undetermined, inconclusive, her future with Keith uncertain.

At least her career was intact. 'Without it I should have been lost, purposeless and bored. I knew now I was Margaret-the-actress first. It had to be that way.' There was a new-found spirit of defiance about her; defiance of Rupert, of Margaret Evelyn, even if necessary of the studio. But, most of all, she could defy her innermost self. She threw herself into playing the Film Star, a role she had never wanted nor particularly enjoyed until now. She seemed to glory in the glamour of the job, the clothes, the jewels, the fan-worship. She was receiving 16,000 letters a week – a rate, one studio statistician calculated, of one letter every 40 seconds.

And this was the Margaret Keith loved. 'He had helped me to learn how to enjoy being a film star because for the first time I had someone with whom I could share *my* life. I looked forward to the gala occasions, the glamorous parties, the heyday and excitement of it all.' With Keith beside her she 'found pleasure in wearing a beautiful gown, exhilaration in dancing till the early hours; fun and companionship in everything. It was good to wake up in the morning knowing each day would start with a telephone call from him and that each evening he would be waiting to hear all the gossip of my day and to tell me all his.'

Reassured and secure in Keith's attentiveness, she didn't pause to question whether it was herself, Margaret, he loved . . . or Margaret Lockwood. 'You're wearing more make-up now,' Rupert had said drily. So she was and now she masked her true self even more heavily behind it, knowing how much Rupert disliked it, knowing how unashamedly Keith revelled in her star persona.

In the freezing New Year of 1947 Margaret embarked on another personal appearance tour. It was the worst winter weather in living memory, aggravated by power cuts and fuel shortages. The party shivered in unheated trains and hotels. 'No one will go to the cinema in this, let alone turn out to see me,' Margaret warned. But people did, in their thousands. The ordeal was made bearable, even enjoyable, by the Rank publicity man in charge, Theo Cowan, who kept spirits up with a continuous flow of jokes and laughs. Patricia Roc, who had made a tour with him a few weeks before, had assured Margaret there wouldn't be a dull moment and there wasn't. In Theo's company she found she could forget her problems for an hour or two.

Her next film began production at the end of March. Based on Flora Sandstrom's novel, *The Milk White Unicorn*, the script came uncomfortably close to home for Margaret. Her role was the warden of a juvenile delinquents' remand institution who recalls, in flashback, the events that led her to take the job: married to a dull barrister, she had fallen in love with someone more dashing, had divorced her husband to marry him . . . and had lost custody of her young daughter. But there the similarity ended, and the producers invited her to let Toots, now six, play the part of the daughter.

There was already a vague thought in Margaret's mind that Toots might conceivably follow in her footsteps. Soon after moving her to London, she had taken her to Miss Grace Cone, whose school was now the Arts Education School, and enrolled her for dancing lessons, despite Margaret Evelyn's disapproval – 'but then, in 1947 she didn't approve of anything I planned for Toots, even to the smallest detail'.

The White Unicorn, as the film was eventually retitled, seemed a serious contemporary subject with wide-ranging emotions calling for contrasting characterisations; the severely dressed sociologist of the present and the carefree, fashionable wife/mistress of the flashbacks. A fancy-dress ball sequence was even infiltrated as a reminder of how good Margaret looked in elaborate period costume.

Joan Greenwood played a troublesome girl whose trust Margaret, as warden, tries to win by confiding her own story. Ian Hunter, the husband in *Bedelia*, took up the same duty again and Margaret's leading man was once again Dennis Price.

Reviewing *The White Unicorn*, Jympson Harman, doyen of the critics, commented: 'I do wish Margaret would do something about her lipstick. They tell me that the heavy make-up is her own idea. But there is no reason why such a pretty girl should do a Joan Crawford with her mouth.'

'A Margaret Lockwood film invariably makes good at the box office, so it may be presumed that showmen will clamour for the latest specimen,' wrote a trade journalist in 1947. Showmen and the public certainly had clamoured for *Hungry Hill* and *Jassy* and in the three years since its release *The Wicked Lady* had been seen by 30 million people and had grossed more than £1 million, a record no other film, British or American, could match.

All in all, it seemed that the only audience capable of resisting Margaret was the critics. It was as though with *The Wicked Lady* she had placed herself beyond their pale. At best they treated her with disdain; at worst they ridiculed her. It became a maxim of the day for them that if a British film failed to measure up to expectation the fault would be laid at the door of the director or the writer; but if it was a Margaret Lockwood film, she was to blame.

Publicly, she put a brave face on the carping but inwardly she was upset and bewildered, sometimes even reduced to tears. It was true that she had never enjoyed an easygoing relationship with the press; she was guarded with journalists, nervous of any deep probing into her personal affairs and when questions were asked about them, she would deftly steer the talk on to Toots and motherhood. The public was hazily aware that she was married but knew nothing of her husband and less than nothing about any other man in her life.

She always did her best to be cooperative and forthcoming but she had the reputation of being a difficult interviewee. 'It was nice being among friends,' she once quipped at the end of a particularly needling press conference, 'even if they are someone else's.' It needled her, too, to realise that there was a grain of validity in much of the criticism. The films Rank were making her do were undistinguished, low-cost, production-line material.

While *The White Unicorn* was in production *Daily Mail* readers again named Margaret their favourite actress, the 166,000 votes tripling her poll of the previous year. If there was any writing on the wall of the Dorchester Hotel the night she accepted her second Silver Star, the print was too small for her or anyone else to bother reading. But *The Wicked Lady* was only the nation's second favourite film. The winner was *Piccadilly Incident* and its star, Anna Neagle, was runner-up to Margaret. New names were now challenging the old order . . . Ann Todd in third place, Celia Johnson in fifth; front-runners of a new, more naturalistic and thoughtful style of film performance and subject-matter. The public was in fact giving notice that its tastes were changing.

For J. Arthur Rank, however, Margaret Lockwood was the leading lady of the moment and he was charting a dazzling programme for her. After her next film, big money was going to be invested in her, a succession of high-profile, showcase roles was being lined up . . . a

Toots was born in 1941, into family conflict.

Despite a busy working life Margaret always made time to play with Toots.

Apprentice film roles for Toots under mother's wing in *Hungry Hill*, 1946 *(above)* and *The White Unicorn*, 1947.

Margaret signing a seven-year contract with J. Arthur Rank.

Britain's favourite stars: Margaret and James Mason receive their Silver Stars from Lady Rothermere in the first *Daily Mail* National Film Award.

A studio crisis: Margaret came to the rescue for *Jassy* in 1947, with Patricia Roc.

James Mason out, John Mills in... but Margaret remained firm favourite at the 1948 *Daily Mail* National Film Award presentations, with J. Arthur Rank.

Margaret chatting with Muriel and Sydney Box at the first Cannes Film Festival in 1946.

Gainsborough glamour in a publicity portrait for *Jassy*, 1947.

Arriving for the premiere of Korda's *An Ideal Husband* with Keith Dobson, 1947.

Margaret and Griffith Jones in *Look Before You Love*, 1948.

life of the nineteenth-century Shakespearean actress Fanny Kemble; Becky Sharp in Thackeray's *Vanity Fair* – this, a role Margaret was specially keen to do; and most imminent was *Elisabeth of Austria*. This had been in preparation since 1946 when unofficial costume and camera tests had been made during the shooting of *Hungry Hill*. For the ball scene in that film she had appeared as an exact copy of the famous Winterhalter portrait of the romantic and tragic Hapsburg empress, complete with jewelled stars in her hair.

But Rank's biggest tempter for Margaret was a project more important to him personally than any other film his companies had produced, the culmination of the missionary conviction that had propelled him into the world of cinema in the first place. She was to play Mary Magdalene in a Biblical epic, *Mary of Magdala*. Rank had initially set his heart on Ingrid Bergman for the part but negotiations with David O. Selznick, to whom Bergman was under contract, had recently collapsed. Now, after endless drafts from countless writers, he had a satisfactory script, written by Clemence Dane. First, though, there was one last little job he'd like her to do for Sydney Box. Then, after that. . . .

The last little job was a comedy called *Roses for Her Pillow*. Margaret read the script and exploded.

It was trite and terrible. Worse, she considered that her own role as the wife of an army officer, who dreams she is having an affair with his batman and wakes up believing it's true, was superficial and cheap.

The strains of the past few months had taken a toll. She had been suffering from septic tonsils which made working on *The White Unicorn* an ordeal. She had rarely missed a single day's work before, even on her wedding day, but production had been held up while she was off sick for two weeks and as soon as the film was finished she went into hospital to have her tonsils removed. Her resistance may have been low but now her temperament was soaring.

She called Herbert and told him she would not do the film. 'I was sick of getting mediocre parts and poor scripts. Since 1945 I'd been sick of it.' Herbert counselled caution but her anger had gone beyond listening to reason. 'I didn't care if they called me temperamental, self-willed, obstinate. I was going to be all of those things for once. I was thoroughly fed up.' Sydney Box was furious when he realised Margaret meant business. 'Sydney was always grateful to her for coming to his aid [over *Jassy*] . . . though his later dealings with her weren't quite so amicable. She was a very difficult lady,' Lady Gardiner remembers. Box refused to release her so, emboldened by her victory over *The Magic Bow*, she went straight to J. Arthur Rank.

This was the new, defiant Margaret Lockwood. 'I had been too docile and too even-tempered for most of my life, I decided. Perhaps I *was* a new Margaret Lockwood. Certainly I felt more alive and more independent than ever before. I wasn't going to live my life in a nice, uncomplaining monotone any more.' But neither was she going to find Mr Rank so amenable this time. She was contracted to him now, not to one of his subsidiaries. Courteously, he reminded her of her obligations and advised her to treat with Sydney Box.

The situation was stalemate. She refused to back down and Box threatened her with suspension. By now the newspapers had got wind of the row. Britain's favourite star, always so modest and so level-headed, was suddenly acting up like a pampered Hollywood goddess. Fleet Street smacked its lips.

In October, a month before *No Roses for Her Pillow* was due to start at Shepherd's Bush, it was announced that Margaret had been put on suspension for six months. Sydney Box told reporters: 'Her decision breaks her contract which calls for two films a year. I think it's a pity that Margaret has come to this decision.' The film world and the fans were agog. These things happened in Hollywood. It was unprecedented for a British star to be put on suspension.

The cost to Margaret of making her stand was going to be £13,000, her fee for the picture, and the cost to Rank was not much less. Production was put back eight months while a replacement for Margaret was sought and it finally went before the cameras in July 1948. Googie Withers was the hapless sacrificial victim chosen to substitute for her opposite Griffith Jones, the original choice for male lead; it would have been his and Margaret's first re-teaming since *The Wicked Lady*. Neither Jones nor Withers had any inkling of the backroom drama in which they had been innocent bystanders until 40 years later. 'Working as a freelance, I was careful to steer clear of studio politics,' Jones explained.

Miss Withers remembers: 'I was called in by Sydney Box who asked me if I would do a little thing for him. He wanted me to test for a film with Ralph Thomas.' Already an established star in such recent hits as *The Loves of Joanna Godden* and *Pink String and Sealing Wax*, she had graduated beyond the need of screen tests. Box was, in fact, testing Thomas for a possible directing debut – he became one of

Rank's most successful directors of the 'fifties and 'sixties, instituting the hugely popular *Doctor* series, with *Doctor in the House*, five years later.

'When I read the script I thought it was a pleasant little thing, so I agreed to do it,' Miss Withers recalls.

To Margaret, seething under the injustice, as she saw it, of being made the public scapegoat in a legitimate grievance, a grand gesture of defiance was called for and the opportunity for one presented itself at the Royal Film Performance in November, three weeks after she was put on suspension. She turned out for the occasion with studied flamboyance, wearing a stunning off-the-shoulder gown of black lace – 'the most spectacular I could find' – and ermine stole . . . 'feeling very much the wicked lady in real life'. The fans, roused by the publicity of the past weeks, mobbed her.

She has never doubted that she was right to defy the almighty Rank. 'If I'd done it earlier or more often, I might have got better scripts,' she said. Arguably, though, had she been more sophisticated politically, she might have emerged from the episode with greater bargaining power. As it was, she had merely labelled herself 'difficult'. When *No Roses* was released, re-titled *Once Upon a Dream*, she had the satisfaction of being proved right. The critics savaged it, the public avoided it.

The last thing Rank was looking for at that time was a prolonged and highly public dispute with its most valuable star.

Britain, virtually bankrupted by the war, was plunging into economic crisis amid draconian austerity measures introduced by the new Labour government. Food rationing was intensified, pleasure motoring and foreign holidays were banned. Government slogans urged 'Export Or Die' and 'Work Or Want'. Swingeing restrictions on imports hit Hollywood's British market particularly hard and a dollar crisis put paid to Rank's expanding agreements for co-productions and star exchanges, but the gravest threat to the film industry came with the imposition of a crippling 38 per cent Entertainments Tax. At one stroke, box-office profits plummeted. Rank's losses on film production alone fell by more than £1½ million that financial year. The industry was in deep trouble and Margaret was an asset Rank could not afford to waste or leave idle for long.

While they re-assessed their future plans for Margaret, Rank, determined to salvage something from the idleness they had forced on her, ordered another personal appearance tour, her second in 1947, this time accompanying *The White Unicorn* to smaller out-of-the-way towns which seldom got the chance of seeing flesh-and-blood film stars.

Margaret was enthusiastic. She wasn't eating humble pie but she hated being in a vacuum. It was a routine chore, one of the bread-and-butter duties of being a film star. So she was totally unprepared for the new friction it suddenly triggered at home.

Margaret Evelyn had been living off and on at the Roehampton flat for most of 1947 and seemed to have learned nothing from previous conflicts, stubbornly refusing to accept the new order Margaret had tried to implement.

'She still wanted to bring Toots up and to treat her as though she were me – her own daughter – and she would brook no interference,' Margaret recalled. 'She didn't like the shoes I bought for her or the way I dressed her. And she always said so. It was useless trying to argue that she would have been the first to resent it if anyone had told *her* how to dress, bring up and look after *me*.' Margaret tried to be understanding and forbearing but a showdown was bound to come.

The preparations for the second tour proved the touch-paper. Upset by the chaotic comings and goings of dressmakers, photographers and studio publicity people at the flat, Margaret Evelyn made her feelings known. 'Absurd . . . rubbish . . . the whole thing's a lot of nonsense.' She could never recognise, much less accept, that all this 'rubbish' contributed to her own income and standard of living as much as to Margaret's. Margaret had given her a home and continued to maintain it. Margaret made her an allowance. She lived for months on end in Roehampton at Margaret's expense.

It all seemed to count for nothing and again Margaret found herself trying to placate her mother. But she didn't intend to be placated. She wasn't going to put up with the disruption any longer. She was going back to Delcott. There were curt goodbyes when Margaret left for the tour. Margaret Evelyn was packing and two days later she slammed the door behind her. She was no more able to accept Keith in her daughter's life than she had been Rupert. The affair was an affront to her puritanism and propriety. It had manoeuvred her into the perverse stance of defending a marriage she had never condoned and she no longer even had Toots for solace.

Margaret threw herself into the tour, travelling like royalty with an entourage of dresser, hairdresser, several publicity aides . . . and

150

Theo Cowan, the comptroller. Theo could make her laugh and help her to forget her troubles. 'We had hilarious train journeys, playing cards and daft games and generally whiling away the travelling time by being as barmy as we could,' she recalled.

She also had the time and opportunity to think, to review her personal situation and, with the objectivity of separation, the meaning Keith had in it. Rupert had convinced her that there would be no question of divorce as long as Keith remained the likely beneficiary of it, and if there was a future for them together, it seemed ill-defined, without direction.

Wherever she appeared the crowds besieged her and she realised now how much they meant to her. 'I met hundreds of people every day. I loved every moment of it – even when one woman ran alongside my car for such a long time that Theo urged me to lower the window and speak to her . . . and she bellowed "I'm an Anna Neagle fan!" '

Gradually, amid the adulation, she found herself edging towards a decision to break with Keith. She told him when she returned home. He couldn't accept it and, distressed, Margaret went to ground at a country hideaway, taking Toots with her. Only Herbert knew where she was for she knew she wouldn't be able to hold out against Keith's arguments and pleadings. For two weeks she stayed away, coming to terms with the knowledge that they must part. 'It wasn't easy for either of us, the lonely way which Rupert had indicated and which I had now chosen.' Those two weeks in hiding were a torment, with Keith desperately trying to locate her, to speak to her, relaying messages. 'He won't leave me alone,' she told Herbert on the telephone, ' and I don't really want him to. It's unfair of him, we agreed to part but I know he's still there.'

Eventually she had to face the return. It was Herbert, steadfast, faithful Herbert, who smoothed it for her. Gently but firmly he convinced Keith that Margaret's decision was irrevocable.

The New Year of 1948 had brought an early warning that Margaret's domination of the screen was far from unassailable. The annual Motion Picture Herald poll of money-making stars named Anna Neagle first among British actresses, with Margaret in second place though still ahead of her closest Hollywood challengers, Bette Davis and Ingrid Bergman. The top money-making film was Neagle's *The Courtneys of Curzon Street*. Margaret could only manage seventh position with *Jassy* – with the knowledge that a new Neagle film, *Spring in Park Lane*, was in the cutting room.

In February Margaret made her debut on television. She had been floating the idea for some time of going back to the stage but Herbert was against it until the timing and the vehicle were perfect. He knew her stage technique would need polishing and that, as a film star going 'legitimate', she would be vulnerable. Margaret already had the perfect vehicle in mind – *Pygmalion* – but George Bernard Shaw kept the rights to it on a tight rein and Gertrude Lawrence had first option on a stage revival. The television rights were another matter and Margaret jumped at the chance to play Eliza Doolittle in what the BBC claimed would be the longest and most ambitious drama production television had ever staged.

It was a challenge and something of an ordeal but it was also a shrewd side-step in her move towards the theatre. Television drama in those early days was live. There was the familiarity of working before cameras in a studio, the comforting routine of filming; but the extensive rehearsals and, on the night of transmission, the pressure of giving a continuous performance before an audience, added the immediacy and momentum of a stage appearance. There could be no re-takes. The production was so successful that the BBC repeated it a few nights later. The critics were generous to Margaret and she faced returning to the film studios at the end of her suspension with a new optimism. Gone, however, were all those seductive promises and roles . . . Elisabeth of Austria, Mary of Magdala, Becky Sharp, Fanny Kemble . . . the recession had seen to that. Still, a punishing programme of three productions was going to keep her busy, almost without a break, for the rest of the year.

The first, with the working title of *I Know You*, later changed to *Look Before You Love*, was for John Corfield, the producer who had offered her sanctuary from her previous confrontation with Rank over *The Magic Bow*.

It was a sophisticated romantic comedy drama which held out promise, in script form. Margaret played a secretary at the British Embassy in Rio de Janeiro who discovers, too late, that the charmer she has just married is a conman. He negotiates to 'sell' her to a millionaire he knows has only a few months to live, with the intention of reclaiming her for himself as a wealthy widow.

The mix of love, laughs and deceit proved an uneasy one. Griffith Jones, cast as the husband, recalled: 'We hoped for a comedy of wit and style, but it wasn't to be.' Production turned out to be as great a confusion as the plot – too many styles, not enough style. 'Maggie would phone me every night to discuss the next day's scenes,' Jones said. 'Her suggestions were pertinent and constructive and I was impressed by her mental and physical resilience.' But the need for these nightly consultations outside studio hours seemed a bad omen.

Few British films of the 1940s received a more devastating barrage of criticism than *Look Before You Love* when it was released in October 1948, and again Margaret was a prime target.

'Some critics have already said that if Miss Lockwood makes any more films as bad as this, her outstanding popularity must end with a bang,' wrote the *Manchester Guardian* reviewer. '*Look Before You Love* may be remarkably bad but it is not remarkably worse than those other films which took Miss Lockwood to her present eminence.' 'Margaret Lockwood displays . . . pretty frocks and less intelligence than in any of her films,' (the London *Star*). 'Miss Lockwood brings to Rio and Monte Carlo the practical passion of Miss Margate 1948,' (the *Daily Mail*).

While the film had been in production Margaret had been awarded the *Daily Mail* Silver Star for the third consecutive year, so the fans were still behind her, but within the industry there was an insidious feeling that her star was in fact on the wane.

She may never have wanted or set out to be that star, never succumbed to the artifice and superficiality of being one, but it was her life now and she didn't take kindly to the idea of relinquishing it. She blamed the films she had been forced to make, the directors who had made them. 'None of those pictures had extended me,' she told an interviewer. 'I felt the need of a director as inspiring as Carol Reed. I'd learned a great deal about the mechanics of the job and there were times when I think the maxim that "Maggie can cope" was used too generously.'

One day, while *Look Before You Love* was shooting at Denham, she casually picked up and read a script which was in preparation.

'I was so intrigued by it and I thought it was so funny, unlike anything I'd ever done before, that I rushed off to find the man who was producing it,' she recalled. The man was Walter Forde, an independent producer. The script was a slapstick comedy called *Cardboard Cavalier*, styled for Sid Field, one of Britain's most original comedians. Three years before Rank had tried to convert Field's music-hall talents into cinema box-office currency with a lavish film musical, *London Town*. It had been an infamous flop, costing Rank dear in cash and credibility and memorable only for introducing a stunning long-legged beauty by the name of Kay Kendall.

Walter Forde, a veteran of screen slapstick, first as a performer in silents, later as a director, was convinced Sid Field had the potential to be as great a comedian on film as he was on the stage but he was astonished when Margaret Lockwood, sovereign lady of the British cinema, tracked him down and pleaded to be allowed to be in his film.

'It threw him into a terrible flap,' she said. 'He did his best to discourage me. "You do realise it's Sid's film, he's got to star in it," he said and I said "I don't give a damn about that." I was perfectly happy to take second billing.'

She finally won a nervous Forde round, then besieged and beseeched her Rank bosses. They were even less enthusiastic than Forde, uneasy about her playing so drastically against type, doubting she had the capacity for foolery. But she was relentless and eventually the part of Nell Gwynn was hers. The film was pure knockabout, down to a statutory custard pie sequence, set in the England of Oliver Cromwell with Field as a cockney simpleton caught up in espionage for the Royalist cause, aided by Margaret's hoydenish Nell.

The critics deemed it a disaster and once again Margaret was pilloried. One poisoned pen wrote that while the sight of Margaret on the receiving end of a custard pie wasn't particularly funny, he had found it very satisfying. 'Margaret Lockwood in a bubbly blonde wig looks like Harpo Marx with curves and a voice,' opined the *Sunday Dispatch*. 'As for Margaret Lockwood as a blonde barmaid, one can only draw an embarrassed veil over the whole enterprise,' (*Sunday Express*). *The Daily Telegraph* at least found her 'an unusually animated Margaret Lockwood' and *The Times* commended her 'surprising gusto', but the general tone of the reviews was devastating. She admitted to breaking down in tears when she read them. The press seemed to have taken over Margaret Evelyn's compulsion to slap her down.

Margaret had gambled her reputation on her own intuition for breaking the Lockwood mould and she had failed but she laid the blame squarely on the critics' personal animosity towards her. 'I still think it's a very funny film but the critics absolutely slaughtered it. I can't think why,' she said recently.

Their reaction only strengthened her determination to prove them wrong on the stage. She was tired and disillusioned with films. 'Towards the end they were handing me out such terrible rubbish. I got so bored with it all. They had a very short-sighted policy.' Looking back from a distance of half a century, Theo Cowan, then in overall charge of Rank's publicity, agreed. 'I would say she was ill-used.'

Theo, tall and good-looking, was a good judge. A year younger than Margaret, he had entered the industry in 1936 as a publicist with Gaumont-British Pictures and after war service joined Rank, working in the Special Services division of the publicity office. His responsibility was to look after the public image of contract artists off the set as distinct from handling their publicity for individual films they appeared in. 'Generally looking after them' was his own job description . . . organising the logistics of personal appearances, attendances at premières, charity events, garden parties, promotional tours like Margaret's.

Everybody liked Theo. He was personable, energetic, easy-going, a diplomatist and a perfectionist in his work. Everybody felt safe in his care. His sense of humour was legendary and it had drawn Margaret to him on two occasions when she needed to laugh aside her troubles.

Theo had known Keith and found him 'youthful and a bit naïve'. Margaret, he believed, had begun to discern for herself where his weaknesses lay. 'She realised he was a loser and a bit of a wastrel. Disenchantment set in.' Theo was in a position to know. He was the new man in her life.

'The biggest cementing factor between us was humour,' he recalled. 'Margaret was a "laugh out loud" lady . . . that roar of a laugh of hers, you could never miss it or forget it. We laughed at the same things. I suppose you could say my entry into her life was well-timed. She was down. And she wasn't exactly fighting off suitors at that point.'

The fates which had brought them together also provided an ideal cover for romance, a professional relationship which threw them into each other's company and raised no eyebrows. As the affair developed it became an open secret among people who knew them but the respect they both commanded helped to shield them from gossip. The industry closed ranks. Not a hint leaked through to the newspapers or fan magazines.

It was not so much an affair, perhaps, as a romantic interlude. Margaret, distressed by two failures in love, was too wary of committing herself deeply a third time but she was lonely, as she had been when she first met Keith, her confidence had been shaken and her spirits needed reviving. No one was better qualified to minister to those conditions than Theo and in the following months they laid the foundations of a lifelong affection that outlasted their intimacy.

Margaret now badgered Herbert to find her a suitable stage play but still he was cautious. For her part Margaret was more than ever determined to repeat her television success as Eliza in its proper context.

Herbert sounded out Henry Sherek, one of the West End's most colourful impresarios who was interested by the sure-fire commercial possibilities of the Lockwood name on a theatre bill and a meeting was arranged over dinner at the Ritz. Sherek, apprised of Margaret's *Pygmalion* ambition, knew that the copyright difficulty and Gertrude Lawrence's option on it made a production for Margaret out of the question. He and Herbert had already worked out an alternative proposition but Margaret arrived at the Ritz believing that the Shaw play was the one they were going to discuss.

Sherek recalled: 'She arrived on the dot, very quietly dressed in black, to my great relief. I had had visions of a film star dressed as I imagined film stars to dress, which would have created quite a stir of the wrong sort at the august Ritz.' He was not prepared, however, for the stir she caused once the introductions had been made and they were seated at their table. He chose that moment to dispense with the *Pygmalion* idea, telling her it was a non-starter.

'Then what are we sitting here for? We're wasting our time!' she blazed, and got to her feet. Skilfully, Sherek calmed her and persuaded her to sit down and listen to some other suggestions.

He and Herbert had agreed on a possible revival of Noel Coward's *Private Lives* – unaccountably, it seemed, the spirit of Miss Lawrence continued to hover over the table; she had created the role of Amanda in the original production. Still, it was a cunning choice. The play was virtually actor-proof; the role, though not without its difficulties, a showy one well within Margaret's acting compass. The more she listened, the more she warmed to the idea. She agreed excitedly to make herself available for a long tour and the prospect of a West End run the following spring, as soon as her next film was completed.

Unbelievably, Rank seemed to have learned nothing from the feuding of the recent past. The subject of *Madness of the Heart* was a throwback to the worst excesses of Gainsborough's pulp-fiction days, giving Margaret little to do except appear vulnerable while the more interesting and effective character went to Kathleen Byron. Based on another novel by Flora Sandstrom, author of *The White Unicorn*, the story was unalloyed women's magazine melodrama. Margaret was cast as a businesswoman who, told she is going blind, enters a convent to take the veil rather than burden the French aristocrat she loves with marriage. Finding out the reason for her retreat, he reclaims her, marries her and takes her, now completely sightless, to the family chateau where she is at the mercy of the ruthless woman who had counted on becoming his wife. Under a guise of friendship, the woman plots her 'accidental' death.

It almost seemed as though Margaret were being made to do penance, an impression amplified by the 'new look' she was given, with her hair cut short and a frumpy wardrobe. Acting blindness, much of the old glamour shorn and much of the old spirit with it, she moved through the film with a colourless personality and a deadpan expression. Even Rank realised they had done her and themselves less than credit. They decided not to show the film to the critics or to give it the showcase of a London première. Instead, it had a semi-official opening in Blackpool, the heartland of her fan following, at the height of the 1949 holiday season.

Earlier in the year Margaret's provincial public had rallied to *Cardboard Cavalier*, transforming it from a London disaster into a respectable hit and now they flocked to her banner again. She attended the Blackpool première and, without knowing anything in advance about the film, crowds lined the three-mile route from her Lytham hotel to the cinema. To everyone's surprise the film turned out a box-office winner but by then Margaret was past caring. She had tasted again the heady excitement of the theatre, the intoxication of applause. She knew now where her future lay.

$\mathscr{S}$HOWDOWN

Private Lives was a triumph and a turning point. Margaret had been excited but nervous at the prospect of returning to the stage for the first time in twelve years. She had to forget the techniques of film acting, adapt herself to disciplines she had never fully experienced or mastered in the relatively small roles she had played a long time ago. But as soon as she launched into the first full rehearsal, she felt 'as though I'd come home'. Peter Graves – Gravyboat in the nickname she coined for him during their films together – was her co-star, and a buttress for her confidence.

The sixteen-week tour opened in April 1949 and played every important theatre city in Britain and some of the largest theatres. Wherever they went the show was a sell-out. Fans waited outside the hotels where Margaret stayed. They laid siege to the stage-doors. They queued round the block at the box offices. Even Henry Sherek, wise and cynical in the ways of audiences, was impressed with her drawing power.

Margaret, accustomed to such public manifestations of her popularity, took it in her stride but privately she was elated. Her personal reviews were flattering and she was proving she could fill theatres as readily as she filled cinemas. Theo travelled to wherever the show was playing to spend each weekend with her and off-stage she kept very much to herself, as always. 'You never really got to know her,' said Graves, who was closer to her than most.

As the end of the tour approached, the company waited eagerly to hear about a West End engagement. The final play date was Brighton in July and it was then that Noel Coward decided to take a look at it. What he saw didn't please him; what he heard infuriated him. One line in the balcony scene contains a famous reference to the Duke of Westminster's yacht. At that time gossip columnists were making much of Stewart Granger's yacht which he was sailing in the Mediterranean, and as a topical in-joke Margaret and Peter Graves had substituted the Granger name for the Duke of Westminster's.

Coward rushed back-stage in the interval and berated the director, Daphne Rye, for tinkering with the text. Making his courtesy call on Margaret after the performance he pressed the point, rather more tactfully, amid some judicious compliments. But she was deflated when he suggested that it wouldn't be 'wise' to take the production into London. More forthrightly, he wrote in his diary that night: 'Peter Graves not bad, but too soft. Margaret Lockwood looked charming but cannot act comedy. Tried to persuade her and Sherek not to bring the play into London. The production is inept and the set is hideous. The whole thing has all the *chic* of a whist drive in Tulse Hill.' The Master's 'persuasion' carried the finality of command. Henry Sherek took the hint and closed *Private Lives* in Brighton.

It was a bitter disappointment for Margaret, who had been savouring the prospect of crowning her provincial triumph with West End success and cocking a snook at her detractors in the film world. But though Coward had denied her the opportunity, the West End was not prepared to lose her. With all its attendant publicity, the theatrical establishment could hardly avoid taking note of her queenly progress round the nation's top theatres. There weren't many 'names' available who could fill 2,000 seaters in a nineteen-year-old play, now slightly dated. Margaret Lockwood was clearly box-office. Herbert now had another canny card to play: an offer to star in the West End's traditional production of *Peter Pan* that Christmas. It was an inspired idea, the first role she could ever recall wanting to play, with all that the story and the character had meant to her early memories and ambitions, and the theatre would be the Scala, where Margie Day had taken those first steps on the road to a professional career and known her first disappointment when she had lost the leading role in *Babes in the Wood*. It almost seemed as though the fates were preparing a soft landing for Margaret as her film career moved into decline.

The public loved her in the part and the critics were admiring. Her 1949 Peter broke all previous records for the show and she ended the year, the first for fifteen years in which she hadn't made a film, flying high – literally.

She had got into a habit of taking Toots to the theatre with her and noticed how enthralled she was by every aspect of life back-stage. 'I could see myself in her all over again,' she said.

Toots, now eight years old, was entered as a full-time pupil with

159

Gracie Cone. Rupert, living at Chiswick, three miles from the Roe-hampton flat, saw her regularly. Since the separation Margaret had been punctilious about allowing him reasonable access and Toots always spent part of the school holidays, as well as regular weekends, with him. Relations between husband and wife were cordial, if distant. To the little girl the arrangement seemed perfectly normal and accept-able. To Margaret it was an uncanny situation of 'seeing myself in her all over again', growing up with hardly any memory of a father's presence, accepting without question that this was how circumstance ordered things. She made sure that she and her daughter were together as often as work allowed and Toots was growing up a happy, natural, loving child.

As the short tour of *Peter Pan* that followed the London run was ending – Toots travelling with her as long as the school holiday lasted – Rank announced Margaret's next film.

In outline, *Highly Dangerous* was just the kind of subject she had been campaigning for; a light, original comedy thriller in the mould of *The Lady Vanishes* and *Night Train to Munich*, scripted by Eric Ambler, a master of the genre. Its plot was a spoof of the currently popular blood-and-thunder serial, *Dick Barton – Special Agent*, with Margaret playing a blue-stocking entomologist addicted to the pro-gramme who is recruited by the British government for a secret mis-sion to an un-named East European communist bloc country to find out if insects are being used in research for bacteriological warfare. Captured and given a truth drug, she takes on the personality of the serial's do-or-die hero, steals the incriminating specimens, blows up the research plant and runs the gauntlet of the secret police in a hair-raising escape. Her leading man, over from Hollywood, was Dane Clark, a reliable but second-division name. Clinching nostalgic links with the earlier films, a part was also written in for Naunton Wayne.

In May 1950 Margaret was back in the studios for the first time in nearly eighteen months. Her absence had not gone unnoticed in the press. Lockwood-baiting, despite her successes on stage, had enjoyed open season in the intervening months, with articles speculating on her future under such headlines 'Lockwood Keeps Her Fingers Crossed' and 'Margaret at the Crossroads'.

A lone voice was raised in her defence. Eve Perrick, an influential *Daily Express* feature writer, devoted a whole article to the injustice of the attacks on her and drew some perceptive conclusions on what had gone wrong with her film career.

I come not to bury Margaret Lockwood but to praise her. If there's any toe-stamping to be done in this column today, Miss Lockwood's already much-trodden toes are immune. Instead, this is aimed at all those who have been hurling unpleasantries at her ever since she graduated from being a sweet young thing to Britain's No. 1 film star. For too long now has Miss Lockwood been a sitting target and general Aunt Sally for every would-be wisecracker.

Too many personal appearances, too many guest spots in radio programmes, too many posed photographs. Her employers worked her too hard and too often in the wrong kind of pictures . . .

But a word to those critics. When you gave her the rave reviews ten or more years ago they were for her performance in a film called *Bank Holiday*. The director of it was a young man named Carol Reed.

Couldn't this imply that you've been shooting at the pianist instead of the offending singer? Isn't there a chance that Margaret Lockwood, well directed in a good picture, could yet prove herself acceptable to you critics as well as to the public?

Of course neither Margaret nor Herbert was entirely blameless. Their judgment of scripts had been erratic and they had both been over-cautious about her popular image, afraid to take risks on any role which deviated too radically from it, and inhibiting her scope to adapt or change or extend her range.

At about this time Margaret rejected two scripts that could have steered her into new, more interesting areas of acting and won her new admirers, even the respect of critics.

The shrewish, adulterous wife in Terence Rattigan's *The Browning Version* was not just another Lockwood lady, a grown-up Jenny Sunley. Superbly written, it powered the entire plot and she could have fashioned it into a potent counterpoint to the character of the broken-spirited schoolmaster, played by Michael Redgrave, despised and deceived by his wife. The second subject, *The Woman in Question*, offered even greater opportunities, portraying a woman found murdered at the outset and seen in flashback by five police witnesses in different and contrasting personalities.

Both roles went to Jean Kent, whose vivid performances have left a pointer to how they might have galvanised Margaret's sagging screen reputation. Looking back, Margaret has always in particular regretted missing the opportunity of *The Woman in Question*. 'I was wrong to turn it down,' she has said. But at that time she had more urgent worries on her mind. Rupert had suddenly announced that he was suing her for divorce.

At first it was a shock and the irony of the situation hurt. She and Rupert had been married for thirteen years, only three of them spent living together as husband and wife. He had thwarted her re-marriage as the price of keeping Toots but now he had met a woman he wanted to marry, and the roles were reversed. 'Possibly I was never cut out to be married to a film star,' Rupert said sadly. 'If we were together now, I think I'd resent your career. I'd want you to stay at home.'

It wasn't the divorce that caused Margaret anxiety. In a sense she welcomed it, clearing as it would the debris of the past. She was more concerned with the possible publicity and its effects on Toots. With this in mind her lawyers advised her not to fight Rupert whatever grounds he cited, pointing out that an undefended suit could not be reported in the newspapers. She would be branded as the guilty party – something which in those days celebrities, particularly film stars, would go to inordinate lengths to avoid – but at least any ill-natured words Rupert's lawyers might choose to bandy about would not be heard in public.

In his petition Rupert alleged that Margaret had deserted him in 1944, the year she had met Keith. This was some relief. He was being civil over the grounds, keeping them as low-key as a successful petition could count on. But then he struck her a body blow by intimating that he would seek custody of Toots and Margaret determined to fight, regardless of publicity. In fact the divorce hearing at the High Court, on 6 November 1950, was straightforward and passed unnoticed, the press attaching no significance to a petition, among many others, which named Leon *versus* Leon.

Granting Rupert a decree, the judge referred custody of the child to chambers for hearing at a later date. The following weeks were an agony of suspense for Margaret. Her lawyers tried to reassure her that she had nothing to worry about: judges invariably awarded custody of a child, especially a daughter, to the mother, but she wasn't convinced, all too aware of Rupert's opposition to her career, of his rooted belief that a working actress could not be a responsible mother. He had left her in no doubt, either, that he disapproved of a possible acting career for Toots. Something warned Margaret that she was facing a hard fight.

She was rehearsing for a return appearance in *Peter Pan*, the first time in its history that an actress had been invited to play the role for a consecutive season. *Highly Dangerous* opened in December, a week after Rupert's decree became absolute and their marriage was legally dissolved. 'The new Margaret Lockwood picture is ready,' the billboards announced, with singular absence of imagination. Rank's lack of enthusiasm was echoed by the critics. 'A film of quite dreadful inanity considering the script is by Eric Ambler,' in the view of *The Times*, with the qualification that 'while Miss Lockwood is engaged in her mildly satirical joke . . . the film is bearable, otherwise not'.

Early in the New Year of 1951 Margaret and Rupert faced each other again in judge's chambers for the custody hearing. Though braced for trouble she had no inkling of the trump card he was about to play. Suddenly she heard the name of Margaret Evelyn Lockwood admitted to the evidence.

Incredulously, she listened as her mother testified on Rupert's behalf that Margaret, her own daughter, was an unfit mother.

All the years of festering grievance and resentment, of possessiveness and jealousy were distilled into this monstrous act of renunciation, a final thrust of revenge by the mother she had defied so many years before to marry the man she loved and who had never been able to forgive what she saw as her own usurpation. Perhaps Margaret Evelyn was motivated by self-interest, by a desperate hope that a legal compromise would restore Toots to her own custody rather than that of the son-in-law she had always despised and refused to acknowledge. The judge ruled in favour of Margaret, but at a terrible cost. She had won her daughter and lost her mother. All her life she had bid for Margaret Evelyn's praise and approval, hardly ever to gain it. To the best of her ability, she had tried to include her mother in her success, made sure she was comfortable and wanted for nothing. 'How often,' she said afterwards, 'I had longed for some spoiling and some praise from her.' All to this end.

In March 1951, three months after his decree nisi became absolute, Rupert, now 36, married Florence Harrison, a 26-year-old farmer's daughter working as a secretary in London. Theo Cowan once said:

163

'Meeting Rupert didn't make much of an impression. You looked at him and wondered what the hell Maggie had ever seen in him.' Margaret herself vowed never to marry again. In an interview she said: 'I am dedicating my life to my daughter. She is all I have now. No woman can say she will never fall in love again. But for me it could never lead to marriage.'

Margaret Evelyn went back to Delcott, the home her daughter had given her, to live out the rest of her years on the allowance Margaret made her. She had become something of the *grande dame* in the tiny community of St Leonards, taking a vicarious pride in her status among the villagers as 'Margaret Lockwood's mother.' Everyone was expected to acknowledge it and show a proper deference. 'She always liked people to know who she was and she was usually very pleasant as long as she felt you were giving her her due,' recalled Mrs Hazel Bartholomew, who served in the general store and post office. 'She was a strong personality, always well dressed. She had lovely clothes. In those days there used to be a chair for customers at the end of the counter. She regarded it as hers. Whenever she came in, she'd go straight to it and sit down. If anyone happened to be sitting on it already she would stand and glare at them until they became uncomfortable and got up for her.'

The rift between 'old Mrs Lockwood' and her famous daughter was common knowledge in the village. 'She made no secret of it,' said Mrs Bartholomew. 'She could be very scathing about Margaret. I remember once overhearing a customer chatting to her about Margaret's films and saying how much she'd enjoyed her in *The Wicked Lady*. Mrs Lockwood said snappishly "That wasn't acting: that was natural." '

Margaret and her mother never spoke to or saw each other again from the moment they left the judge's chambers.

PART THREE

RECOVERY

Nineteen fifty-one was a year of clean breaks, with marriage, with her mother – and with Rank. She asked to be released eighteen months early from her contract and Rank, with nothing lined up for her, obliged.

It was a sad, muted end to her reign. 'Films have given me a raw deal,' she said in a magazine interview after she'd broken with Rank. It wasn't the whole truth. They had also given her unprecedented success, made her Britain's best-known actress and brought her riches she'd never dreamed of that first day on a film set at Elstree sixteen years before. But if her day was done, hers was not an isolated case. All the stars Rank had created and who had brought such lustre to their studios were drifting away, James Mason and Stewart Granger to Hollywood, Phyllis Calvert and Patricia Roc to freelance. Britain's studio star system, like Hollywood's, was breaking up under the onslaught of television.

Margaret had no regrets. She was free now to build her home life, to extend her horizons, to choose the work she really wanted to do. Perfectly on cue, the chance to play Eliza Doolittle on stage suddenly presented itself: *Pygmalion* was the main drama production that summer at the Edinburgh Festival.

'It was a severe test for me in the legitimate theatre,' she admitted. 'Again, I was extremely nervous and I don't think I gave my best performance on the first night. It took me several weeks before I really got into my stride.'

The production was not an unqualified success but her personal notices were generally favourable. 'There were times when her Eliza was good and times when it was not so good,' reported *The Scotsman*. But her star quality overrode any deficiencies the critics might find. Audiences in Edinburgh and on the tour that followed clamoured for curtain calls.

Towards the end of the year, while she was still touring, news that she had signed to make a picture for Herbert Wilcox and Anna Neagle sent a frisson of surprise through the film world. The idea of the former No. 1 screen star setting foot in the production camp of the arch-rival who had deposed her had a certain piquancy, and the press scented a promising prima donna confrontation.

'Even in the studio there were people who expected the sparks to fly when Margaret Lockwood arrived,' Dame Anna's secretary Joyce Wright recalled. 'They didn't, of course. These were highly professional, hard-working actresses. They never thought of themselves as rivals. That was just press talk.'

The film was *Trent's Last Case*, based on E. C. Bentley's creaky and dated detective story published in 1913 and first filmed in 1920.

Michael Wilding, who had been Anna Neagle's inseparable co-star in the series of romantic comedy hits with which she had supplanted Margaret in the public's affections, now changed partners, adding a further titillating twist to press speculations. But as the story's reporter-sleuth hero, he was not required as a romantic partner; rather, to suspect Margaret of murdering her millionaire husband so as to leave the field clear for her affair with his male secretary.

Herbert Wilcox had updated the plot, hingeing on a sequence of inspired deductions to demonstrate that the husband had not, as believed, committed suicide. It was a fundamental error. Margaret herself tried to convince him that the mechanics of the story, taken out of their period, were no longer plausible – modern forensic science made a nonsense of the circumstances – but the film went ahead, complete with inconsistencies and Margaret had to admit that apart from Alexander Korda, Herbert Wilcox was Britain's only producer with pretensions to Hollywood-style flair and a sense of its glamour. 'He runs a film studio in the way most people outside the profession imagine a film studio is run,' she enthused. 'I'd never worked in such an atmosphere before.'

During production Wilcox announced that he was signing Margaret to a three-year contract. Signing a contract with J. Arthur Rank had been an austere ceremony of putting pen to paper amid an explosion of flash-bulbs. With Herbert Wilcox it was a gala occasion of bouquets, gifts and champagne followed by a celebration dinner. To find herself being so pampered was a novel experience for Margaret and she loved it.

'From that day I was never allowed to forget I was a really bright and dazzling star on their horizon. They were going to look after me as no one else had done before.'

To the press Wilcox announced that 'apart from her outstanding ability as an actress, she has top world star quality'. He described Margaret as 'a director's joy who can shade a performance or a character with computer accuracy'. That statement gave a coded intimation of his plans for her. He had recently concluded a deal with Hollywood's Republic Pictures, a company not best renowned for the quality of its product – its considerable fortunes had been founded on an output of B-pictures interspersed with an occasional prestige feature, the latest of which, *The Quiet Man* starring John Wayne, had proved a gigantic box-office hit. But Wilcox had his sights on Republic's distribution network which would guarantee a valuable American outlet for his own productions. His intention for Margaret was to orchestrate that 'top world star quality' for the US market. The production values he built into her three films were a revelation, glossier, more polished than anything she had done under Rank's tight-fisted economic constraints. She could at last feel that she had placed herself in the hands of a producer who realised and was willing to exploit her true value.

Production on *Trent's Last Case*, which started in February 1952, was troubled but not without its share of humour, largely unintentional. On 21 February Michael Wilding was married to Elizabeth Taylor. He reported for duty on the set after an eight-day honeymoon, somewhat the worse for wear. Herbert and Anna had welcomed him back at the airport like fond foster parents.

'He was on his knees,' Margaret recalled. 'He couldn't do a thing. He never turned up before noon and then he'd have to be given brandy or champagne to get him back on his feet. Poor chap, he was worn out.'

On one occasion Margaret went to the couple's suite at the Dorchester to rehearse an act she and Michael were contributing to a 'Night of a Hundred Stars' charity show – sentimentally for her, it was the *Titanic* shipboard scene from Noel Coward's *Cavalcade*. Much to Margaret's embarrassment the door suddenly opened and the twenty-year-old bride came in wearing nothing except a transparent *peignoir* and, heedless of their guest, started to vamp her husband. Elizabeth haunted the set, prolonging the honeymoon, never taking her love-hungry violet eyes off Michael and keeping her hands off him only when he was called away for a take.

Wilcox had pulled off a considerable coup in persuading Orson Welles to play the millionaire husband in the film, a cameo role. But Welles spelt trouble. Always self-conscious about his small snub nose, he insisted, as he did in every film, on wearing a false one. It was patently false and looked so incongruous that Margaret had difficulty keeping a straight face in their scenes together. At one point he stalked off the set in a huff and out of the studio. No one could track him down, so Wilcox decided to shoot over the shoulder of a double wearing his clothes. Welles had outsmarted him, however, and taken his entire wardrobe with him.

Unluckily, more of the irritants than the humour of production worked their way into the completed film. Though handsomely mounted, it was flat-footed and unexciting – 'a placid, satisfying film' in the view of the *Daily Herald* – yet it turned the critical tide for Margaret. More serious attention was paid to her performance than in any of her films since *The Stars Look Down* twelve years before.

Leonard Mosley of the *Daily Express* wrote: 'Margaret Lockwood's future depends on *Trent's Last Case*. She makes no secret of the fact that if critics and public fail to like her in this film she will concentrate on television and the stage in future.' He quoted her as saying: 'Even critics praise my television performances. No one is horrid to me. Yet whenever I play in films there is always someone waiting to say something beastly, knowing only too well that it hurts, hurts, hurts.'

Mosley made some effort to compensate: '*Trent's Last Case* is the first film where Margaret has quietly, calmly and painstakingly gone through her part and by sheer skilful acting made it hit right home. You could almost give the nickname Deadpan Lockwood to the new Margaret, she uses facial expression so sparingly. But she is more than expert in conveying practically all the emotions through the medium of her eyes.' There were still some, however, who couldn't resist sniping. The respected Richard Winnington of the *News Chronicle* sneered at 'her glum suburban elegance untouched by the years' and the *Sunday Chronicle* spoke loftily of 'a tasteful little comeback'. But she still had her admirers in high places. The film's unofficial première, a few weeks before its London opening, took place at Balmoral Castle by command of Queen Elizabeth II, just six months into her reign and eager to see it during her summer holiday.

A perceptive writer in the London *Star* had noted: 'There is an assurance about her acting now that theatregoers and TV viewers have already spotted but which has not always been apparent in her

170

films.' It was true. Subdued as her performance was in *Trent's Last Case*, it marked a new-found maturity in her screen acting. At 36 and approaching the notoriously difficult middle-age of a film actress, Margaret was acquiring a new authority and depth of character.

That summer she appeared in two important television productions, H. G. Wells's *Ann Veronica* and Shaw's *Captain Brassbound's Conversion*, and with Toots joined Herbert de Leon and his wife Mary for a holiday in Holland where she savoured the freedom of going about unrecognised despite the belated post-war release of earlier films that was beginning to make her a favourite in the Low Countries.

There was a flurry of press interest when Herbert Wilcox announced plans to reunite her with James Mason in a co-production with Republic of the Daphne du Maurier bestseller *The King's General*. The film rights to this romance of the English Civil War had originally been bought by David O. Selznick, who, envisaging a British *Gone with the Wind*, had planned a joint production with Alexander Korda in 1948 and pencilled in James Mason for the role of Sir Richard Grenville, commander of the Royalist army in Cornwall. Mason turned it down. 'I liked *The King's General* as a book but it was not a good script,' he said. In reality his reasons probably had more to do with the litigation he was involved in with Korda over certain terms in the contract under which he would have made the film.

Wilcox had bought the rights from Selznick but the idea of storming the box office on a sure-fire Mason-Lockwood ticket was fanciful. Mason had an aversion to working in Britain now that he had established himself in Hollywood and after the initial announcement nothing more was heard of it.

Margaret was offered *Laughing Anne* instead. Based on a Joseph Conrad short story, *Because of the Dollars*, and set in the Java Seas of the 1890s, it gave her the strongest, most emotionally challenging role she had had for years as a French cabaret singer washed up in the tropics and torn between her crippled ex-prizefighter lover and a sensitive sea captain whose life she wrecks. Two Republic stars were imported from Hollywood, Forrest Tucker to play the prizefighter, Wendell Corey the skipper, neither of a standing to complement her own.

Carol Reed had recently directed another Conrad story, *An Outcast of the Islands*, with a similar background and the coincidence wasn't lost on Margaret. She had watched covetously as Carol's post-war films brought him a prestige no other British director could rival. His next film – one which would bring James Mason back to England – was to be *The Man Between*. Fifteen years earlier Margaret would have been his first choice for the female lead in it. Now it was awarded to the 22-year-old Claire Bloom . . .

Another factor conspired to cast her mind back in 1953 to her own years of aspiration. Toots, now twelve and determined to be an actress, auditioned for a BBC children's television serialisation of *Heidi* and, to Margaret's delight and pride, won the part. Always known publicly by her childhood nickname, she now insisted on reverting to her given name and on being billed as Julia Lockwood. She was growing into an attractive, well-balanced young lady. Margaret, mindful of Rupert's objections to an acting career for her, was careful to maintain an even-handed position on Julia's ambitions, remembering only too vividly how Margaret Evelyn had cramped her own so insensitively. So she praised Julia, encouraged her, yet corrected or criticised kindly – 'not with the abruptness that my mother used when she minimised everything with her favourite comment "rubbish" '. She was scrupulous, too, about letting Rupert, now beginning to flourish in business, maintain his place in his daughter's life and affections. He and Florence had two children of their own and Julia enjoyed regular visits to her 'other' family at their Chiswick home, becoming particularly attached to her little half-brother and half-sister.

With the release of *Laughing Anne* in September 1953 the critics finally discovered the true actress in Margaret and sheathed their knives. She 'emerges as an actress of remarkable distinction', declared the *News of the World*, while the influential C. A. Lejeune of *The Observer* commended 'a beautifully flexible performance'. The film itself didn't find quite the same level of favour with them but they were unanimous in hailing a new Margaret Lockwood and the public, taking their cue from them, made it a substantial hit.

They were exhilarating weeks. A month later *Heidi* went out live and the critics hailed a new Lockwood. One wrote: 'Move over Margaret . . . your daughter has arrived.' Inimitably, Herbert Wilcox made Julia feel a real star, sending her flowers and telegrams for her 'first night' on the day of transmission.

Margaret had just started shooting her third film for the Wilcoxes. *Trouble in the Glen* was modelled unashamedly on Republic's hit, *The Quiet Man*, designed to do for Scotland what the John Wayne film had done for Ireland. Wayne had originally been announced as her co-star but dropped out, to be replaced by Forrest Tucker. The screenplay was the work of the same team responsible for *The Quiet Man* – story by Maurice Walsh, script by Frank S. Nugent, the former film critic of the *New York Times*. Victor McLaglen, who had been nominated for the best supporting actor Oscar in *The Quiet Man* earlier that year, now learned a Scottish accent for a replica role and again Wilcox prevailed on Orson Welles to put in an appearance. It was probably the nadir of his career. He played a South American tycoon arriving in the Highlands to claim his inheritance as laird and proceeding to divide the clannish community with his alien ways and behaviour. Margaret, 'swathed in tartan' according to one reviewer, was cast as his daughter.

Trouble in the Glen proved a misbegotten film, shot in the Trucolor process which 'gave faces an orange peel look', though *The Daily Telegraph* found it 'superbly photographed'. It divided the critics, some finding it 'charming', others 'curdled whimsy', but the film-goers were united in giving it a wide berth. Margaret was mere decoration, her role largely superfluous, her impact negative.

Her contract with the Wilcoxes had been for three films and now she had discharged it they decided to part company. Herbert Wilcox wrote later: 'I went to exceptional lengths in the three films we made together to find the deep, sympathetic understanding I had with Anna. Not Margaret's fault, I'm sure, but it did not come off. Perhaps Anna, with her fair loveliness, blue eyes and beautiful skin, plus her innate integrity as an actress, sublimated, both as woman and artist, my spiritual and physical needs and ideals, and I had subconsciously developed a blind spot for brunettes! It could well be.'

He added, perhaps with Margaret still in mind: 'Whether it is the toughness of being at the top or the fear that the higher you go the harder you fall has any significance I cannot say, but seldom have I met a star, particularly a woman star, who has enjoyed her success to the full and maintained a reasonable perspective.' They were ambiguous observations and, for Herbert Wilcox, uncharacteristically edged with discourtesy to Margaret. Joyce Wright denies that there had been any animosity in their relations before the split.

'Herbert and Anna were both great admirers of Margaret; I never heard anyone speak more highly of her than Anna. As far as any of us were aware it was a perfectly amicable agreement not to renew the contract.'

Early in 1954 Margaret broke new ground – for her sex as well as herself – by becoming the first woman to chair a panel game on British television. *Down You Go* was a quiz game based on a crossword principle. An avid crossword puzzler herself, it could not have been a more appropriate vehicle.

'Margaret Lockwood conquers TV,' ran the headline on a *Daily Express* news story the morning after the first show went out in January, declaring her debut 'a great personal triumph'. She'd started nervously with 'restless hands and a tiny quaver in her voice. But within two minutes everything was under control and TV's first Madam Chairman sent the game galloping along at a cracking pace.'

After the series ended a few weeks later, she took the spring and summer off, enjoying the longest period of inactivity she'd known since making *Lorna Doone*, apart from the six months' break when Julia was born. Her life had reached a quiet plateau, focused on Julia but with Theo still discreetly in the background, always on hand to make her laugh and take her out. They had become an acknowledged twosome in their own circle. She had lost interest in filming. Offers and ideas percolated through Herbert but she turned them all down. She could afford to. Agatha Christie was writing a play for her.

Thrillers were in vogue on the West End stage and for some time Margaret had been asking Herbert to look out for a suitable one for her. Behind the vogue was Peter Saunders, a producer relatively new to the West End scene who had made his name three years earlier by converting Agatha Christie's novel *The Hollow* into a play. It had long been a pipe-dream of the Queen of Crime to have the book dramatised and by obliging her where previous producers had declined Saunders won her lasting gratitude. Moreover, the production was a success. As a result Mrs Christie had entrusted all dramatic rights in her work to him and now, in 1954, he had two of her plays, *The Mousetrap* and *Witness for the Prosecution* running simultaneously in the West End. Herbert de Leon – 'one of the shrewdest and nicest of theatrical agents' – had become a personal friend and when Herbert broached the idea of an Agatha Christie play specially written for Margaret, Saunders was keen.

The first move was to have author and actress meet. Over lunch the two women immediately warmed to each other. They were mutual admirers of each other's work: Margaret had read every Christie book; Mrs Christie thought her 'a wonderful actress and a delightful person'.

With the idea safely off the ground, Margaret herself suggested what she had roughly in mind – a comedy whodunnit. She wondered, too, if there could be a part in it for Wilfrid Hyde-White, another of Herbert's clients. Mrs Christie went back home and set to work on what was to become *Spider's Web*, the only play she ever wrote to a commission and tailored for a specific star. So taken was she with her star that she wrote into it a sizeable part for a fourteen-year-old girl, anticipating that Margaret would like to have Julia appear with her.

When Mrs Christie delivered the script in the early summer of 1954 Margaret was thrilled with both the play and her role as Clarissa Hailsham-Brown, a woman, in the author's stage directions, 'with a very vivid imagination' who was not above embroidering the truth. This propensity for telling little white lies triggered the plot and its comedy. Clarissa, finding the body of a man in her drawing-room, believes the fatal blow must have been dealt by her teenage step-daughter (the role intended for Julia). She persuades two respectable elderly gentlemen and a young admirer to help her conceal the body, none of them, implausibly, foreseeing the embarrassments and dangers in store.

An eleven-week provincial tour opened at Nottingham in September 1954. Disappointingly, Julia, her own career burgeoning, was not available to play her mother's step-daughter: she was making a television film and later rehearsing for the title role in a Christmas production of *Goldilocks and the Three Bears* at the Q Theatre where Margaret first trod the boards as a professional actress. Nor was Wilfrid Hyde-White able to take the role Margaret had hustled for him. It went instead to Felix Aylmer who had played the faithful old retainer she had murdered so memorably in *The Wicked Lady*. The tour was the familiar story of packed theatres and enthusiastic audiences. Theo couldn't get away to join her as regularly as he had during *Private Lives* but every Monday when she arrived in a new city there would be a telegram from him waiting for her.

Then, the Savoy Theatre, 14 December 1954 . . . the London opening night, the one Margaret had been waiting for for five years; her 'legitimate' debut in the West End. She didn't count *Peter Pan*, playing to a Christmas audience in a festive frame of mind. She needed to be judged as an actress, not as a story-book legend.

The combination of Margaret Lockwood and a new Agatha Christie play had stoked feverish interest from the press. She gave interviews at home and during the previous day's dress rehearsal. Her dressing-room was filled with bouquets, her mirror wreathed with telegrams.

'People were popping their heads round the door wishing me luck and I seemed to be . . . thoroughly in control of myself, but all the time my heart was thudding and I was thinking: only another twenty minutes to go . . . fifteen . . . ten . . .'

The West End first-nighters gave her a rousing welcome, unlike the critics, who paid scant attention to her in a generally lukewarm reception for the play: 'As a whole [it] is the least exciting and not the most amusing of the three Agatha Christies now running in London,' thought *The Times* and even the monthly *Theatre World*, normally generous to a fault in its appraisals, found it 'entirely devoid of excitement except for a moment in the final scene'. However, the critic had the grace to add: 'If this new Agatha Christie play achieves an equal success with her other two current record-breakers, it will be largely due to Margaret Lockwood . . . [who] dominates the scene with her unexpected gift for comedy.'

Margaret was disappointed for herself and for Mrs Christie but they knew from the box office that they had a hit, cemented in the early weeks of the run by the presence of the Queen, who took a private party to see it. Julia, sitting just behind the royal party, reported that everyone had been totally absorbed.

Spider's Web ran for two years, with Margaret starring for fifteen months of them. 'She was a wonderful person to have in a company,' Peter Saunders recalled, 'always punctual, never complaining if she was kept hanging around. She rather disconcerted a cast because, having a photographic memory, she used to come to the first rehearsal knowing her lines.'

The *Theatre World* reviewer had been close to the mark in saying that Margaret would be largely responsible for any success *Spider's Web* could expect. It was one of the few Agatha Christie plays that failed to stand the test of time. Revivals have been rare. The public paid to see Margaret, a star who had somehow survived all vicissi-tudes. The fans were her power-base . . . and fans love a survivor.

'How she survived such films as a personality is a mystery,' a *Picturegoer* columnist wrote during the play's run. 'For she has sur-vived. The tinsel on this star is only slightly tarnished. Her theatre and television successes prove that.' But perhaps it wasn't such a mystery. 'The public', added *Picturegoer*, 'always spotted in her the magic qualities of a real top-liner.'

And suddenly she was once again being inundated with scripts. 'After her success in the theatre and on TV, she can call her own film tune,' the article disclosed. One of the offers was an adaptation of a recent West End thriller called *Murder Mistaken* by Janet Green, now writing screenplays for Sydney Box. Rank's hottest young star, Dirk Bogarde, an actor Margaret admired, had already been cast and the title changed to *Naked is the Flame*. The director was Lewis Gilbert who would later make two of the James Bond movies, *You Only Live Twice* and *The Spy Who Loved Me*.

Bogarde was cast as a pathological charmer, married to a wealthy elderly woman, who murders her when he mistakenly believes she is about to alter her will and makes her death look convincingly like an accident. He next charms a blowsy, moneyed, middle-aged ex-bar-maid, recently widowed, into marrying him but she is more than a match for him in guile, and when an easier prospect arrives on the scene he sets the stage for another murder.

The part of the no-nonsense second wife was a ripe one, interest-ingly shaded; warm-hearted, assertive but vulnerable, slightly vulgar, not a character Margaret could remotely see herself playing and she added the script to her pile of rejections. But she reckoned without Dirk Bogarde. Convinced she was ideal for it, he nagged and cajoled her until she finally relented. The chance to work with him chiefly persuaded her but she was uneasy about her casting and always remained so. 'Totally miscast,' she would say. 'It was meant for someone like Diana Dors.' Not even the most laudatory notices of her entire film career would make her change her view.

She began shooting *Naked is the Flame*, later re-titled again to *Cast a Dark Shadow*, in April 1955, four months into the run of *Spider's Web*. Nearly 30 years had passed since she had been subjected to the rigours of filming by day and appearing on stage by night and, now in her fortieth year, she found it arduous. Nevertheless, when the film opened five months later in September, Margaret's performance astonished the critics. They found her acting her age and looking it, with few concessions in make-up or lighting. It was a brave perform-ance and, for the first time since *Bank Holiday*, she was accorded unreserved credit.

'This role is a triumph of talent over vanity. It reveals for the first time that inside the glittering star there is a real actress struggling to get out.' (London *Evening Standard*)

'The best performance of her career; the performance of a genuine actress, not a star.' (*Daily Sketch*)

'The film is worth seeing for her performance alone.' (*Daily Mail*)

'In her long career Margaret Lockwood has never been so well suited in a part, nor can I remember her getting so convincingly into the skin of a character.' (*The Daily Telegraph*)

'Margaret Lockwood will surprise you. She plays the coarsely humorous wife with a razor-sharp tongue and a shrewd eye for cash with outstanding authority.' (*Picturegoer*)

The Observer's C. A. Lejeune thought it 'a shattering performance', the *Sunday Dispatch* a 'vivid' one.

With her forty-fourth film she had finally won the regard and respect she had always craved as an actress, but *Cast a Dark Shadow* was a box-office disappointment despite all the acclaim. People were turning away from the cinema for the home comforts of television and Margaret Lockwood, for all the potency the name still carried, was yesterday's film star, on her way to becoming a symbol of silver screen nostalgia.

The rising star was Julia. Under Herbert's management and carefully guided by her mother, she was emerging as a star in her own right and spent the summer of 1955 playing her first featured role in a movie, another Wilcox production.

The romantic floss which had borne Anna Neagle to the topmost place in public popularity had run its course. The Wilcoxes had tried to prolong the cycle with two lavish but vapid extravaganzas starring Anna with Errol Flynn who, bankrupted by his own disastrous bid to produce a film of *William Tell*, desperately needed Wilcox cash. *Lilacs in the Spring*, in which Sean Connery found work as an extra, and the Ivor Novello stage musical, *King's Rhapsody* had both cost money and prestige. A new direction was needed for Anna and Herbert found it in contemporary social issues.

My Teenage Daughter was the first in a series of titles exploring grittier themes, this one dealing with the generation gap and the currently controversial topic of teenage rebellion. Sylvia Syms made her screen debut as the problem child and Julia, now fourteen, was cast as her younger sister.

'Anna was slightly worried at the thought of using Margaret's daughter,' Joyce Wright recalled. 'She had visions of Margaret acting

Left: Cardboard Cavalier, 1948, left Margaret with critical egg on her face. *Right:* in *Highly Dangerous* with Dane Clark, 1950.

The ball scene in *Madness of the Heart,* with Paul Dupuis, 1949.

Keeping a straight face under Orson Welles's false nose in *Trent's Last Case*, 1952.

Margaret, Herbert Wilcox and Anna Neagle on the set of *Trent's Last Case*.

'An actress of remarkable distinction': Margaret in 1953 as *Laughing Anne* with Forrest Tucker.

Margaret recording songs from *Laughing Anne*. She wasn't allowed to sing on the soundtrack.

Dirk Bogarde 'bullied' Margaret into appearing with him in *Cast a Dark Shadow*, 1955.

Agatha Christie directing a rehearsal for *Spider's Web*, 1954, with Herbert de Leon 'standing in' for the body.

Mother and daughter celebrating Margaret's pledge that they should play *Peter Pan* together.

Margaret as Peter in 1950.

Above left: 'Far too much rouge and not enough clothes…' as Mrs Cheveley in 1965 in *An Ideal Husband*, with Richard Todd. *Above right:* Margaret's first meeting with John Stone was prophetically romantic in *And Suddenly It's Spring*, 1959.

Fourteen years on… and John and Margaret are a partnership at home as well as on television in *Justice*, 1973.

At last... in wig and gown for television's *Justice is a Woman*, 1969.

'The best-known and most elegant wicked lady of them all': Margaret's final screen performance as the Stepmother in *The Slipper and the Rose*, 1976.

The last picture: Margaret, with grandchildren, outside Buckingham Palace after receiving her CBE from the Queen.

the typical stage mother, having her say and popping up on the set to keep her eye on things. It was quite the opposite, in fact. The only time we ever saw her during production was on the final day when she came down to collect Julia and take her home. Everyone was terribly impressed with Julia; her charm, her professionalism, her beautiful manners. She was always making herself useful, running round the studio, fetching and carrying for people when she wasn't on call. I remember Anna saying what a wonderful job Margaret had done with Julia because in her circumstances it couldn't have been easy.'

Anna herself later wrote in her autobiography: 'Julia made an enormous impression on me right from the start. I marvelled that Margaret managed to bring her up so beautifully while making such a fine career for herself at the same time.' The film did its job well, restoring Herbert's finances and setting Anna on a new road that kept her profile high for the next six years.

Margaret's fifteen-month commitment to *Spider's Web* ended in March 1956. She rested for the summer and in October re-learned her role in *Cast a Dark Shadow* for a BBC television production under the original title *Murder Mistaken*. In a blonde wig, she co-starred with Derek Farr playing the Dirk Bogarde part, with whom she had last worked in the dark days of the Battle of Britain on 'The first Blitzkrieg film', *Quiet Wedding*.

She had been replaced in *Spider's Web* by Anne Crawford, a beautiful blonde former Rank star as popular with her colleagues in the business as she was with the fans. She took over the role knowing that she was incurably ill with leukaemia and that October she died, still in harness, at the age of 36. Her understudy, Elizabeth Bird, stepped into the role for the short time remaining of the West End run and the provincial tour that followed but with only two dates left on the tour, she was forced to withdraw on health grounds, leaving Peter Saunders in crisis. No other actress was available to learn and play the part at such short notice.

Margaret was holidaying in the south of France. Unknown to Saunders, Herbert de Leon phoned her, explained the situation and Margaret immediately flew home to offer her services to an astounded Saunders for the remaining weeks of the tour. It was an action he never forgot. 'I know of very few stars who would have done that,' he said.

He already had a new play lined up for her. *Subway in the Sky* took her back to the Savoy Theatre in February 1957, playing a woman who shelters an American army officer deserter trying to clear his name of a murder he hasn't committed. While falling in love with him she begins to suspect him of being the killer. There were vestiges of Clarissa Hailsham-Brown in the character . . . '[She] skilfully suggests not only the attractiveness of the lady who has to lie her way from pillar to pillar but also a certain natural foolhardiness,' noted *The Times*. Even with a Hollywood name, Zachary Scott, for her co-star, the play was only a moderate success, though they carried a respectable run through the spring and summer.

Margaret and Julia were now emerging as a professional mother-and-daughter team. During the run of *Subway in the Sky* they worked together for the first time since the brief scene they had shared in *The White Unicorn* on a television play, *Call It a Day*, and the BBC had been impressed enough to consider expanding it into a drama series, one of the earliest instances of the television 'spin-off'. *The Royalty* speedily evolved and started transmission in October 1957, a four-part serial about a former Cochrane revue star running a small exclusive West End hotel while coping with the demands of bringing up a lively teenage daughter.

One thing seemed to be leading to another . . . and what had been perhaps the Lockwood ladies' most fanciful ambition became a reality that Christmas. Back in 1950 when Margaret had been playing *Peter Pan* and nine-year-old Julia had spent most of her school holidays with her backstage at the Scala, she had given her stage-struck daughter a pledge: 'As soon as you're old enough you shall play Wendy if we can arrange it – and I'll be Peter.'

Now, seven years later, she kept her promise. Margaret's hat-trick in the role was 'a thoroughly friendly performance', *The Times* thought, while 'She has a tall, graceful, motherly Wendy in her daughter.'

That Peter was Margaret's last stage work for a year. She was in demand for television, appearing on game panels and in an adaptation of Arnold Bennett's *The Great Adventure* with Alec Clunes, but the theatre – her kind of theatre – had little to offer. The Angry Young Men had usurped it, the Osbornes, the Weskers, the Pinters. In the cinema, too, the new cult was youth and neo-realism – Laurence Harvey in *Room at the Top*, Richard Burton in *Look Back in Anger*, Albert Finney in *Saturday Night and Sunday Morning*. There might be a place in the new order for the character-actress Margaret of *Cast a Dark Shadow*, but the prevailing mood wasn't her style and she surveyed it with distaste. Had she been more amenable to change she might have recognised the new trends as an opportunity to widen her acting horizons and diversify. She had the capability and, with her showing in *Cast a Dark Shadow*, the credentials, but not the will. It was her nature – and Herbert's as advisor – to play safe.

There was certainly safety in one of the scripts he forwarded towards the end of the year, a thriller called *Murder on Arrival*. This, she decided, was *her* kind of play. She persuaded Peter Saunders to produce it for her and a provincial tour with the West End in view at the end of it opened early in 1959. Saunders, indulging Margaret's whim rather than following his own instincts, was uneasy.

'After the first performance I realised I would never bring it into London – and I didn't,' he said. Again Margaret's and Herbert's judgement had played them false.

Saunders was aware of the impasse she was creating for herself. When, in the late summer, he recommended a role for her in a new comedy he was planning, he saw it as being mildly but not too drastically daring, a divergence from the characters the theatre-going public had come to expect from her. She allowed herself to be persuaded.

In *And Suddenly It's Spring* she played a drab, strait-laced business-woman who, at the age of 35 (Margaret herself was now 43) realises that love has passed her by, a state of affairs for which she has only herself to blame. To make up for lost time, she sets about reforming and glamorising her image to attract a middle-aged Lothario. Instead she dazzles an American naval officer much younger than herself and unexpectedly finds herself falling genuinely in love for the first time.

To boost the play's publicity, Saunders decided to gamble on an idea that had been in his mind for several years. *And Suddenly It's Spring* opened in November 1959 not with the traditional first night, but with a novel first afternoon. Far from being a gimmick, there was sound commercial and artistic reasoning behind the move. He had long had a theory that the usual first-night audience – critics, professional first-nighters, ticket agency representatives – was untypical of the paying public on whom a successful run depended. The man-in-the-street theatre-goer was more likely to attend an afternoon 'first night' and the critics, who would still be invited, should get a more realistic impression of the production's impact on an average audience.

His gamble only partially paid off. The novelty of the occasion did garner a lot of valuable publicity in the news pages but . . . 'to my horror, I saw the same first-night faces in the same seats and the thought that they might be a better audience was quickly dispelled. The play went through in near-silence. At the end, as the curtain came down, there was some modest applause, but as it went up again there was the loudest booing from the gallery I had ever heard in any theatre.'

The reviews next day were 'terrible'. The cast, headed by Margaret, Yolande Donlan and Frank Lawton, had not been in favour of Saunders's innovation from the start; they gritted their teeth and soldiered on, turning disaster into a reasonable six-month run. Those months also turned Margaret's world upside down, so dramatically and unexpectedly that her life would never be the same again. Reality gradually took over from the fiction she was playing nightly. She found herself falling in love, as she did on stage, with the young actor playing her leading man.

AN IDEAL HUSBAND

His name was John Stone and he was one of that legion of good-looking, competent, reliable actors who hover, eternally hopeful, in the no-man's-land between regular employment and the high ground of recognised stardom; valuable to producers but just another face the the public.

Born John Hailstone in Cardiff in 1924, he was eight years younger than Margaret. His father had been a regular army officer who had worked his way up from the ranks, never quite overcoming his lower middle-class origins to feel wholly at ease in the officers' mess. John's earliest years, like Margaret's, had been spent in India where Major Hailstone had been posted soon after the boy was born. He was seven when the family had finally returned to England. They found they had still more in common. He, too, had begun his acting career at the Q Theatre. After several years in provincial repertory, he had arrived in the West End in 1948 with a small part in a long-running farce, *One Wild Oat*, and thereafter he was never out of work for long, always well down the cast list but gainfully employed in front-rank productions including, in 1955, the British première of Arthur Miller's controversial *A View from the Bridge*.

Firm-jawed, he was handsome in a strong, quiet, unexceptional way. Like Rupert and Keith, he was fair-haired; like Theo, everyone liked him. He had a laconic sense of humour, a laid-back attitude and an aura of dependability. He was patently masculine with a refreshing absence of 'actorish' affectation and he was also a self-avowed ladies' man. The ladies who caught his eye were invariably dark-haired ones.

He had been married twice, the first time, at 21, to a woman called Elizabeth Taylor, known as 'Blackie'. That marriage had broken up in 1953 when he met a Chinese opera singer, Lian Shin Yang. Shin Yang had all the temperament of her calling but after living together

183

for six years they were married in 1959, following his divorce from 'Blackie'.

'It was a disaster,' he later recalled. Marriage only served to intensify Shin Yang's jealousy. By the time he joined *And Suddenly It's Spring* and met Margaret, marriage had degenerated into a succession of fights and scenes. One of the most embarrassing occurred backstage at the Duke of York's Theatre soon after the play had opened, and was witnessed by members of the company. Shin Yang stormed through the stage door and provoked a quarrel which quickly became a physical assault. Dodging her blows, John ran out into St Martin's Lane and down to Trafalgar Square watched by astonished bystanders as a diminutive Chinese woman chased after him, trying to beat him with a shoe.

Margaret, like her character in the play, had begun to sense a lack of romance in her life. Her relationship with Theo, still at her disposal as companion and escort, had slipped into affectionate friendship. It was ten years since she had known the delights and comforts of being in love. And hadn't she once said: 'No woman can say she will never fall in love again'? It was John's quiet strength of character as much as any other quality about him that attracted Margaret. He had a way of taking control of a situation without fuss, without needing to assert himself. And he was his own man. He showed her respect as a great star but he wasn't awed by her. They could laugh together – an element in a relationship that was always important to her – and there was a security about him, the supportive factor she had always needed.

In due course John moved into the Roehampton flat. It was a discreet arrangement, Margaret's innate sense of the proprieties still governing her conduct, although she was not now quite so conscious of 'image' in her private life as she had once needed to be. Times had changed. The permissive 'sixties were dawning and she was no longer the public's goddess, the exemplar, as she had been in the years when she had loved Keith. Nor did she now have to be mindful of Margaret Evelyn's feelings and remonstrations, and as for Rupert's sensibilities, well, Julia was eighteen now, a celebrity in her own right and, though still living at home, free to make her own judgements and choices.

The new situation called for some domestic re-organisation. For some time, she had been toying with the idea of investing in a place of her own: apart from Delcott she had always rented, never owned, her home. She and John began looking at properties, to all appearances a couple laying the foundations of a settled life together.

She had found a new comedy, *Milk and Honey*, which she pressed Peter Saunders to produce. It developed into a 'family' affair, with parts for John and Julia as well. The Lockwood ladies, mother and daughter, made good copy for the provincial newspapers on the touring circuit, but the added news factor of John's presence in the cast and the Lockwood household escaped them. The play, which opened in Newcastle upon Tyne in February 1961, was another of Margaret's miscalculations and the tour was quickly abandoned. Back home again she and John finally found a house they liked in Kingston upon Thames on the far side of Richmond Park which had been Margaret's 'back garden' for so long. Soon after moving in she granted an interview to the local Kingston paper, the *Surrey Comet*.

'I like it here because it's so quiet,' she told the reporter, who went on to describe how the 'eau-de-nil walls and a soft blue fitted carpet set off a raspberry suite in the lounge. The setting has a touch of the theatrical about it but it is not bizarre.'

Margaret was still adroitly shifting the emphasis of her domestic life on to Julia: 'Margaret Lockwood and her daughter have no staff living at their new home although they do have daily help in the house. "We live quietly and privately," Miss Lockwood told me. "We don't have enormous parties but we like to have friends in." The two appear to be inseparable but Miss Lockwood maintains, "We're really quite independent although we enjoy each other's company. We're more like sisters than mother and daughter. At one time I looked after Julia but now the position seems to have been reversed." ' There was no hint of a man about the house.

Kingston has been her home ever since; an unpretentious 1920s house in a quiet cul-de-sac, detached but crowded by its neighbours, set back behind a tiny front garden.

The move ushered in a long period of serenity and security. At 45 Margaret had become a sophisticated woman, still glamorous, with a commanding presence, who had preserved her figure remarkably well. She could have her imperious moments but John, friends noticed, knew how to handle her, taking the heat out of any approaching flashpoint with a quizzically raised eyebrow and a gently mocking word or two. He set about refurbishing their home with more enthusiasm than Margaret, who had never been a natural home-maker. It was faintly ironic that the posed photograph accompanying the *Surrey Comet* article showed her duster in hand, as though pausing in her housework, under a glamorous oil painting of herself in her Gainsbor-

185

ough heyday. Anyone who knew her could recognise the false
impression it gave. She had rarely concerned herself with cleaning
chores any more that she had with cooking. There was always paid
help to deal with it.

Her run of theatrical ill-luck was staunched in February 1962 with
Signpost to Murder at the Cambridge Theatre under the auspices of
Emile Littler, the first time she had ventured away from Peter Saunders. The plot mechanics were routine but the thrills they sprang were
enterprising enough to keep the box office busy for a year. They
concerned a woman held hostage in her remote cottage by an escaped
murderer with whom she develops a strangely close and sinister
relationship leading to a series of ingenious psychological twists. 'Margaret Lockwood rarely falters in her presentation of the complex
character of this woman, forced at pistol point to pass nightmare
days with an overwrought and dangerous stranger,' reported *Theatre
World*. Derek Farr co-starred and there was a small part for John
Stone as an attendant at the institution for the criminally insane from
which the killer has absconded.

While she was settled in the West End Saunders was working
long-term to the formula which had earlier resulted in *Spider's Web*.
Margaret had developed a whim to play a barrister in a courtroom
drama and Saunders was nursing along a new play by Jack Roffey, a
lawyer-playwright, which he was planning to produce for her as soon
as she was free of *Signpost to Murder*.

Hostile Witness fulfilled all the criteria she anticipated . . . except
one. The central character was a woman barrister and the entire action
took place in court, but the lawyer was in the dock, on trial for
murder, and therefore she wouldn't wear a wig and gown – so she
rejected it. Instead she pressed Saunders yet again to stage a play she
had read and liked herself. Yet again he humoured her and yet again
the results were dire.

Re-worked from a successful Paris farce, *Every Other Evening* was
tired froth about a middle-aged lover (Derek Farr) who moves into
his mistress's apartment where his wife – Margaret – and teenaged
children promptly join him. The plot, said *The Times*, was 'flaccid'
with 'witless gibes at the Common Market and the Channel Tunnel'
and 'Margaret Lockwood brings her own style of down-to-earth artificiality to the part of the wife.' *Every Other Evening* didn't run for
long.

Meanwhile Saunders pressed ahead with *Hostile Witness*. With a little judicious re-writing Jack Roffey effected a sex-change on the leading character and the play went on with Michael Denison in the dock. It packed the Haymarket Theatre for a year.

In January 1965 Margaret Evelyn died. Her health had been failing for some time but although in the final months of her life her son Lyn and his wife Sheila had moved in with her at Delcott, at the last it was to her niece, Betty Lait, the surrogate daughter she had brought up after her sister Kitty's death, that she turned. Betty had her moved into her own home at Bourne End, Hertfordshire and nursed her through repeated cerebral haemorrhages until she died peacefully, at the age of 83. There had been no reconciliation with Margaret.

Long before, Margaret had forced herself to come to terms with the rejection she had suffered from both her parents: the father she had hardly known, who had stayed in India and died there in the late 1950s; the mother whose love and approval were everything she had once wanted in life but which had been callously withheld. Margaret Evelyn had made her will two years before her death. Margaret no longer appeared to exist for her; neither she nor Julia was remembered with so much as a token trinket. She left her entire estate, valued at £5,500, to Lyn, including Delcott. So many people Margaret worked with would say: 'You never really got to know her,' unaware of the forces which had conditioned her, which had helped structure the protective reserve, the reluctance to stand up for herself, and the reticence that made it so difficult for her to reveal herself to any but the closest friends.

Two months later Margaret and Julia appeared in the first episode of a television series called *The Flying Swan*, developed from *The Royalty* of eight years before. Margaret's character, Mollie Manning, was again running a hotel – the Flying Swan – this time on the banks of the Thames outside London, with Julia as her air hostess daughter. Each episode was a self-contained story, most of them featuring a guest star, and was screened at Saturday night peak viewing time, replacing the BBC's then most popular drama series, *Dixon of Dock Green*. It ran for the next two years.

That summer of 1965 Margaret was offered the chance to play a classical role on stage for the first time. She had once told an interviewer that she didn't rule out the possibility of trying her hand at Shakespeare, preferably Juliet or Rosalind, her favourite parts, but no producer had taken the hint. The role of Mrs Cheveley in Oscar Wilde's *An Ideal Husband* may not have been of quite the same order but it was an acceptable compromise for an actress with ambitions to be taken seriously.

The approach came from Dulcie Gray, an admirer of Margaret's ever since she had made her film debut in *A Place of One's Own* more than twenty years before. 'Maggie had been tremendously kind to me then,' she said. 'I was very much the new girl at Gainsborough and she'd made me feel welcome. There was a distinct pecking order at the studios in those days. I was fairly low in it, Maggie was right at the top. She found out I was living at Dolphin Square and travelling to and from work by public transport. After that she insisted on giving me a lift home in her car every evening. I've always had the most affectionate feelings of warmth for her.'

Dulcie Gray was herself now at the top of a pecking order and with her husband, Michael Denison, whose run in *Hostile Witness* had just finished, was using her influence to help two old producer friends through a bad patch.

Peter Donald, who had given her the break which launched her career and later teamed her with her husband professionally for the first time, had gone into partnership with Peter Bridge, a brilliant though erratic Young Turk in West End production. That summer business had slumped for them, so the Denisons came up with a suggestion for an all-star revival of *An Ideal Husband*, offering to play the Chilterns – 'the least exciting parts' – themselves. It was Miss Gray who envisaged Margaret as the glamorous, blackmailing Mrs Cheveley who, in Wilde's lines, wore 'far too much rouge and not quite enough clothes . . . always a sign of despair in a woman'.

Margaret wasn't familiar with the play and after reading it, she slightly stunned the Denisons by turning it down. 'She didn't think Cheveley was a very good part for her,' Miss Gray recalled, 'because she didn't appear in the final scene, and Margaret was used to being on for the whole of a play.'

Peter Bridge asked Dulcie Gray to take the role but she was adamant that Margaret was the perfect actress for it and also the 'name' the production needed to fulfil its 'all star' promise, so she set to work making Margaret change her mind. Subjected to relentless persuasion, Margaret eventually allowed herself to be talked round.

As preparations went ahead for a tour preceding a West End season, the theatre world thought Peter Bridge was indulging another of his fortunes of the two Peters, Donald and Bridge, were triumphantly restored, their reputation for success and daring vindicated.

Margaret was happy in the company but her behaviour off-stage still puzzled even those who were familiar with it.

'Everyone remarked on her dress during rehearsals,' said Richard Todd. 'It seemed curious that such a big star and such a glamorous one in public seemed to care nothing for her appearance out of the public's eye. She would wear very little make-up, trousers and very ordinary clothes. I always remember her wearing an old black balaclava when we were rehearsing *An Ideal Husband*. The next time we were in a play together, years later, she turned up at rehearsal in the same old balaclava. We often stayed in the same hotels on the *Ideal Husband* tour but the only times I ever seemed to see her outside the theatre was if I popped into the lounge for a pot of tea. She'd sometimes be sitting by herself at a table doing *The Times* crossword. But she'd never offer to join me or invite me to join her.'

Her solitariness worried the Denisons. Although she didn't appear in the last scene, she had to remain in the wings to take her curtain-call and they noticed how anxious she was every night to leave the theatre. 'We used to ask her to join our table for supper after the show,' said Michael Denison, 'but we'd have to race out of the theatre to catch up with her. She dashed away as soon as the tabs came down and was out of the stage door before any of us to avoid the crowds who would be waiting for her. She always seemed shy of her public.' And Dulcie Gray added: 'I always had the feeling she wasn't a very happy person.'

While *An Ideal Husband* was in the West End, Jack Roffey, undaunted by her rejection of *Hostile Witness*, tried again and towards the end of her year's run at the Strand Peter Saunders triumphantly presented her with a script he was sure she couldn't resist. Writing jointly with Ronald Kinnoch, Roffey had fashioned a courtroom drama, *Justice is a Woman*, which fulfilled all the criteria she had found wanting in his previous play, in addition to which the main character, a woman barrister, was given ample opportunity to don wig and gown.

She was interested but told him she preferred to stay with *An Ideal Husband* for its transfer to the Garrick. Disappointed, Saunders decided he wasn't going to wait for her and went ahead with his plans for a four-week tour before opening in the West End. Dame Flora Robson had agreed to play the role.

A week before the start of the tour at Brighton – where Dame Flora lived – she was taken ill and with only three days to go had to withdraw. Her doctors couldn't guarantee that she would be fit enough to play any of the touring dates or the London opening. The understudy took over, but, good as she was, Saunders knew he had to have a star name if the production were to be saved. Desperately, he again appealed to Margaret, remembering no doubt how nobly she had flown to his rescue in similar circumstances with *Spider's Web*.

Unable to see the play for herself because of her commitments in *An Ideal Husband*, she dispatched Herbert instead. His report was highly favourable and he strongly advised her to change her mind. Other voices, friends she'd also asked to monitor the play for her, counselled against. Probably for the first time in her long association with Herbert, she disregarded his advice and gave Peter Saunders a second 'no'. Constance Cummings stepped in. The play arrived in the West End to indifferent reviews and a brief run, although Saunders has always considered it one of the three best productions in his career up to that point.

A few months later the allocation of new licences for Independent Television companies came up for renewal. Early in 1967 the Independent Broadcasting Authority considered bids for a new franchise to cover the Yorkshire area and Peter Saunders was a member of the consortium awarded the licence. One of his first contributions, once Yorkshire Television was in business, was to suggest that *Justice is a Woman* should be adapted as a television play and that it should star Margaret Lockwood.

JOHN AND JUSTICE

The film industry had not totally forgotten her. Offers kept coming in but she brushed them aside with the contempt most of the scripts deserved. One of them, an Italian production called *L'Avventuriero*, was based on Joseph Conrad's novel *The Rover* and must have awakened memories of *Laughing Anne*. Her co-star, they said, would be Anthony Quinn. 'I'm not on the breadline yet and I don't have to do rubbish like that,' she told Herbert after reading it. Rita Hayworth, in the dying fall of her career, finally played the part and for once Margaret's judgement had been sound. The film received a single screening in New York before it was dumped.

True to form, she was also turning down scripts which could have given her acting interesting new facets and directions, most famously the film version of Joe Orton's controversial black comedy, *Entertaining Mr Sloane*. And turning them down for the usual reasons. She was indignant that the very idea could be entertained of Margaret Lockwood playing a middle-aged women with lecherous designs on a youthful lodger, horrified that in one scene the character would be seen removing dentures from her mouth; afraid, perhaps, of what people would say.

Almost immediately after finishing in *An Ideal Husband* she was back on the provincial rounds with *The Others*, a two-character ghost play co-starring Donald Houston which opened a three-month tour at Glasgow in June 1967. 'A limp, morbid piece of work,' according to one critic, about a married couple marooned by a snowstorm in a remote cottage where the woman keeps hearing ghostly children's voices singing nursery rhymes. 'Miss Lockwood, her eyes slithering into their corners to catch a glimpse of some unspeakable horror at her back occasionally lifts this exercise in *Petit Guignol* on to the grand scale,' *The Times* conceded. She wasn't however, able, to lift

192

it into a successful run when it arrived in the West End at the Strand Theatre.

She returned to Peter Saunders's fold in the summer of 1969 for *On a Foggy Day*, in which mourners at a funeral feast 'peeled away the veils of their own stunted lives'. She seemed to be edging gingerly into Ortonesque black comedy as the deceased's 'randily bigoted' mistress, matching memories and grief with his widow, played by Siobhan McKenna. *The Times*, conjuring images of *Cast a Dark Shadow*, reported: 'Margaret Lockwood, swinging between surface sympathy and granite self-interest, torturing her vowels with the relish of an old music-hall queen, gives a magnificently vulgar display of middle-aged sexual aggression.'

The play received, in Peter Saunders's own admission, 'the most ghastly set of reviews imaginable'. After reading them he agonised over whether to take it off immediately or let it try to weather the worst. He phoned each of his stars to sound out their views. Margaret was in favour of cutting their losses; Siobhan McKenna insisted that they should 'battle on', citing the encouraging notices the play had received on tour. Miss McKenna prevailed and within a month they were all out of work. Saunders conjectured afterwards how differently the sorry tale might have worked out had his first choice for the male lead materialised: he had originally offered it to Charles Chaplin.

While Margaret was 'battling on' that month, she finally appeared on television in wig and gown as the formidable barrister, Julia Stanford, in *Justice is a Woman*. All the harmless little conceits that had led up to her performance were vindicated. Reaction to her was so favourable that Yorkshire TV programme chiefs decided to expand the character into a series. Work would begin in about eighteen months.

In the summer of 1970 she was touring as Somerset Maugham's *Lady Frederick*, another scheming society woman, distantly related to Mrs Cheveley. Griffith Jones was in the audience on one of the provincial stop-overs. He hadn't seen or met Margaret since *Look Before You Love* and he was struck by the regal authority of the actress with whom he had 'giggled' through *The Wicked Lady* a quarter of a century ago.

'She was still beautiful. Her voice had deepened and her personality filled the theatre,' he said. Afterwards, thinking of old times, he went round to her dressing-room to share memories with the happy, fun-loving star who had jogged alongside him on her studio horse, but

'Sadly we were rather shy with each other. The years had ironed out the giggles.' They didn't meet again.

The critics applauded again when *Lady Frederick* reached London. 'Convincing us throughout that at heart she is a thoroughly nice woman as well as an extremely intelligent one, she gives one of the few impressions I have ever seen in recent years of a great beauty at the height of her powers,' commented John Barber in *The Daily Telegraph* under the headline 'Margaret Lockwood saves Maugham play.' He added: 'Her sparkling performance makes it perfectly possible to accept that three men would propose to her on a single morning. What she cannot do is make it for a moment credible that the lovelorn lordling would finally reject her, when she decides to throw him over, because she allows him to see her without wig and rouge. This is the play's big scene and without make-up Miss Lockwood looks an impish darling. Her long, lying explanation of how this eye-pencil adds roguishness and that pot of paste adds youth is delivered with such a world of humour that it drew applause. But if it makes nonsense of the play, it made something splendid of it.'

Throughout the spring and summer of 1971 Margaret worked on *Justice*, the series evolved from *Justice is a Woman*. When it was aired for the first time in October, she found herself overnight with a major hit. Within weeks her fan mail soared to the kind of volume she had known in her Gainsborough days.

Each episode was a self-contained drama, skilfully juggling the case-load of Harriet Petersen, a barrister on the Northern Circuit, with the problems and stresses of her private life. The man in that life was a doctor, Ian Moody, down-to-earth, dependable, a counterpoint to the emotional demands of Petersen's professional existence, relating to her much as John Stone did to Margaret Lockwood.

John in fact played the part on screen too and it was Margaret herself who had recommended him for the role.

'The full-blooded vigour that long ago marked her performance in *The Wicked Lady* still seems undiminished,' reported *The Daily Telegraph*, which went on to commend her 'imperious professionalism'. The same notice noted that: 'Dr Moody never seems to attend to his patients. He is forever slaving over a hot stove or up to his armpits in detergent for Harriet's benefit as if he had been set a penance by Germaine Greer.'

One of the most devoted viewers of the series was Dame Anna Neagle. 'She hardly missed an episode', said Joyce Wright, 'and she was full of admiration for Margaret. "I don't know how she manages to keep up the standard," she would say.' Two more *Justice* series followed, keeping Margaret and John busy for the next two years. It was a perfect arrangement domestically; they were able to travel between Kingston and Leeds together, work together, they could count on their free time more or less together. In the public's eye they became a team but purely a professional one. In the huge expanse of column inches *Justice* and its stars filled over the three years of its popularity, there was never any hint that their partnership extended beyond the studios.

They themselves extended it to the stage in 1972, appearing in a revival of Noel Coward's *Relative Values*, first on tour and then, after a break, in the West End. From then on, for the next six years, virtually any work they accepted, they did together. According to Richard Todd, for whose Triumph Productions they both at one time worked, 'You learned to think of Maggie and Stone as a package. If you wanted Lockwood, it was taken for granted that you had to take Stone, too.'

On 18 December 1972, during the break between the tour and the West End opening of *Relative Values*, Julia was married. The suddenness of her decision and her choice of husband took friends – and the press – unawares.

Many years before, when Julia was still a teenager, Margaret had written: 'I have made one promise to myself which I may find very hard to keep . . . that no matter who Toots wants to marry, I will never let myself become an antagonist towards my child's husband.' Margaret Evelyn had still been alive when those words were written and they must have been heavy in her heart at Richmond Registry Office when Julia married the actor Ernest Clark. She was 31. He, at 60, was nearly twice her age and more than four years older than the woman who was now his mother-in-law. He was divorced and had children older than his bride. They had first met two years earlier when both were appearing in William Douglas Home's comedy *The Jockey Club Stakes*.

Margaret's pledge was put to the test. As any mother would be in such circumstances, she was concerned about the difference in their ages but she kept her promise. She welcomed Ernest into the family and, with time, found in him a staunch support when she herself was most sorely in need of the love and loyalty of those dearest to her.

The marriage proved successful and lasting and Margaret has always played her role in it with sensitivity and understanding. In October 1973 the first of the Wicked Lady's four grandchildren was born.

The third and last series of *Justice* ended in August 1974 with a registry office wedding between Harriet, who had become increasingly dominant as the scripts progressed, and her doctor boy-friend, who had become, in the words of one commentator, increasingly 'boring, dull and colourless'. The marriage proposal had come, in character, from her.

Over the three years Harriet had exceeded any fanciful ambition of Margaret's to play a barrister. Towards the end Harriet took silk: Margaret Lockwood QC! Several profile writers during that period saw fit to revive and perpetuate the old fiction that her 'grandfather' had been a celebrated member of that fraternity. She loved the part and didn't want to relinquish it. For a time she tried to talk the producers into commissioning a further series, suggesting that Harriet should enter politics and become a Member of Parliament but wisely, perhaps, it was decided to drop the series while it was still riding high in the ratings. Harriet had served her well. The task of sustaining a role on television, the exposure it brought and her undeniable popularity bore fruit. Twenty years after her last film, *Cast a Dark Shadow*, her return to the cinema was announced.

It fell to Bryan Forbes, one of the most persuasive voices in the industry, to coax her back before the film cameras for his nearly £3 million musical version of the Cinderella story, *The Slipper and the Rose*. There was, in his mind, only one actress eligible and fitted to play the part of the Stepmother, though the traditional qualifying adjective 'wicked' was judiciously omitted from the character and from the film's credits. Nevertheless, it was a word that hovered over his conception of the role. 'Possibly subconsciously there was an element of tongue-in-cheek in casting Margaret,' he now admits.

On a more practical level, he had been a life-long admirer of Margaret's and 'always regretted that there had never been an opportunity of working with her'. A rumour persists that he and Richard Attenborough had been anxious to cast her, ten years before, in their highly acclaimed drama *Seance on a Wet Afternoon*, a role which brought Kim Stanley an Academy Award nomination, but that the idea had been blocked by the film's backers because Margaret was then considered 'box office poison'. Forbes denies she had ever been fantasies by taking such a high-powered cast into the provinces where commercial theatre was struggling to survive: in addition to Margaret and the Denisons, the cast now boasted Richard Todd, returning to the stage for the first time since rocketing to screen stardom in *The Hasty Heart* sixteen years earlier; Roger Livesey, with whom Margaret had last worked in *Midshipman Easy* 30 years before, and Ursula Jeans.

But Bridge was his usual confident self, banking on the drawing power of the names and booking the largest theatres available. What the sceptics didn't realise was that, thanks to the Denisons' intercession, he was getting his stars at bargain-basement prices: each of them agreed to take a paltry £60 a week plus a percentage of the profits, if any. Just three weeks into the tour, the gamble paid off: the production recovered its costs and started to make money.

An Ideal Husband was Margaret's finest hour in the theatre. All the craft she had accumulated over the years, the commanding presence, the vocal authority, the grace of poise and movement, converged into a glittering interpretation. When the production arrived in the West End at the Strand Theatre in December 1965 it failed to stir the critics . . . but Margaret succeeded.

'Who would have thought the day would come when she would sweep the board in a comedy dependent on bubble-light wit?' asked Mary Holland in *Plays and Players*. 'Here she seems to be the only one to have real control of her part from the moment she swaggers on, resplendent in strapless velvet, beauty spots and wicked lady hairdo. She laughs with menace, glances murderously, relishes her lines and plays with a high gusto.'

The Times called it a 'voluptuous performance' and noted: 'Thanks largely to the poise, style and cool insolence with which Margaret Lockwood plays the villainous Mrs Cheveley the melodramatic element comes off surprisingly well.'

The author Michael Thornton, reviewing at that time for the *Sunday Express*, recalled: 'Her performance was a revelation. All I could remember during the evening was how often Noel Coward had told me that "Maggie Lockwood simply can't play comedy." In *An Ideal Husband* she proved him very wrong. She not only dominated the stage from the moment of her first entrance but cornered every laugh of the evening, playing in a gloriously sardonic, mocking style.'

The production ran for nearly eighteen months, outlasting its allotted span of a year at the Strand and transferring to the Garrick. The under consideration. 'And she would certainly not have been turned down on the grounds that she was no longer a box-office name. I remember that we approached Simone Signoret who rejected us, and then, at one point, I rewrote the script completely for two male characters and approached Sir Alec Guinness and Tom Courtenay. We were again rejected and we finally decided on Kim Stanley.'

Margaret enjoyed making *The Slipper and the Rose* and being back in the studios, even taking a two-week location trip to Austria in her stride, the first time she had travelled overseas for a film since her Hollywood excursion 36 years before.

'It feels as if I've never been away,' she told an interviewer on the Pinewood set. 'Things haven't changed much.' Nor had some of the faces working with her . . . Michael Hordern, who had made his screen debut in *The Girl in the News* and had a small part in *Highly Dangerous*; and 'dear old Gravyboat' – Peter Graves. She granted a lot of interviews on the set. Margaret Lockwood as Cinderella's stepmother was a neat association of ideas that was no more lost on the press than it was on her fans. There was a nice piquancy in finding her portraying, as one magazine writer put it, 'the best-known and most elegant wicked lady of them all'.

Her part was not large but it was flamboyant, the perfect frame for a comeback. 'It turned out to be an inspired piece of casting,' said Bryan Forbes. 'She gave a glorious performance, without any hint of parody or pantomime, and it was my privilege to have her in the film.'

While she was working on it, the fortieth anniversary of the first day she had ever stepped on to a studio stage, for the dance sequence in *Lorna Doone*, passed unremarked. *The Slipper and the Rose* was Margaret's forty-fifth film and it was her last. In the spring of 1976 it was chosen for the Royal Film Performance in the presence that year of Queen Elizabeth the Queen Mother. Then the memories did flood back, across 30 years to the time when a six-year-old Toots had presented Queen Elizabeth with a bouquet and Margaret Evelyn, 'quite excited for once', had looked on. Margaret herself had been the unchallenged queen of British films then.

In that spring of 1976 she was back on stage for Peter Saunders in *Double Edge*, 'one of the cleverest whodunnits for years' according to *The Daily Telegraph*. She was cast opposite Paul Daneman and Barrie Ingham as an Oxford don caught up in an assassination attempt on a British Prime Minister, in which the wife of the Home Secretary has been killed. All three of the play's characters had a motive for murder but 'Miss Lockwood is too gracious, too beautiful and too intelligent a woman to be acceptable as a killer, and she was filling the theatre with all these qualities,' (*The Daily Telegraph*). After a year-long run at the Vaudeville Theatre, Margaret took the play on tour with two new co-stars, one of them John Stone, replacing Paul Daneman as the Home Secretary. 'I generally play doctors or army officers,' he once told a reporter. 'I must look professional.'

They were playing Wimbledon, just down the road from their Kingston home, when Margaret celebrated her sixtieth birthday. The following week's attraction at the theatre was a West End-bound comedy called *Out on a Limb*, starring Julia Lockwood.

That birthday was not surprisingly something of a psychological watershed for Margaret. She was now eligible to draw her old-age pension. Though still looking marvellous and in her measurements barely changed from her youth, she was made aware of the passage of the years, and she didn't care to acknowledge it. But she had much to be grateful for. Her career and her fame were as strong as ever. Her private life was tranquil and well ordered; she and John enjoyed a placid, companionable relationship. Julia, settled and happy in her marriage, and with the bonus of her own continuingly successful career, was living nearby in Barnes and there were now three grandchildren for Margaret to dote on. The years of family anguish and recrimination were long passed. Only the unwanted prospect of advancing age, when she dwelt on it, seemed to cloud her horizons.

In the spring and summer of 1977 she and John toured in a revival of Noel Coward's 1951 romantic comedy, *Quadrille*. Richard Todd's Triumph Productions company was producing it and he was her leading man, astonished, at rehearsals, to see the old balaclava he remembered from twelve years before.

The tour reached Guildford for a three-week run in July. Cheryl Goodman, a young actress with a minor role in the production under the stage name Cheryl van Hoorn, had developed a special regard for Margaret as they travelled from city to city. In Wolverhampton Miss Goodman had been mugged one night and admitted to hospital. For a star with a reputation among her lesser colleagues for being standoffish, Margaret had been very solicitous, sending her flowers and a Snoopy cuddly toy. Miss Goodman saw something of Margaret's private side. 'She and John appeared to have a good relationship, friendly and relaxed,' she remembers. 'He tended to send her up a little, but in an affectionate way. Sometimes she would lay down the law a bit

198

and he would just raise his eyebrows or make some amusing remark or other. She liked to think she was the boss . . . and he let her.'

But Miss Goodman also noticed a vague restlessness in John. 'I got the impression he was just hanging around and wanted to be moving on to bigger and better things. It was as though his style was being cramped, though I never knew him to show any outward signs of resentment. He was always very pleasant, very charming, a "hail fellow well met" sort of guy. We all realised, once we'd got to know him, that he had an eye for the ladies. It seemed harmless. He obviously liked women and treated them in a very charming way.'

At Guildford, settled into the Yvonne Arnaud Theatre for three weeks, a longer engagement than at any of the other theatres on the tour, John's eye was caught by a particular lady, a member of the Yvonne Arnaud's permanent staff. That might have been all there was to it – a passing eye flirtation – had not Chance taken a hand.

Guildford was the last date on the *Quadrille* tour. Margaret was going to take a rest but John already had his next play lined up – he was to play Friar Lawrence in *Romeo and Juliet* for a production originated by the Yvonne Arnaud. Two weeks after the final performance of *Quadrille*, he was back at Guildford to start rehearsals. In the light of subsequent events, it became an in-joke with the company that the production in the background should have been, of all plays, *Romeo and Juliet*.

Patricia Wingfield was the theatre's wardrobe mistress. At 47, she had come late to theatre work; previously she had been a seamstress at Debenham's department store in Guildford. She was married, with an adolescent son. Like his two ex-wives, like Margaret, Patricia was dark, 'almost gipsy-ish', according to one of the people working with her in those days. She was a 'fairly large' woman, her features not particularly striking, but with her flair for clothing she cut a conspicuously stylish figure. She had a strong personality and could be formidable in argument and in the discipline with which she managed her department. Men, her colleagues conceded, found her attractive.

During the three weeks of rehearsal and three more of performances, she and John fell in love, the burgeoning affair common knowledge in the closeted intimacy of the theatre. It quickly became a favourite topic of company gossip but it took much longer for Margaret to find out.

When the production ended, John and Pat continued to meet – with Guildford only a fast 30-minute drive down the A3 from Kingston they could do so without too much risk of rousing suspicion – but as the weeks passed and the affair became more rooted, John faced up to the decision that he would have to leave Margaret.

'Actors are vagabonds and shouldn't have ties,' he remarked in an interview some months later.

When the confessions and revelations finally came, Margaret was shattered. They had been together for more than seventeen years, a long, stable 'marriage' in all but the formalities, which she had had every reason to believe would continue into the evening of their lives.

'He preferred someone younger,' was all the explanation she would give later to people who had known the situation. Beneath the words lay unspoken loss and hurt and the dignity of an abandoned woman conscious of her years. In September she would be 62, a time of life at which no woman, least of all a great star celebrated for her beauty, can be expected to come to terms philosophically with the humiliation of being abandoned for a much younger rival.

Solitary, insular by nature and inclination, Margaret now faced a future alone. She had never sought consciously to attract the men who had shared her life; Rupert, Keith, Theo, John . . . all of them had strayed into it by chance. It was too late now, and she was too hurt, to think that somewhere, at some future time, chance might be holding someone else in waiting. John had gone. He had moved in with Patricia, sharing a flat she owned in Guildford. But their happiness was brief and poignant. Soon after they set up home together Patricia was found to have incurable cancer and given only a few more years to live. John devoted himself to caring for her, at the expense of his career, until her death in 1984 at the age of 54. In her will Patricia left him the flat they had shared for so little time and he continued living there.

In the meantime Margaret turned to the only constant there had ever been in her life, the only certainty of fulfilment and forgetfulness over which she had mastery – work. Triumph Productions wanted her for a revival of Noel Coward's *Suite in Two Keys*, originally staged as three one-act plays adding a third 'key' to the title, but pared down to two for this production. Phyllis Calvert was going to be in it, the first time the two long-ago screen rivals had appeared together since *The Man in Grey* 36 years before. There could not have been a more therapeutic balm. In the first play, *Come into the Garden, Maud*, Margaret played Maud Caragnani, a widowed Italian princess. She is encountered by a hen-pecked American millionaire on the night his wife (Phyllis) is holding a dinner party, and he persuades her to elope with him. In *A Song at Twilight*, originally regarded as the finest of the three, she was Carlotta Gray, the long-time mistress of a writer whom his wife (Phyllis) nobly summons to his death-bed to share their last hours together. Margaret loved doing the play and afterwards looked back on the Carlotta role as one of her favourites, but in her private moments she was heart-sick.

Phyllis was a great comfort, always trying, with some success, to take her out of herself and make her laugh. They would rake over old times and names, exasperated but amused by mutual attacks of amnesia.

The assistant stage manager on the tour, an aspiring young actress, Sam Clarke, recalled: 'Everyone knew about the John Stone business but, of course, it was a forbidden area. She never talked about it – she was never the sort to talk about herself – but we all realised things weren't going well for her. She would walk around the theatre in curlers, with a cigarette dangling from her mouth. Anyone who didn't recognise her would have thought she was one of the cleaners. Then she'd come out on stage, the total star. She was magnificent. I remember how much I admired the way she kept up this front, always self-controlled, always the absolute professional, always pleasant to us all. It couldn't have been easy for her. At the same time, she was a sad figure. We all sensed it. At weekends she would never go home, like the rest of us who couldn't wait for the curtain to come down on a Saturday night. She would stay in the hotel and the following Monday when we met up again in a new town, she would already be there. It was as though she didn't have a home to go to.'

One night, in Newcastle upon Tyne, Miss Clarke threw a party for her company friends. Out of politeness she tentatively invited Margaret too, never expecting her to turn up. 'But to my surprise she came, and was very charming. She didn't stay long, but it was unusual for her to come to that type of party. Normally she didn't mix very much with the rest of us.'

For some weeks during the tour Margaret had been feeling unwell. At first she attributed it to her generally run-down condition but at Eastbourne she suddenly began to suffer dizzy spells, accompanied by noises in the head. Doctors found that she was suffering from a viral infection of the middle ear known as vestibulitis, probably caused by a virus she had picked up from sea water during a recent holiday in Greece. The symptoms were disturbing. The condition affected the twin nerves which control balance and hearing. In extreme cases the spells of dizziness it caused could lead to vertigo, a sensation of spinning either in the victim or in her surroundings and, when balance was lost, a sense not so much of falling as of the ground rising up. And all this to an accompaniment of intermittent whooshing and whistling noises in the head. 'You go whirling off into space – it's ghastly,' she told friends.

She struggled on with the tour, not missing a performance, but it was obvious to everyone in the company that she was under great strain. Antibiotics cleared up the infection in a few weeks but the doctors couldn't do anything to alleviate the after-effects: her hearing was impaired.

When the tour ended Margaret shut herself away at home and for the rest of the year hardly dared to venture far from the house. Without John it was a silent house of memories, of loneliness and grieving for seventeen years which had crumbled to ashes. Her deafness and the problem of coming to terms with it only served to heighten her sense of isolation.

Julia and Ernest did all they could to make life easier for her, though they were in the throes of moving house from nearby Barnes to a village in Somerset 140 miles away. They offered Margaret a home with them and their three children there and for a time she considered it. But she was not a countrywoman at heart and would never settle into rural retirement, far from London, forfeiting her independence. It was frustrating enough that even in Kingston her illness had robbed her of much of her freedom. Ever since Rupert had taught her to drive and she had acquired her first car she had been a keen and skilful driver. Now she lacked the confidence to take the car out.

Phyllis, since their reunion in *Suite in Two Keys*, had become her closest friend and she would drive over from her home in the same Barnes road as Julia's and persuade Margaret out of the house for a change of scene, shopping or visiting a garden centre. Occasionally one or other of them would be recognised and asked for an autograph. It amused them that the fan seldom seemed to realise that two famous signatures were there for the taking, and when the identified star had obliged, she would say: 'Wouldn't you like Margaret Lockwood's/ Phyllis Calvert's as well?' They would both have a laugh over the supplicant's expression of dawning incredulity.

202

Late in 1979 Herbert sent Margaret the script of a new play with a powerful and challenging role – Queen Alexandra, the long-suffering wife of Edward VII.

Motherdear was the work of Royce Ryton whose earlier play, *Crown Matrimonial*, dealing with the Abdication crisis of 1936, had stirred controversy with its portrayal, for the first time on the stage, of living members of the royal family. The new piece, spanning a period of 34 years, explored the relationship between the charming and beautiful but capricious and domineering Alexandra and her daughter Princess Victoria, who sacrificed her youth, marriage chances and happiness to remain her mother's sorely tried companion until the old lady's death.

Royce Ryton had not written the play originally with Margaret in mind but from the time its production was first under consideration she was the actress he envisaged for the Alexandra role. 'I wanted a strong actress,' he recalled. 'Alexandra was a strong woman, all sweetness and charm to people who were not a threat to her but wilful and demanding with those closest to her. I thought immediately of Margaret Lockwood. She would be ideal. I also thought it would give her career a fillip. Here was a fine actress, a great star, but she had allowed herself to become an uninteresting one. For the past twenty years she'd been too cautious, encouraged by Herbert, doing little else but thrillers and routine comedies. Her regular fans were ageing – old ladies in charabancs going to matinees of her latest whodunnit – and she hadn't made any new ones because, to be frank, she'd become predictable and boring.'

Herbert strongly recommended the play to Margaret but she was hesitant, her confidence undermined by her illness, her emotions drained by the events of the past year, but under Herbert's gentle coaxing, she agreed to consider it.

'She seemed unable to take a step without consulting Herbert,' Ryton said. 'As a preliminary we invited her to dinner at our home to talk things over.' Ryton and his actress wife Morag Kennedy lived a couple of miles down the road from Margaret in the village of Ham. They were astonished later to discover that, unwilling to commit herself even to an informal social occasion, she had even sought Herbert's advice on whether to accept their invitation.

Herbert himself had been in declining health for some time and just as negotiations were getting under way over *Motherdear* he died suddenly, on 8 December. He was 74.

To Margaret he had been indestructible, working right to the end, the one dependable presence in her life through all its vicissitudes, all the 45 years since she had nervously climbed the stairs to his Shaftesbury Avenue office the day after her RADA performance in *Hannele*. Herbert, who had created her, orchestrated her career, who had managed her affairs, supervised her finances, cushioned her against the pinpricks of everyday living. Herbert, the guide, counsellor, confidant and helpmeet; the shoulder to cry on and the strength to lean on. Herbert, virtually the father she had never had . . .

She was inconsolable. Without Herbert, she was alone, bereft. As one friend said afterwards: 'Margaret had gone through life never really having to lift a finger for herself.' There had always been someone to smooth the path . . . Margaret Evelyn, Rupert, John, the studios, nannies, daily helps . . . and always Herbert.

At the funeral, weeping uncontrollably, she barely seemed capable of supporting herself. Nobody had ever seen the reserved, contained Margaret Lockwood betray such naked emotion in public before. Dame Anna Neagle, distressed as much by Margaret's state as by her own sorrow, went home and told Joyce Wright: 'She was utterly distraught. It was very upsetting to see her like that.'

She felt completely alone. A deeply concerned Phyllis Calvert urged her to give up the Kingston house and move into a service flat where she would not need to worry about many of the petty organisational details of living. Unknown to Margaret, Phyllis contacted Peter Graves who lived at Dolphin Square and they discussed how Margaret could be persuaded to return there, but nothing came of it. Herbert's widow, Hazel, whom he had married in 1975, took over the agency. She had originally joined it in 1961, and had become a partner in 1963, sharing fully in all his undertakings. The negotiations for *Motherdear* had reached a crucial phase but with Herbert's death Margaret no longer had the will to continue them – she seemed to have lost interest in most things. Phyllis now took her in hand. The play, she said, was the best thing Margaret could do for herself, for Herbert, and she bullied and badgered her into doing it.

Margaret hedged herself with conditions and stipulations, Royce Ryton remembered. She insisted on, and was granted, the right to approve the director and cast and let it be known that the deal was off unless the director she wanted, Frith Danbury, was available. He was. She insisted on all rehearsals being held close to Kingston so that she wouldn't have to travel into London. They were. Rehearsal space was found in Richmond and the rest of the company had to make their way out there.

'We didn't regard it as a case of her being "difficult",' said Ryton, 'rather, knowing what she had been through recently, we all wanted to make things as simple and easy as possible for her.' She refused to tour the play – 'a pity, for her sake; it would have given her more confidence' – so a compromise was agreed to open it in Birmingham, then bring it straight into the West End.

There was a tellingly sad moment towards the end of rehearsals when members of the cast were discussing the move up to Birmingham. Someone asked Margaret how she intended travelling. Suddenly bewildered, she said she didn't know. 'Will you be driving up?' another asked.

Ryton recalled: 'She went ashen. "I can't drive up, I can't," she whispered. It was rather pathetic.'

Everyone treated her with sympathy for the difficulties they knew about, but nobody realised the unacknowledged strain the role must have placed on her. Playing the part of a domineering mother, blighting her daughter's life with her demanding need for loyalty and sacrifice, came too close to home.

'I wasn't right for it,' she would say afterwards, and she remarked to one interviewer in Birmingham: 'How Alexandra hung on to her daughter!' The personal resonances were disturbing. During the three-week run in Birmingham, she passed each long day alone in her hotel room, watching TV and reading.

As a play, *Motherdear* was tepidly received by the critics when it opened at the Ambassadors Theatre in May 1980 but her performance drew respectful mentions, summed up by *The Times*: 'Margaret Lockwood revels in Alexandra's complexity, ranging instantaneously from charm to tears, baring a loathing of sexuality, then turning flirtatious for gain.' It could have been, Royce Ryton believes, a truly great performance under a different director from the one she herself had appointed.

'She needed a tough young director who would storm down and beat the performance out of her. Frith Danbury showed too much respect for her stardom.' Even so, no one who saw the brief run could doubt her powers; beautiful, mercurial, fascinating and in total command of her character, effortlessly spanning a sweeping range of emotional expression and technique. Nor could anyone have suspected that the exercising of those powers masked a broken spirit.

The play ran for six weeks, defeated finally by an inflation-imposed box-office slump in the West End and a down-turn in the volume of American tourists. With the final curtain, Margaret took her last bow on the same stage where she had taken her first in the West End 46 years before. She never worked again.

The following year her long, unique service to the stage and screen was recognised by the Queen. She was appointed a Commander of the Order of the British Empire in the New Year's Honours of 1981. Her first call, congratulating her on New Year's Day, was from Phyllis Calvert. Two months later she went to Buckingham Palace for her investiture. Julia had just made her a grandmother for the fourth time by giving birth to a third son. Ernest was Margaret's escort and she took the three other grandchildren with her.

The Queen, she was told afterwards, had spent longer talking to her than to anyone else she invested that day. Outside the palace she posed for the cameramen, displaying her insignia and surrounded by the children. They were the last photographs taken of her in public.

Ernest drove her home to Kingston and she walked up the short path to her front door, went inside and closed it on the world.

&PILOGUE

In January 1982 the director Michael Winner announced that he had bought the rights to *The Wicked Lady* from Rank, and intended to re-make it with the Oscar-winning Hollywood star Faye Dunaway as Barbara. In his view it 'was the most famous and probably the most successful film in British cinema history', and he confessed to having seen it at the under-age of ten, defying the censor's prohibition by returning again and again to enjoy it.

Newspapers delved into their picture files for 36-year-old stills of Margaret in the role of Lady Skelton, bold, insolent and challenging, their caption writers conferring the accolade of 'classic' on a movie which many of those same papers had dismissed so scathingly a generation before.

Within a month the BBC rushed out a television re-run and Margaret told the *Daily Mail* on the day of the screening: 'You wouldn't have believed the furore about that film . . . but really it was just a rollicking romp.' The re-make, she thought, would be 'fun' but she wasn't amused by a news item floated by the new film's publicists that Winner was going to offer her a cameo role 'for old times' sake'. No such offer reached her 'and, in any case, what on earth could he expect me to play? One of the dotty old ladies in it? Nonsense.'

Nor, as the première approached, did she take kindly to another widely circulated story that Winner was proposing to invite her and place her on a special dais of honour . . . 'Like a fairground sideshow! Not, I think, in the best of taste.' Wisely, she distanced herself from the hype when *The Wicked Lady*, 1980s-style, complete with nude wenches and explicit love-making, opened in April 1983.

Though faithful, virtually word for word, to Leslie Arliss's script and scene for scene to the screenplay, Winner and his actors conspicuously failed to recapture the uninhibited, defiant spirit of the Lockwood-Mason partnership, partly of course, because it no longer seemed outrageous. A new generation of critics scoffed, but this time in order to refer back nostalgically to the merits of the original for unfavourable comparisons.

The National Film Theatre chanced to be showing a major retrospective of Gainsborough films that April and in the same week that Winner's *The Wicked Lady* opened, *Bank Holiday, The Lady Vanishes* and *A Girl Must Live* were screened; a purposeful corrective, it almost seemed.

As the 'eighties passed, Margaret retreated deeper into anonymity. Stage and television offers continued to reach her via Hazel de Leon; she would consider them, seek advice from friends and turn them down.

'Too much bother,' she would say. 'It's not as though I need the money.'

Gradually she acquired the press label of 'Britain's Greta Garbo' and a reputation as a recluse, refusing all requests for interviews or invitations to film industry functions.

In September 1986 the National Film Theatre honoured her 70th birthday with a season of eleven films covering the glory days of her career from *Dr Syn* to *Jassy*. Ronald Bergan, in an introduction, wrote: 'Margaret Lockwood's film career, stretching uninterrupted from 1935 to 1955, covered a wide range, ample evidence as to why *the* Gainsborough Lady was one of the most popular and loved stars during the heyday of British cinema.' Newspapers, television and radio chat-shows, the NFT itself, begged Margaret for appearances but she remained resolutely silent behind the firmly closed door of the Kingston house.

'Who's interested?' she would say. 'I'm old hat now.'

But emphatically she was not, as her postbag would testify every time one of her old films was revived on television. Nor were the letters exclusively from ageing fans: to her surprise she found that the young generation recognised something of the glamour, the personality, that had captivated their parents. Every letter, every birthday card, would always be acknowledged with a hand-written note.

She is remembered with enormous affection. Once, going to visit her, I bought flowers from a middle-aged stall-holder in Kingston Market Place. Her face lit up when she heard who they were for, and she snatched up a second bunch. 'Give her these from me. I used to love her films,' she said.

EPILOGUE

The famous raven hair is white now, invariably covered by a chiffon scarf. The beauty spot is still there high on the left cheek bone, but no longer painted. The voice is deep and commanding. She lives modestly and unpretentiously, as she always has, though she must be a relatively wealthy woman. Taxation during her highest-earning period, during and immediately after the Second World War, was punitive at 19s 6d in the pound but, as one of her contemporary colleagues commented: 'Don't forget Maggie was making good money before the war and Herbert de Leon managed it very shrewdly for her.' She watches television avidly, rarely missing one of her own films. She admires Clint Eastwood and Paul Newman but is not greatly impressed by any modern screen actresses, comparing them unfavourably with Katharine Hepburn for talent and Hedy Lamarr for beauty. She rarely ventures from the house now, unless it is down to the local parade of shops to replenish her stock of cigarettes. Julia and Ernest keep in regular touch and the grandchildren come up for occasional visits, otherwise for company she can turn to loyal and long-standing neighbours who shield her from prying outsiders. 'I just potter around. I'm happy doing nothing,' she says. Phyllis Calvert is the only colleague from her own generation of stars with whom she keeps in touch.

She is neither lonely nor unhappy but she carries, as she always has, an air of solitariness and isolation tinged, one senses, with an elusive sadness. There are no evident mementoes in her home of the great years, the great star; no trophies, no scrapbooks, no reminders.

'That's all in the past,' she will say. 'What's the point of hanging on to it?'

$\mathcal{F}$ILM ROLES

Lorna Doone, 1934. Associated Talking Pictures; produced and directed
by Basil Dean; screenplay by Dorothy Farnum, Miles Malleson,
Gordon Wellesley, based on the novel by R. D. Blackmore.
Cast: Victoria Hopper, John Loder, Margaret Lockwood, Roy
Emerton, Edward Rigby, Mary Clare, Roger Livesey, George
Curzon, D. A. Clarke-Smith, Lawrence Hanray, Amy Veness,
Eliot Makeham.

The Case of Gabriel Perry, 1935. British Lion; produced by Herbert Smith;
directed by Albert de Courville; screenplay by L. du Garde Peach,
based on the play *Wild Justice* by James Dale.
Cast: Henry Oscar, Olga Lindo, Margaret Lockwood, Franklin
Dyall, Raymond Lovell, John Wood, Martita Hunt, Rodney Ackland, Percy Walsh, Ralph Truman, Lawrence Anderson, Mark
Lester, Alastair Sim.

Some Day, 1935. Warner Bros; produced by Irving Asher; directed by
Michael Powell; screenplay by Brock Williams based on the novel
Young Nowheres by I. A. R. Wylie.
Cast: Esmond Knight, Margaret Lockwood, Henry Mollison,
Sunday Wilshin, Raymond Lovell, Ivor Barnard, George Pughe,
Jane Cornell.

Honours Easy, 1935. British Independent Pictures; produced by Walter C.
Mycroft; directed by Herbert Brenon; based on the play *Honours
Easy* by Roland Pertwee.
Cast: Patric Knowles, Greta Nissen, Margaret Lockwood, Chili
Bouchier, Ivan Samson, Robert Rendel, George Graves, W. H.
Berry, Wallace Douglas.

Man of The Moment, 1935. Warner-First National; produced by Irving
  Asher; directed by Monty Banks; screenplay by Guy Bolton,
  Roland Pertwee, A. R. Rawlinson, based on the play *Water
  Nymph* by Yves Mirande.
  Cast: Douglas Fairbanks Jr, Laura La Plante, Margaret Lock-
  wood, Claude Hulbert, Donald Calthrop, Monty Banks, Peter
  Gawthorne.

Midshipman Easy, 1935. Associated Talking Pictures; produced by Basil
  Dean; directed by Carol Reed; screenplay by Anthony Kimmins,
  based on the novel *Mr Midshipman Easy* by Captain Marryat.
  Cast: Hughie Green, Roger Livesey, Margaret Lockwood, Harry
  Tate, Robert Adams, Lewis Casson, Dennis Wyndham, Tom Gill,
  Frederick Burtwell, Desmond Tester, Dorothy Holmes-Gore,
  Esme Church.

Jury's Evidence, 1936. British Lion; produced by Herbert Smith; directed
  by Ralph Ince; screenplay by Ian Dalrymple from the play by
  Jack de Leon and Jack Celestin.
  Cast: Hartley Power, Margaret Lockwood, Eve Gray, Nora Swin-
  burne, Sebastian Shaw, Tracy Holmes, Jane Millican, Patrick
  Ludlow, Charles Paton, W. E. Holloway, Dick Francis, Philip
  Strange, Aubrey Fitzgerald.

The Amateur Gentleman, 1936. Criterion; produced by Marcel Hellman;
  directed by Thornton Freedland; screenplay by Clemence Dane
  and Sergei Nolbandov, based on the novel by Jeffrey Farnol.
  Cast: Douglas Fairbanks Jr, Elissa Landi, Gordon Harker, Hugh
  Williams, Basil Sydney, Irene Brown, Athole Stewart, Margaret
  Lockwood, Frank Pettingell, Esme Percy, June Duprez.

The Beloved Vagabond, 1936. Toeplitz; produced by Ludovico Toeplitz;
  directed by Kurt (Curtis) Bernhardt; screenplay by Hugh Mills,
  Arthur Wimperis, Walter Creighton, based on a novel by W. J.
  Locke.
  Cast: Maurice Chevalier, Betty Stockfeld, Margaret Lockwood,
  Desmond Tester, Austin Trevor, Peter Haddon, Charles Carson,
  Cathleen Nesbitt, Barbara Gott, D. J. Williams, Denier Warren.

Irish for Luck, 1936. Warner-First National; produced by Irving Asher; directed by Arthur Woods; based on a story by L. A. G. Strong.
Cast: Athene Seyler, Patric Knowles, Margaret Lockwood, Gibb McLaughlin, Edward Rigby, Eugene Leahy, George Dillon, Terry Conlin.

The Street Singer, 1937. British National; produced by Dora Nirva; directed by Jean de Marguenat; screenplay by Reginald Arkell, based on a story by Paul Schiller and Jean de Marguenat.
Cast: Arthur Tracy, Margaret Lockwood, Hugh Wakefield, Ellen Pollock, Arthur Riscoe, Emil Boreo, Wally Patch, Ian MacLean, John Deverell, Rawicz and Landauer, Lew Stone and His Band, the Carl Hyson Dancers.

Who's Your Lady Friend?, 1937. Dorian; produced by Martin Sabine; directed by Carol Reed; screenplay by Anthony Kimmins, from a story by Julius Hoest, based on the play *Der Herr ohne Wohnung*.
Cast: Frances Day, Romney Brent, Margaret Lockwood, Betty Stockfeld, Vic Oliver, Sarah Churchill, Marcelle Rogez, Muriel George, Frederick Ranalow.

Dr Syn, 1937. Gaumont-British; produced by Michael Balcon; directed by Roy William Neill; screenplay by Roger Burford with additional dialogue by Michael Hogan, based on the novel by Russell Thorndike.
Cast: George Arliss, Margaret Lockwood, John Loder, Roy Emerton, Graham Moffat, Frederick Burtwell, George Merritt, Athole Stewart, Wally Patch, Meinhart Maur, Muriel George, Wilson Coleman.

Melody and Romance, 1937. British Lion; produced by Herbert Smith; directed by Maurice Elvey; screenplay by L. du Garde Peach, Maurice Elvey, based on a story by L. H. Gordon.
Cast: Hughie Green, Margaret Lockwood, Jane Carr, Alastair Sim, Garry Marsh, Denier Warren, Julien Vedey, Margaret Scudamore, Hughie's Gang, Joyce Cannon and Geraldine, Rex Roper and Maisie, Bobby Price.

Owd Bob, 1938. Gainsborough; produced by Edward Black; directed by Robert Stevenson; screenplay by J. B. Williams, Michael Hogan, based on the novel *Owd Bob* by Alfred Ollivant.
   Cast: Will Fyffe, Margaret Lockwood, John Loder, Moore Marriott, Graham Moffat, Wilfrid Walter, Elliot Mason, A. Bromley Davenport, H. F. Maltby, Edmund Breon, Alf Goddard, Wally Patch.

Bank Holiday, 1938. Gainsborough; produced by Edward Black; directed by Carol Reed; screenplay by Rodney Ackland and Roger Burford from a story by Rodney Ackland and Hans Wilhelm.
   Cast: Margaret Lockwood, Hugh Williams, John Lodge, Garry Marsh, Linden Travers, Jeanne Stuart, Wilfrid Lawson, Rene Ray, Merle Tottenham, Wally Patch, Kathleen Harrison, Felix Aylmer, Alf Goddard, Michael Rennie, Angela Glynne.

The Lady Vanishes, 1938. Gainsborough-Gaumont-British; produced by Edward Black; directed by Alfred Hitchcock; screenplay by Frank Launder and Sidney Gilliat with additional dialogue by Alma Reville, based on the novel *The Wheel Spins* by Ethel Lina White.
   Cast: Michael Redgrave, Margaret Lockwood, Paul Lukas, Dame May Whitty, Cecil Parker, Linden Travers, Mary Clare, Naunton Wayne, Basil Radford, Emil Boreo, Googie Withers, Philip Leaver, Catherine Lacey, Charles Oliver, Sally Stuart.

A Girl Must Live, 1939. Gainsborough-Twentieth Century-Fox; produced by Edward Black; directed by Carol Reed; screenplay by Frank Launder, based on a novel by Emery Bonet.
   Cast: Margaret Lockwood, Lilli Palmer, Renee Houston, George Robey, Hugh Sinclair, Naunton Wayne, Moore Marriott, Mary Clare, David Burns, Kathleen Harrison, Drusilla Wills, Wilson Coleman, Helen Haye, Frederick Burtwell, Martita Hunt, Muriel Aked, Joan White, Merle Tottenham, Michael Hordern.

Susannah of the Mounties, 1939. Twentieth-Century-Fox; produced by Kenneth MacGowan; directed by Sidney Lanfield; screenplay by John Taintor-Foote and Philip Dunne.
   Cast: Shirley Temple, Randolph Scott, Margaret Lockwood, J.

213

Farrell MacDonald, Maurice Moscovitch, Moroni Olsen, Victor Jory.

Rulers of the Sea, 1939. Paramount; produced and directed by Frank Lloyd; screenplay by Talbot Jennings, Frank Cavett, Richard Collins.
Cast: Douglas Fairbanks Jr, Margaret Lockwood, Will Fyffe, Montagu Love, George Bancroft, Mary Gordon, Alan Ladd.

The Stars Look Down, 1939. Grafton; produced by Isadore Goldsmith; directed by Carol Reed; screenplay by J. B. Williams, based on the novel by A. J. Cronin.
Cast: Michael Redgrave, Margaret Lockwood, Emlyn Williams, Nancy Price, Edward Rigby, Alan Jeayes, Cecil Parker, Linden Travers, Milton Rosmer, George Carney, Ivor Barnard, Olga Lindo, Desmond Tester, David Markham.

Night Train to Munich, 1940. Twentieth Century-Fox; produced by Edward Black; directed by Carol Reed; screenplay by Frank Launder and Sidney Gilliat, based on a story by Gordon Wellesley.
Cast: Margaret Lockwood, Rex Harrison, Paul von Hernried (Paul Henreid), Basil Radford, Naunton Wayne, James Harcourt, Felix Aylmer, Wyndham Goldie, Roland Culver, Eliot Makeham, Raymond Huntley, Austin Trevor, Kenneth Kent, C. V. France, Morland Graham, Billy Russell, Fritz Valk, Irene Handl.

The Girl in the News, 1940. Twentieth Century-Fox-MGM; produced by Edward Black; directed by Carol Reed; screenplay by Sidney Gilliat, based on a novel by Roy Vickers.
Cast: Margaret Lockwood, Barry K. Barnes, Emlyn Williams, Roger Livesey, Margaretta Scott, Wyndham Goldie, Basil Radford, Irene Handl, Mervyn Johns, Betty Jardine, Kathleen Harrison, Felix Aylmer, Roland Culver, Edward Rigby.

Quiet Wedding, 1941. Conqueror; produced by Paul Soskin; directed by Anthony Asquith; screenplay by Terence Rattigan, Anatole de Grunwald, based on the play by Esther McCracken.
Cast: Margaret Lockwood, Derek Farr, Athene Seyler, Marjorie Fielding, A. E. Matthews, Margaretta Scott, Peggy Ashcroft,

Frank Cellier, Roland Culver, Jean Cadell, David Tomlinson, Sydney King, Michael Shepley, Bernard Miles, Roddy Hughes, Muriel Pavlow, Margaret Rutherford, Martita Hunt, Muriel George, Peter Bull, Ivor Barnard, Esma Cannon.

Alibi, 1942. Corona; produced by Josef Somlo; directed by Brian Desmond Hurst; screenplay by Lesley Storm, from the French screenplay by Jacques Companeez, Justine and R. Carter, based on the novel by Marcel Archard.
Cast: Margaret Lockwood, James Mason, Hugh Sinclair, Raymond Lovell, Enid Stamp-Taylor, Jane Carr, Hartley Power, Rodney Ackland, Edana Romney, Elisabeth Welch, Olga Lindo, Muriel George, George Merritt, Judy Grey, Philip Leaver, Derek Blomfield.

The Man in Grey, 1943. Gainsborough; produced by Edward Black; directed by Leslie Arliss; screenplay by Margaret Kennedy, Leslie Arliss, Doreen Montgomery, based on the novel by Lady Eleanor Smith.
Cast: Margaret Lockwood, James Mason, Phyllis Calvert, Stewart Granger, Raymond Lovell, Nora Swinburne, Helen Haye, Martita Hunt, Amy Veness, Diana King, Beatrice Varley, Roy Emerton, A. E. Matthews.

Dear Octopus, 1943. Gainsborough; directed by Harold French; screenplay by R. J. Minney, Patrick Kirwan, based on the play by Dodie Smith.
Cast: Margaret Lockwood, Michael Wilding, Helen Haye, Celia Johnson, Frederick Leister, Roland Culver, Basil Radford, Athene Seyler, Jean Cadell, Nora Swinburne, Antoinette Cellier, Kathleen Harrison, Madge Compton, Ann Stephens, Muriel George, Graham Moffat.

Give Us the Moon, 1944. Gainsborough; produced by Edward Black; directed by Val Guest; screenplay by Val Guest, based on a novel by Caryl Brahms and S. J. Simon.
Cast: Margaret Lockwood, Peter Graves, Vic Oliver, Roland Culver, Jean Simmons, Max Bacon, Frank Cellier, Eliot Make-

215

ham, Iris Long, George Relph, Gibb McLaughlin, Irene Handl, Henry Hewitt, Jonathan Field, John Salew.

Love Story, 1944. Gainsborough; produced by Harold Huth; directed by Leslie Arliss; screenplay by Leslie Arliss, Doreen Montgomery, Rodney Ackland, based on a short story by J. W. Drawbell.
Cast: Margaret Lockwood, Stewart Granger, Patricia Roc, Tom Walls, Reginald Purdell, Moira Lister, Dorothy Bramhall, Vincent Holman, Joan Rees, A. E. Matthews, Beatrice Varley.

A Place of One's Own, 1945. Gainsborough; produced by R. J. Minney; directed by Bernard Knowles; screenplay by Brock Williams, based on a story by Sir Osbert Sitwell.
Cast: Margaret Lockwood, James Mason, Barbara Mullen, Dennis Price, Ernest Thesiger, Helen Haye, Michael Shepley, Dulcie Gray, Moore Marriott, Gus MacNaughton, O. B. Clarence, Muriel George, Aubrey Mallalieu.

I'll Be Your Sweetheart, 1945. Gainsborough; produced by Louis Levy; directed by Val Guest; screenplay by Val Guest, Val Valentine.
Cast: Margaret Lockwood, Michael Rennie, Peter Graves, Moore Marriott, Vic Oliver, Jonathan Field, Frederick Burtwell, Maudie Edwards, Garry Marsh, George Merritt, Muriel George, Eliot Makeham, Ella Retford, Alf Goddard, Barry Lupino, David Crowley, Joss Ambler, Wendy Toye.

The Wicked Lady, 1945. Gainsborough; produced by R. J. Minney; directed by Leslie Arliss; screenplay by Leslie Arliss, Aimee Stuart, Gordon Glennon, based on the novel *The Life and Death of the Wicked Lady Skelton* by Magdalen King-Hall.
Cast: Margaret Lockwood, James Mason, Patricia Roc, Griffith Jones, Michael Rennie, Enid Stamp-Taylor, Felix Aylmer, Martita Hunt, David Horne, Emrys Jones, Jean Kent, Amy Dalby, Beatrice Varley, Helen Goss, Ivor Barnard, Muriel Aked.

Bedelia, 1946. John Corfield; produced by Isadore Goldsmith; directed by Lance Comfort; screenplay by Isadore Goldsmith, Vera Caspary,

Herbert Victor, Moie Charles, Roy Ridley, based on the novel by Vera Caspary.
Cast: Margaret Lockwood, Ian Hunter, Barry K. Barnes, Anne Crawford, Jill Esmond, Barbara Blair, Louise Hampton, Ellen Pollock, Julien Mitchell, Kynaston Reeves, Beatrice Varley, Olga Lindo, John Salew, Claude Bailey.

Hungry Hill, 1946. Two Cities; produced by William Sistrom; directed by Brian Desmond Hurst; screenplay by Daphne du Maurier, Terence Young, Francis Crowdy, based on the novel by Daphne du Maurier.
Cast: Margaret Lockwood, Dennis Price, Dermot Walsh, Cecil Parker, Michael Denison, F. J. McCormick, Jean Simmons, Peter Murray, Eileen Herlie, Siobhan McKenna, James Robertson Justice, Guy Rolfe, Patrick Holt, Dan O'Herlihy, Julia Lockwood.

Jassy, 1947. Gainsborough; produced by Sydney Box; directed by Bernard Knowles; screenplay by Dorothy and Campbell Christie, Geoffrey Kerr, based on the novel by Norah Lofts.
Cast: Margaret Lockwood, Patricia Roc, Dermot Walsh, Dennis Price, Basil Sydney, Nora Swinburne, Linden Travers, Ernest Thesiger, Cathleen Nesbitt, Esma Cannon, Jean Cadell, John Laurie, Grey Blake, Beatrice Varley, Susan Shaw.

The White Unicorn, 1947. John Corfield; produced by Harold Huth; directed by Bernard Knowles; screenplay by Robert Westerby, A. R. Rawlinson, Moie Charles, based on the novel *The Milk White Unicorn* by Flora Sandstrom.
Cast: Margaret Lockwood, Ian Hunter, Dennis Price, Joan Greenwood, Guy Middleton, Catherine Lacey, Mabel Constanduros, Paul Dupuis, Eileen Peel, Julia Lockwood, Lilly Kann, Valentine Dyall, Stewart Rome, Bryl Wakely, Elizabeth Maude, Noel Howlett, Joan Rees.

Look Before You Love, 1948. Burnham; produced by John Corfield, Harold Huth; directed by Harold Huth; screenplay by Reginald Long, based on a story by Ketti Frings.
Cast: Margaret Lockwood, Griffith Jones, Norman Wooland,

Phyllis Stanley, Michael Medwin, Maurice Denham, Frederick Piper, Violet Farebrother, Bruce Seton, Peggy Evans, June Elvin, Joan Rees, Nigel Lawlor, Alan Adair, Giselle Morlais, Stanley Quentin.

Cardboard Cavalier, 1948. Two Cities; produced and directed by Walter Forde; screenplay by Noel Langley.
Cast: Sid Field, Margaret Lockwood, Mary Clare, Jerry Desmonde, Claude Hulbert, Brian Worth, Anthony Hulme, Edmund Willard, Irene Handl, Miles Malleson, Joan Young, Jack McNaughton.

Madness of the Heart, 1949. Two Cities; produced by Richard Wainwright; directed by Charles Bennett; screenplay by Charles Bennett, based on a novel by Flora Sandstrom.
Cast: Margaret Lockwood, Paul Dupuis, Kathleen Byron, Maxwell Reed, Thora Hird, Raymond Lovell, Maurice Denham, David Hutcheson, Cathleen Nesbitt, Peter Illing, Jack McNaughton, Pamela Stirling, Marie Ault, Marie Burke, Patricia Cutts.

Highly Dangerous, 1950. Two Cities; produced by Antony Darnborough; directed by Roy Baker; screenplay by Eric Ambler.
Cast: Margaret Lockwood, Dane Clark, Marius Goring, Naunton Wayne, Wilfrid Hyde White, Eugene Deckers, Olaf Pooley, Gladys Henson, Paul Hardtmuth, Michael Hordern, George Benson, Eric Pohlmann, Joan Haythorne, Patric Doonan, Anthony Newley, Jill Balcon, Anton Diffring.

Trent's Last Case, 1952. Wilcox-Neagle; produced and directed by Herbert Wilcox; screenplay by Pamela Wilcox Bower, based on the novel by E. C. Bentley.
Cast: Michael Wilding, Margaret Lockwood, Orson Welles, John McCallum, Miles Malleson, Hugh McDermott, Jack McNaughton, Sam Kydd, Eileen Joyce, Kenneth Williams.

Laughing Anne, 1953. Republic/Wilcox-Neagle; produced and directed by Herbert Wilcox; screenplay by Pamela Wilcox Bower, based on the story *Because of the Dollars* by Joseph Conrad.

Cast: Margaret Lockwood, Forrest Tucker, Wendell Corey, Ronald Shiner, Robert Harris, Jacques Brunius, Daphne Anderson, Helen Shingler, Danny Green, Harold Lang, Maurice Bush, Dave Crowley, Sean Lynch, Edgar Norfolk.

Trouble in the Glen, 1954. Republic/Wilcox-Neagle; produced and directed by Herbert Wilcox; screenplay by Frank S. Nugent, based on a story by Maurice Walsh.
Cast: Margaret Lockwood, Orson Welles, Forrest Tucker, John McCallum, Victor McLaglen, Margaret McCourt, Eddie Byrne, Archie Duncan, Ann Gudrun, Moultrie Kelsall, Alex McCrindle, Mary Mackenzie, Jack Watling, Peter Sinclair, Janet Barrow.

Cast a Dark Shadow, 1955. Frobisher; produced by Herbert Mason; directed by Lewis Gilbert; screenplay by John Cresswell, based on the play *Murder Mistaken* by Janet Green.
Cast: Margaret Lockwood, Dirk Bogarde, Kay Walsh, Kathleen Harrison, Robert Flemyng, Mona Washbourne, Walter Hudd, Philip Stainton, Myrtle Reed, Lita Roza.

The Slipper and the Rose, 1976. Paradine; produced by David Frost, Stuart Lyons; directed by Bryan Forbes; screenplay by Bryan Forbes, Robert and Richard Sherman.
Cast: Richard Chamberlain, Gemma Craven, Kenneth More, Michael Hordern, Edith Evans, Annette Crosbie, Margaret Lockwood, Christopher Gable, Julian Orchard, Lally Bowers, John Turner, Peter Graves.

*S*TAGE ROLES

House on Fire, June 1934. Q Theatre, Kew Bridge. (Professional debut; one week only.)

Family Affairs, August 1934. Ambassadors Theatre, London; by Gertrude Jennings; with Lilian Braithwaite, Jack Livesey, Athene Seyler, Archibald Batty, Robert Eddison.

Repayment, January 1936. Arts Theatre, London (two weeks only); by John Beanes and Evan John; with Marius Goring, Joyce Bland, Margery Phipps-Walker, Margaret Emden, Douglas Jefferies, Sydney Tafler, John Abbott, Eugene Leahy, Ethel Coleridge, Beckett Bould, Julian D'Albie, Edward Gee.

Miss Smith, July 1936. Duke of York's Theatre, London; by Henry Bernard; with Olga Lindo, Dora Gregory, Julien Mitchell, Phyllis Konstam, Rex Arden, Sylvia Hammond, John Hepworth, Anthony Bruce, Nona Saffell, Beckett Bould, John Boxer, J. B. Rowe. (Margaret Lockwood joined the cast in September 1936, replacing Enid Morgan.)

Ann's Lapse, July 1937. Q Theatre, Kew Bridge; by Kenneth Horne; with Anthony Hawtrey, Eliot Makeham, Iris Hoey, Vernon Kelso, John Wood, Sydney Malcolm, Godfrey Baxter, Vernon Harris, Yvonne Cadwallader.

Private Lives, April 1949. Tour; by Noel Coward; with Peter Graves, Jack Allen, Josephine Stuart.

STAGE ROLES

Peter Pan, December 1949. Scala Theatre, London, and tour; by J. M. Barrie; with Christina Forrest, John Justin, Jane Welsh, Philip Ray, Perlita Neilson, Desmond Carrington, Iain Scott.

Peter Pan, December 1950. Scala Theatre, London, and tour; by J. M. Barrie; with Shirley Lorimer, Alan Judd, Jane Welsh, Russell Thorndike, Jane Wren, Iain Scott.

Pygmalion, August 1951. Edinburgh Festival and tour; by George Bernard Shaw; with Alan Webb, R. Stuart Lindsell, Charles Vance, Beatrice Varley.

Spider's Web, December 1954. Savoy Theatre, London; by Agatha Christie; with Felix Aylmer, Harold Scott, Myles Eason, Margaret Barton, Judith Furse, Campbell Singer, Desmond Llewellyn.

Subway in the Sky, February 1957. Savoy Theatre, London; by Ian Main; with Zachary Scott, Nigel Stock, Valerie White, Joseph Wise, Reed de Rouen.

Peter Pan, December 1957. Scala Theatre, London, and tour; by J. M. Barrie; with Julia Lockwood, Michael Warre, Jane Welsh, Melvyn Baker, James Ray, Jane Wren, Russell Thorndike.

Murder on Arrival, February 1959. Tour, opened Royal Court Theatre, Liverpool; by George Batson; with Joy Shelton, Cyril Raymond.

And Suddenly It's Spring, November 1959. Duke of York's Theatre, London; by Jack Popplewell; with Yolande Donlan, Frank Lawton, John Stone, Graham Payn, Pat Pleasance, John McCarthy.

Milk and Honey, February 1961. Tour; by Philip King; with Derek Farr, Patrick Cargill, Sheila Steafel.

Signpost to Murder, February 1962. Cambridge Theatre, London; by Monte Doyle; with Derek Farr, Cyril Raymond, John Stone, Stanley Beard.

Every Other Evening, November 1964. Phoenix Theatre, London; by Jack Popplewell; with Derek Farr, Diane Hart, Julia Lockwood.

An Ideal Husband, December 1965. Strand Theatre/Garrick Theatre, London; by Oscar Wilde; with Richard Todd, Michael Denison, Dulcie Gray, Roger Livesey, Ursula Jeans.

The Others, September 1967. Strand Theatre, London; by Richard Lortz; with Donald Houston.

On a Foggy Day, July 1969. St Martin's Theatre, London; by John Kerr; with Siobhan McKenna, Kenneth Connor, Saeed Jaffrey.

Lady Frederick, June 1970. Vaudeville Theatre, London; by W. Somerset Maugham; with Tony Britton, Heather Chasen, Ellen Pollock.

Relative Values, April 1972. Initial tour; September 1973, Westminster Theatre, London; by Noel Coward; with Gwen Cherrill (Patricia Hayes on tour), Joyce Blair, John Stone.

Double Edge, September 1975. Vaudeville Theatre, London; by Leslie Darbon and Peter Whelan; with Paul Daneman, Barrie Ingham (Peter Byrne, John Stone on tour).

Quadrille, May 1977. Tour; by Noel Coward; with Richard Todd, Anne Rogers, John Stone, Vyvian Hall, Daphne Newton, Cheryl Van Hoorn, John Larsen, Alfred Hoffman, Margaret Inglis, Hilary George, Nan Munro, Edwin Walters.

Suite in Two Keys, May 1978. Tour; by Noel Coward; with Phyllis Calvert, Robert Flemyng, Alan Gifford, Reynold Silva.

Motherdear, May 1980. Ambassadors Theatre, London; by Royce Ryton; with Polly James, Sheila Burrell, Frank Barrie, Norma Streader, William Eedie, Dorothy Primrose, Chris Johnston, Francis Lloyd, Margaret Diamond, Zulema Dene.

ᏴIBLIOGRAPHY

BARR, Charles (ed.): *All our Yesterdays: 90 years of British Cinema* (British Film Institute, London, 1986).

BOX, Muriel: *Odd Woman Out* (Leslie Frewin, London, 1974).

CONNELL, Brian: *Knight Errant: A biography of Douglas Fairbanks Jr* (Hodder and Stoughton, London, 1955).

CROSS, Robin: *The Big Book of British Films* (Sidgwick and Jackson, London, 1984).

CURRAN, James and Vincent PORTER (ed.): *British Cinema History* (Weidenfeld and Nicolson, London, 1983).

DENISON, Michael: *Overture and Beginners: The story of Dulcie Gray and Michael Denison* (Gollancz, London, 1973).
———— *Double Act* (Michael Joseph, London, 1985).

ENSER, A. G. S. (ed): *Filmed Books and Plays* (André Deutsch, London, various editions).

FAIRBANKS Jr, Douglas: *The Salad Days* (Collins, London, 1988).

FALK, Quentin: *The Golden Gong: Fifty Years of the Rank Organisation, Its Films and Its Stars* (Columbus, London, 1987).

GRANGER, Stewart: *Sparks Fly Upwards* (Granada, London, 1981).

GREENE, Graham (ed. John Russell Taylor): *The Pleasure Dome: The collected film criticism 1935–40* (Secker and Warburg, London, 1972).

HALLIWELL, Leslie: *Film Guide* (Granada, London, various editions).
———— *Filmgoer's Companion* (Granada, London, various editions).

HARRIS, Robert A. and Michael S. LASKY: *The Films of Alfred Hitchcock* (Citadel, New York, 1976).

HARRISON, Rex: *Rex: an autobiography* (Macmillan, London, 1974).

HENREID, Paul (with Julius FAST): *Ladies' Man: an autobiography* (St Martin's Press, New York, 1984).

HIRSCHHORN, Clive: *The Films of James Mason* (Citadel, New York, 1977).

KATZ, Ephraim: *The International Film Encylopaedia* (Macmillan, London, 1980).

LODER, John: *Hollywood Hussar* (Howard Baker, London, 1977).

LOW, Rachael: *Film Making in 1930s Britain* (George Allen and Unwin, London, 1985).

KELLEY, Kitty: *Elizabeth Taylor: The Last Star* (Michael Joseph, London, 1981).

LOCKWOOD, Margaret: *My Life and Films* (World Film Publications, London, 1948).
——— *Lucky Star: the autobiography of Margaret Lockwood* (Odhams Press, London, 1955).

MASON, James: *Before I Forget* (Hamish Hamilton, London, 1981).

MOSLEY, Leonard: *Zanuck: The Rise and Fall of Hollywood's Last Tycoon* (Granada, London, 1984).

MOSS, Robert F.: *The Films of Carol Reed* (Macmillan, London, 1987).

NEAGLE, Anna: *There's Always Tomorrow: an autobiography* (W. H. Allen, London, 1974).

NOBLE, Peter: *British Film Yearbook* (British Yearbooks, London, 1947).
——— *British Film Yearbook 1947–48* (Skelton Robinson British Yearbooks, London, 1948).

PERRY, George: *The Great British Picture Show* (Hart Davis/MacGibbon, London, 1974).

POWELL, Michael: *A Life in Movies: an autobiography* (Heinemann, London, 1986).

BIBLIOGRAPHY

QUINLAN, David: *British Sound Films: The Studio Years 1928–1959* (Batsford, London, 1984).
————— *Wicked Women of the Screen* (Batsford, London, 1987).

REDGRAVE, Michael: *In My Mind's Eye: an autobiography* (Weidenfeld and Nicolson, London, 1983).

SAUNDERS, Peter: *The Mousetrap Man* (Collins, London, 1972).

SHEREK, Henry: *Not in Front of the Children* (Heinemann, London, 1959).

SHIPMAN, David: *The Great Movie Stars: The Golden Years* (Hamlyn, London, 1970).

SPEED, F. Maurice: *Film Review* (Macdonald and Co., London, 1944–52).

VICKERS, Hugo: *Vivien Leigh* (Hamish Hamilton, London, 1988).

WALKER, Alexander: *Vivien: The Life of Vivien Leigh* (Weidenfeld and Nicolson, London, 1983).

WARREN, Patricia: *Elstree: The British Hollywood* (Elm Tree Books/ Hamish Hamilton, London, 1983).
————— *The British Film Collection: 1896–1984* (Elm Tree Books/Hamish Hamilton, London, 1984).

WILCOX, Herbert: *Twenty-Five Thousand Sunsets: an autobiography* (The Bodley Head, London, 1967).

WILEY, Mason and Damien BONA: *Inside Oscar: The unofficial history of the Academy Awards* (Columbus, London, 1986).

WOOD, Alan: *Mr Rank: A study of J. Arthur Rank and British films* (Hodder and Stoughton, London, 1952).

Newspapers, Magazines, Periodicals, etc.

Daily Express, Daily Herald, Daily Mail, Daily Mirror, Daily Sketch, The Daily Telegraph, Manchester Guardian, News Chronicle, The Scotsman, The Times, London Evening News, London Evening Standard, The Star, Sunday Chronicle, Sunday Dispatch, Sunday Express, Sunday Graphic, Sunday Times, Mail on Sunday, News of the World, The Observer, The People.

Films and Filming, Films Illustrated, Film Pictorial, Film Weekly, Kinematograph Weekly, Monthly Film Bulletin, Picturegoer, Picture Show, Plays and Players, Theatre World, Today's Cinema, Variety.

Los Angeles Times, New York Times, New York World-Telegram, Radio Times, TV Times, Surrey Comet.

BFI Dossier 18: Gainsborough Melodrama (British Film Institute, 1983).
The Basil Dean Collection (British Film Institute Library).
The Carol Reed Collection (British Film Institute Library).

The Daily Mail Film Award Annual (Winchester Publications, London, various editions).

$\mathscr{I}$NDEX

INDEX

229

INDEX

INDEX

INDEX

INDEX

INDEX

INDEX